IMAGES
of America

KEYPORT
VOLUME II

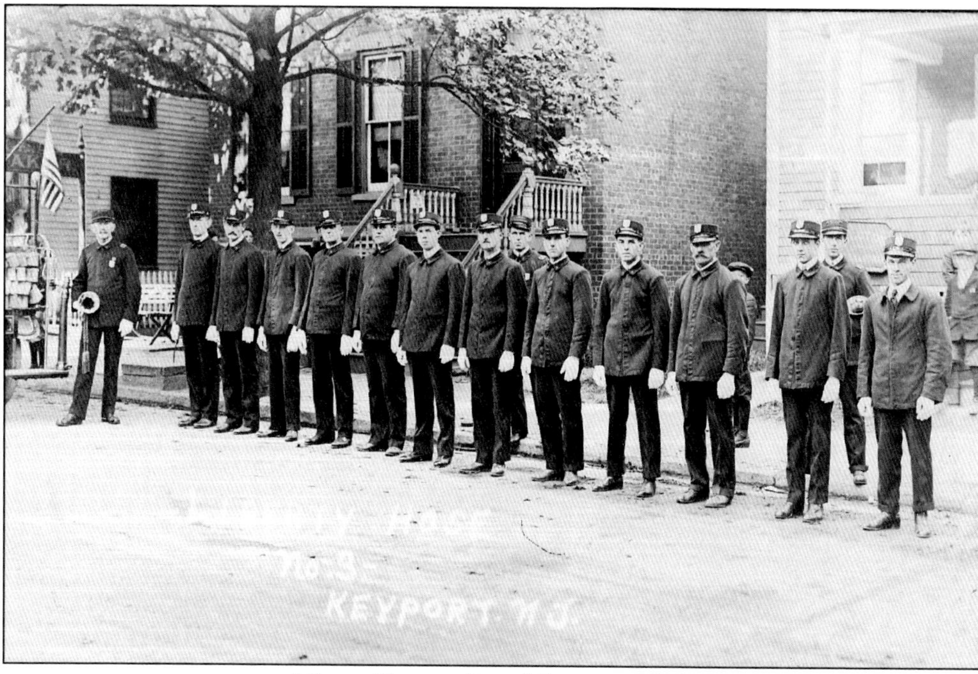

Liberty Hose on Broad Street, *c.* 1920.

IMAGES
of America

KEYPORT
VOLUME II

Timothy E. Regan

ARCADIA
PUBLISHING

ISBN 978-0-7385-6434-0

Published by Arcadia Publishing
Charleston, South Carolina

Printed in the United States of America

For all general information contact Arcadia Publishing at:
Telephone 843-853-2070
Fax 843-853-0044
E-mail sales@arcadiapublishing.com
For customer service and orders:
Toll-Free 1-888-313-2665

Visit us on the Internet at www.arcadiapublishing.com

This book is dedicated to my grandparents, Stafford and Mae Dibble, and in memory of Francis "Junior" VanPelt (1935–1996)

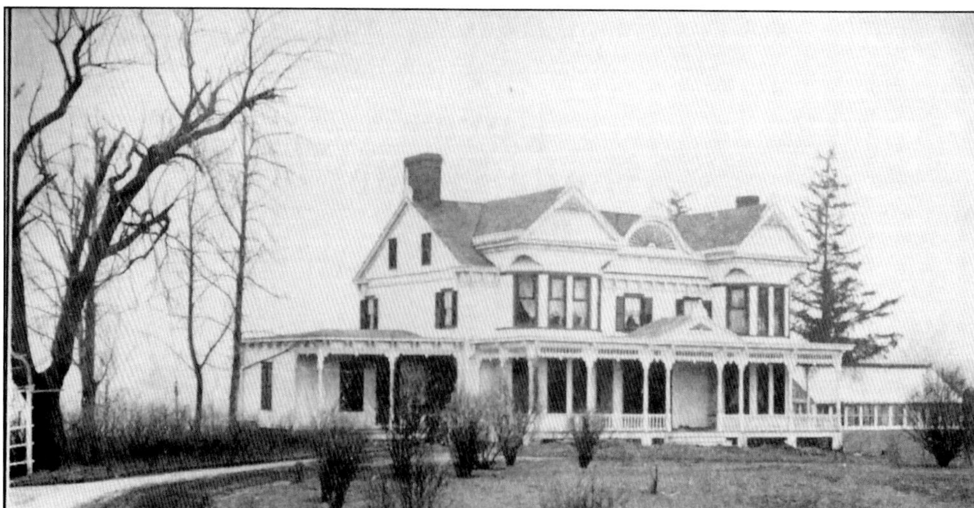

KEYGROVE MANSION, 1910. This impressive structure stood from 1714 to 1972.

Contents

Acknowledgments

At the close of the *Keyport Volume I*, I had no intention of doing a second volume. However, it seemed that everyone wanted a second book and I knew that there was plenty of information out there to complete it. So here it is, and only with the help of the following people could it have been completed.

About a third of the photographs in this book were lent by Bert Morris. Bert was born and raised in Keyport, down in Mechanicsville. He has gone out of his way time after time to help me with this venture as well as others and is a great friend.

Another person to whom I owe much thanks is Les Horner of Hazlet. Les provided me with some of the best images in this book, and it is his contribution that truly rounded out this pictorial history.

Next I would like to thank the Keyport Historical Society for their great contribution. I would also like to thank the following members of the society: President Eloise Schanck, Curator Norrine Schanck, and Jack and Angel Jeandron.

In addition, I would like to thank the following friends for their help and others who donated many of the fine photographs contained herein: Dave Galloway, Frank Currier, John Reith, Randy Stout, Charles McCue, Bill Cerase, Larry and Linda Schleicher, the staff of the Keyport Post Office, the staff of the Keyport Public Library, Jim Poling, Roger and GayLee Benedict, and fellow historian Jim McTernan, for all his assistance.

Of course, I can't go without giving my thanks once again to my future wife, Patricia Schleicher, who proofread and corrected this entire book for the big mistakes.

Finally, a thank you to my parents Betty and Gene. I know that I couldn't have succeeded without their constant support and encouragement (and my father's memories of old Keyport). Thanks Mom and Dad (and my brother Dan too!).

Introduction

"Keyport (ke´port,-pôrt'), *n*. a town in E. New Jersey. 6440 (1960)." This is the official definition of the town as it appears on p. 784 of *Webster's Encyclopedic Unabridged Dictionary* of the English language. But those who know the town know that such a small definition does not do it or its great history justice. For an exact definition of Keyport, you must look to the individual, and ask what the town means to them.

Keyport is a place of little change, where families have lived in the same houses for generations, a place where a stroll through town or to the post office is impossible to complete without waving to a half dozen people, all of whose lives you know intimately. Streets and buildings are lonely places without the faces, personalities, and lives of the various people who have resided here since 1830, when Keyport became an "official place" on national maps and in international dictionaries. Memories of the recent and distant past abound: hanging out at Stanley's Diner on Friday nights, Soap Box derbies, spending cold autumn days playing high school football, Keyport Days, and Halloween parades. Everyone has memories, thousands of them, which alone could fill up a hundred volumes of a book this size. Years from now people will wonder what the twentieth and twenty-first-century Keyporters passed their time doing, just as we think about those who came before us. Keyport is a very special place for those who know it today, knew it yesterday, and will know it in the future. I hope that with *Keyport Volume I*, and now *Keyport Volume II*, have succeeded in painting an accurate portrait of the people, places, and memories of life in this small town along the Jersey Shore.

One

A Fine Place to Live

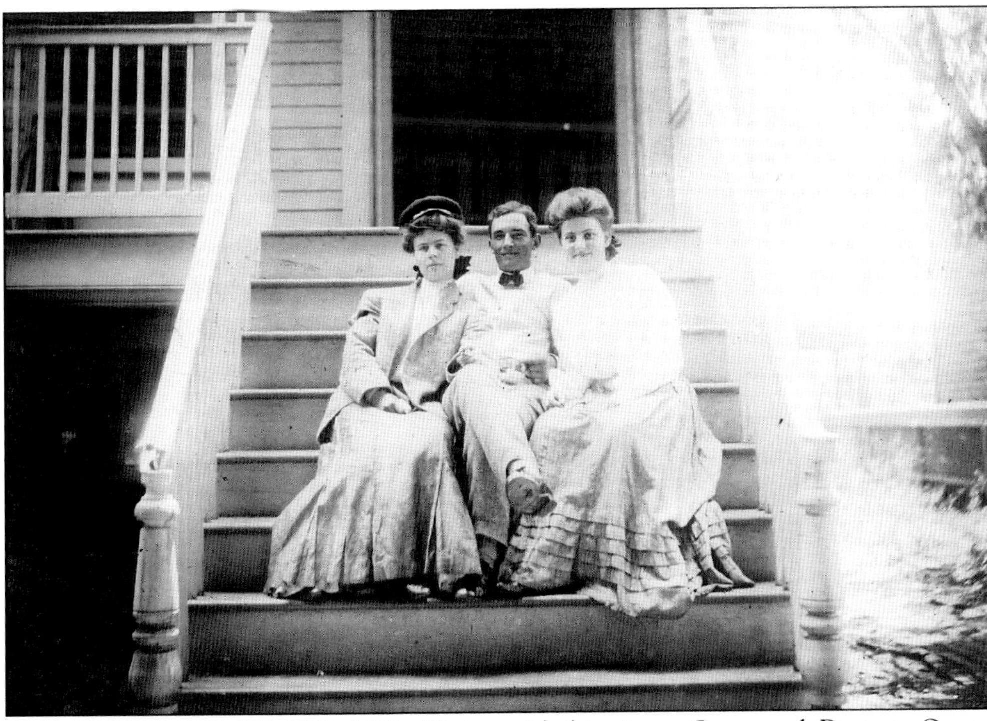

THE APPLEGATE FAMILY, 1890. Sitting with his sisters Grace and Decient, George Applegate relaxes at the family homestead in the summer of 1890.

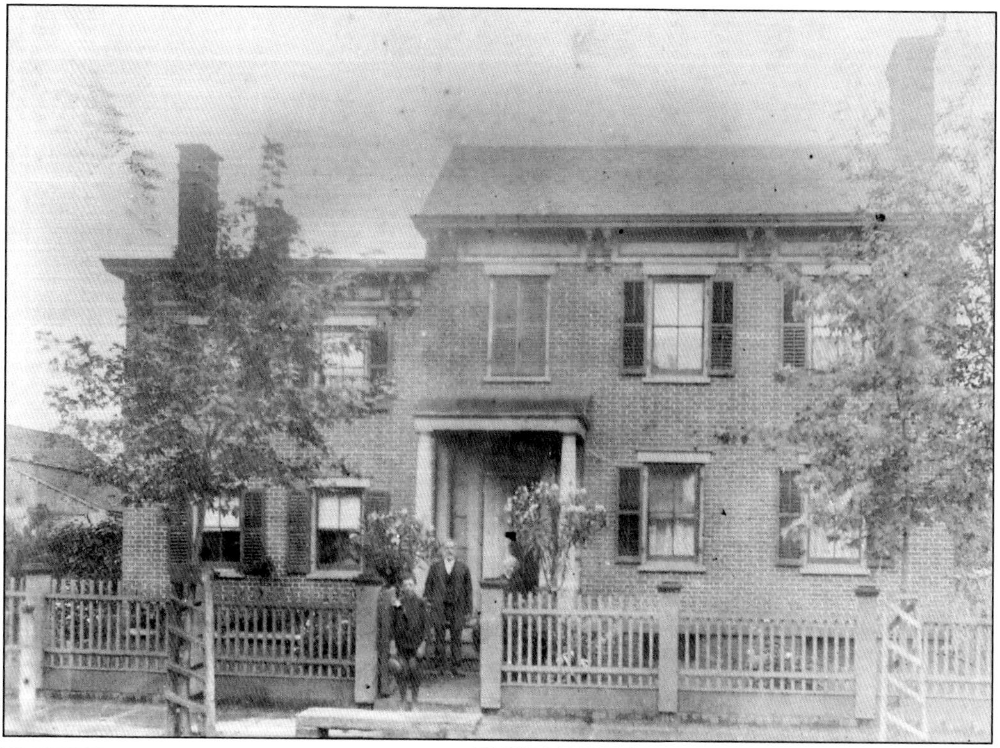

THE VANBRAKLE HOUSE, 1840. Built by George Vanbrakle in 1840, this fine brick home at 72 First Street has remains unchanged. The two-bay extension to the left in the photograph was added around the time of the Civil War. The house was nearly destroyed by fire in 1976 when the West Furniture Showroom burned less than 4 feet away.

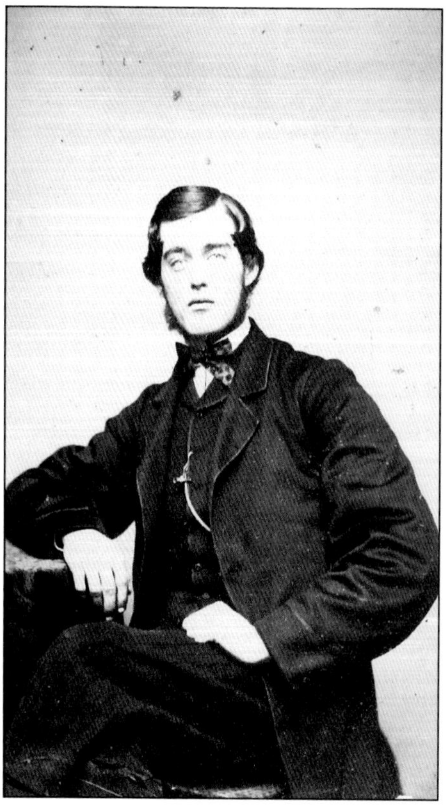

GUS CHEEVER, 1893. It is believed that this photograph was taken in Massachusetts, where Mr. Cheever often visited his relatives. The long trip from the Keyport Railroad Station would have taken about two days and cost around $14 round trip.

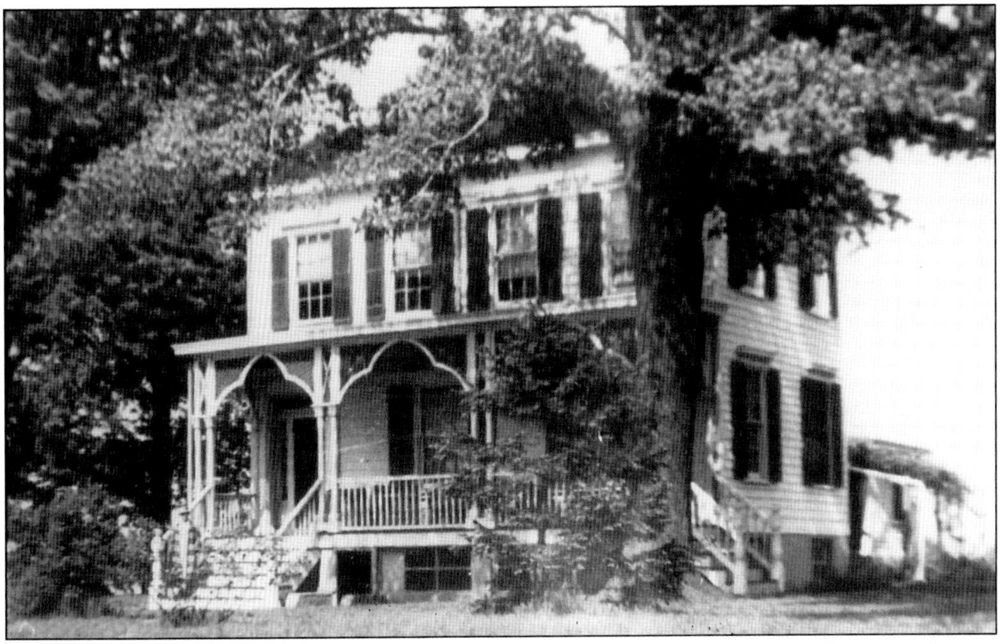

THE MOSES CHERRY HOMESTEAD, *c.* 1855. Mr. Cherry was born on July 7, 1833, about 2 miles south of Keyport. After his first wife's death he purchased 40 acres in South Keyport along Beers Street. Over the next sixty years Moses and his second wife, Hannah (Dorsett), farmed here and raised six children. In 1957 the building was destroyed by fire and is now the site of Tom's Ford.

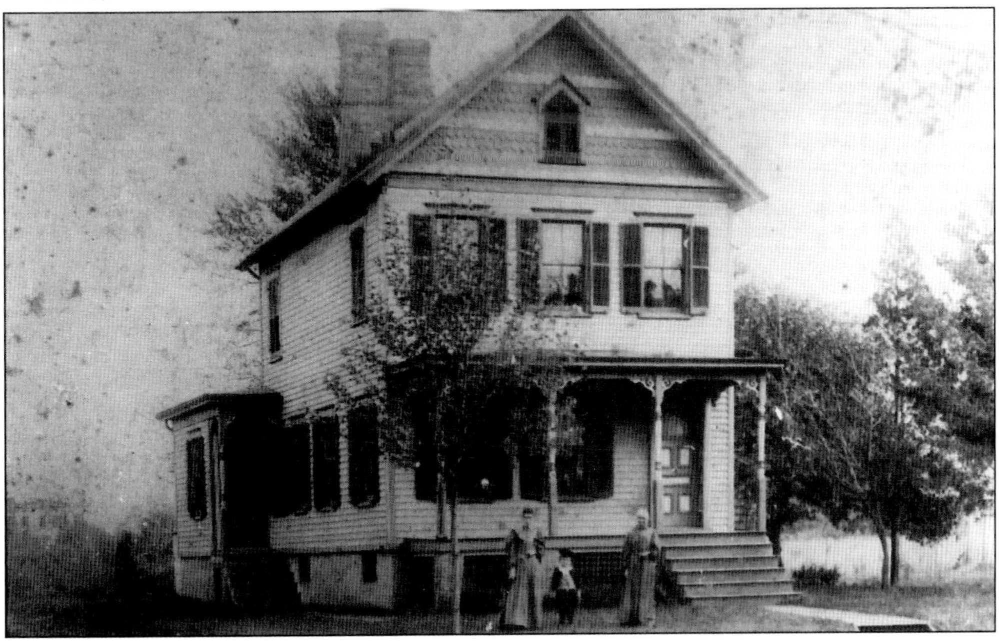

A BROAD STREET HOUSE, *c.* 1885. Three generations of this family have gathered at one of the first houses built "on the other side of tracks." Located on the southeast corner of Broad and Hurley Streets, this house was typical of many gable-front houses in town. The house also has heavy Victorian accents, and an interesting side porch and entry.

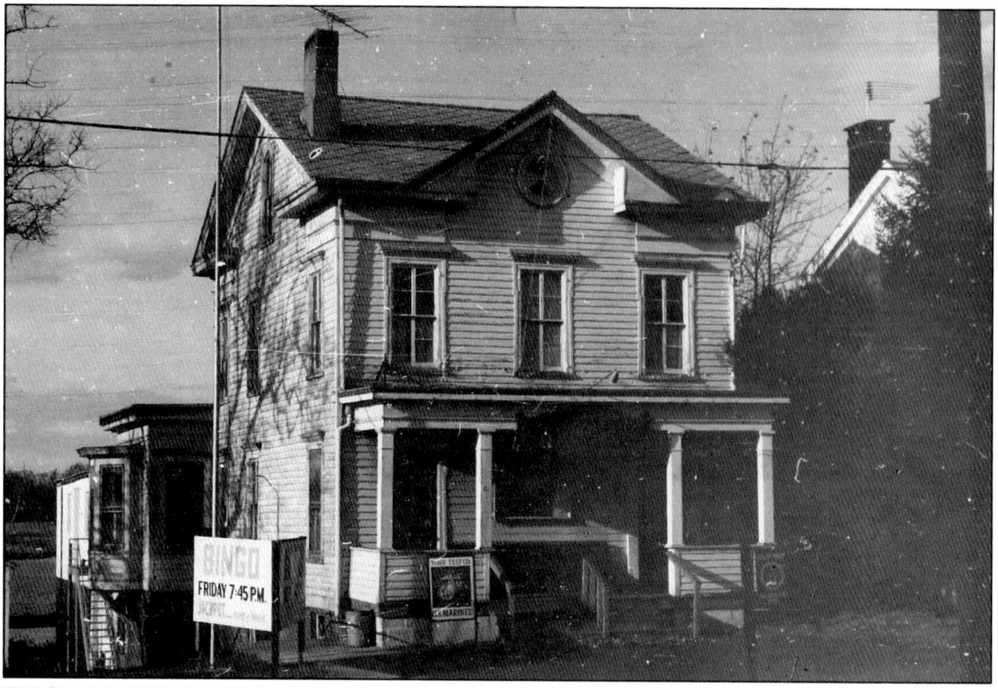

THOMAS BURROW'S HOUSE, c. 1960. Built around 1849, this house served as the residence of Thomas Burrow and the office of the T & J Burrows Lumber and Coal Co. The business opened on the north side of Front Street and soon began selling coal and building supplies to area contractors. In 1930 the American Legion Post 23 purchased the building and remodeled it (as shown in the lower photograph) into a one-story structure, totally robbed of its former elegance.

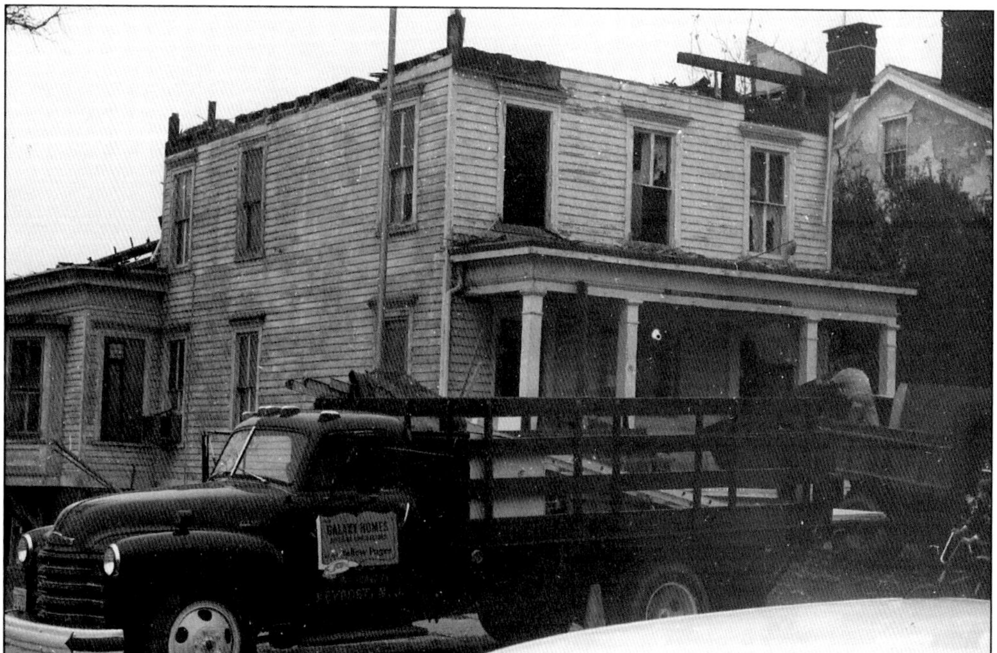

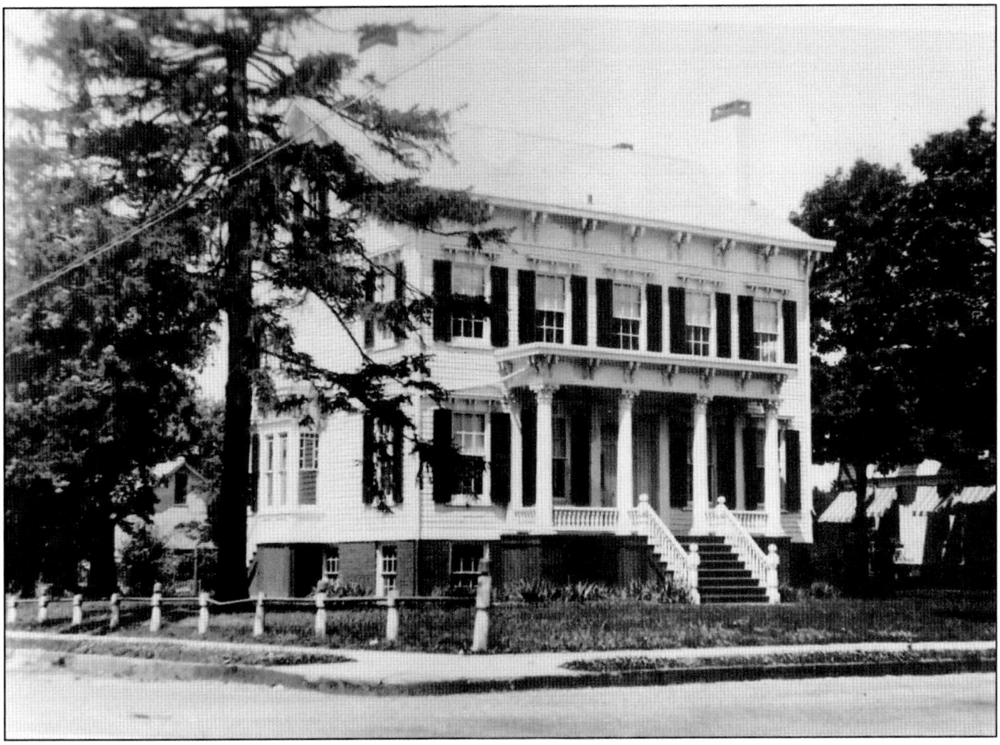

THE CORNELIUS ACKERSON HOUSE, 1935. One of Keyport's most graceful Greek Revival houses was completed on the corner of Main and Elizabeth Streets in 1865 by Joseph Beers. This house, with its fine porch and multiple fireplaces, was nearly destroyed by fire in 1932. Although heavily damaged, it was later remodeled. During the remodeling the house was lowered onto a new foundation, the porch was removed, and a small doctor's office was added to the south side.

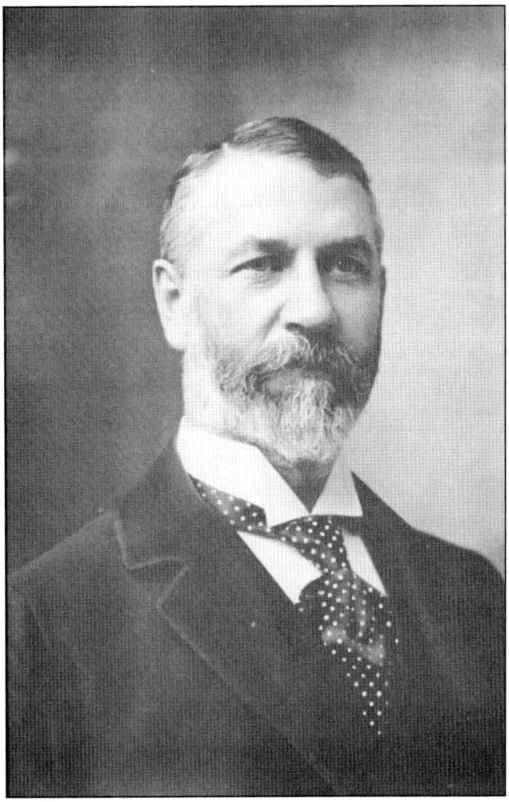

CORNELIUS ACKERSON, 1912. Born on September 11, 1852, to Captain Henry Ackerson, who was the pilot of the steamboat *Holmdel* (see Volume I), Cornelius moved to Keyport around 1874 and purchased the house shown above from the Reif Estate. Mr. Ackerson organized the People's National Bank in 1889, served as a water commissioner, and later spent thirteen years on the board of education. He died at his Main Street home on June 23, 1921, leaving a wife and two sons behind.

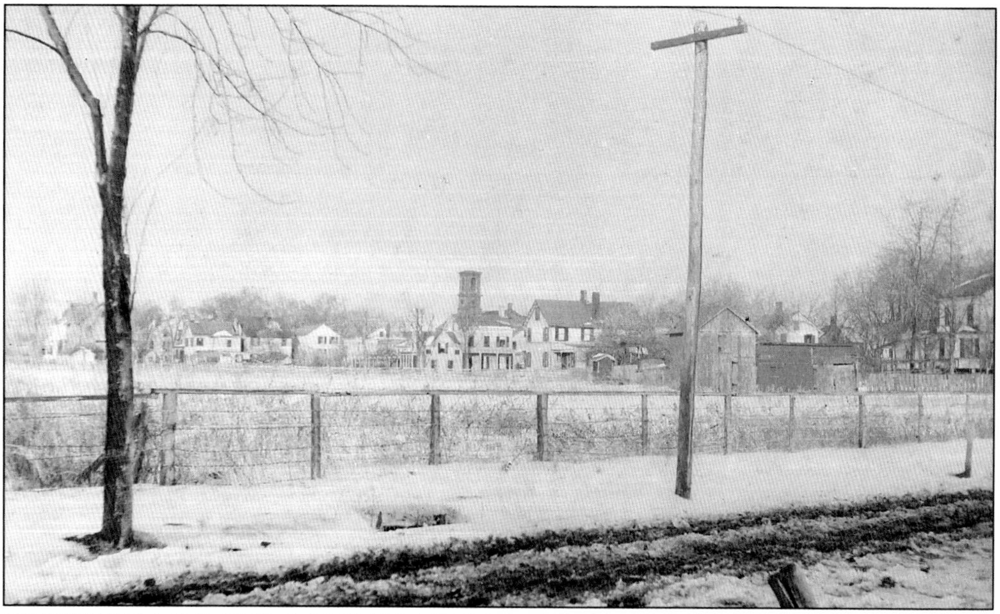

THE BROWN LUMBER COMPANY FIELD, 1900. Snow still piles up on Green Grove Avenue, though the mud isn't such a problem anymore since the streets were paved in the 1930s. This view, taken from about 80 Green Grove, looks across the lumber company's field toward Atlantic Street. Both the lumber company and the field have disappeared and been replaced by a new street, Coluco Place, and about ten new homes.

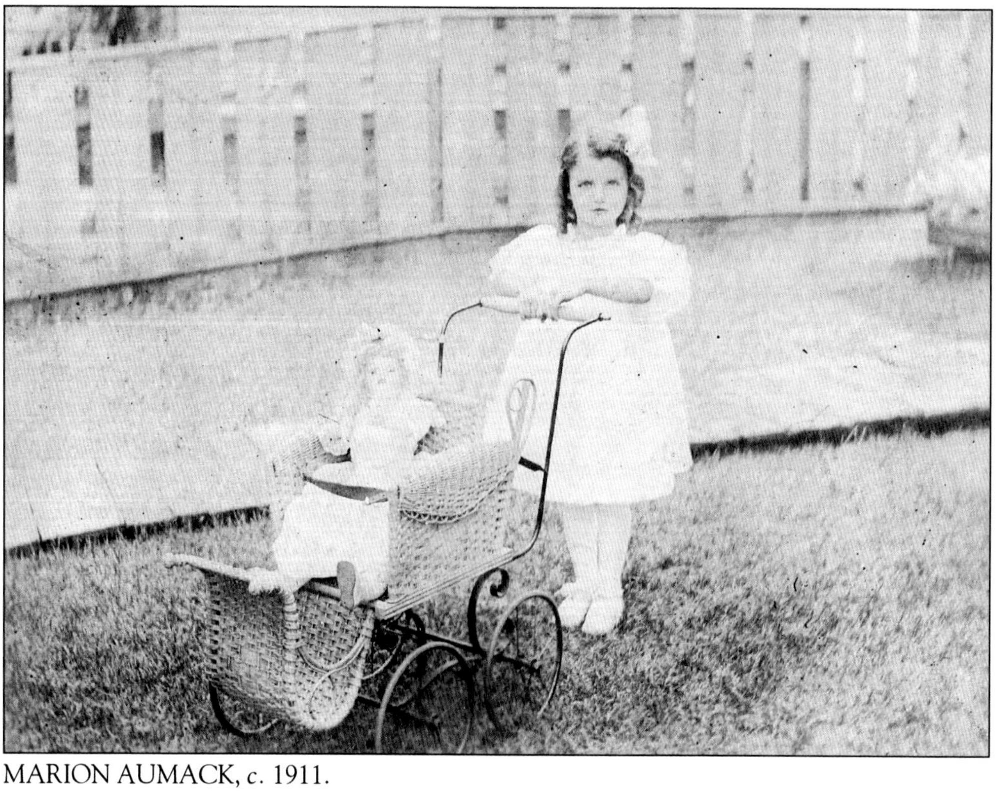

MARION AUMACK, *c.* 1911.

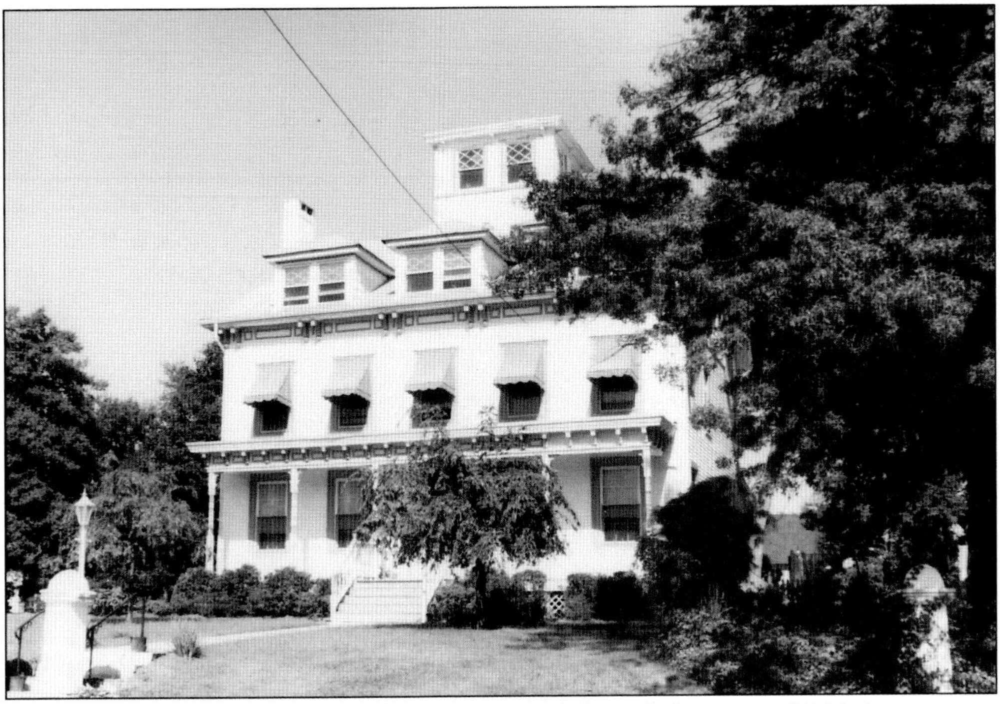

THE H.P. MOLLER HOUSE, *c.* 1880. It is rumored that sideshow legend P.T. Barnum once owned this house on Main Street. When built it was one of only three houses south of the railroad on Main Street. Only recently was the vast property sub-divided.

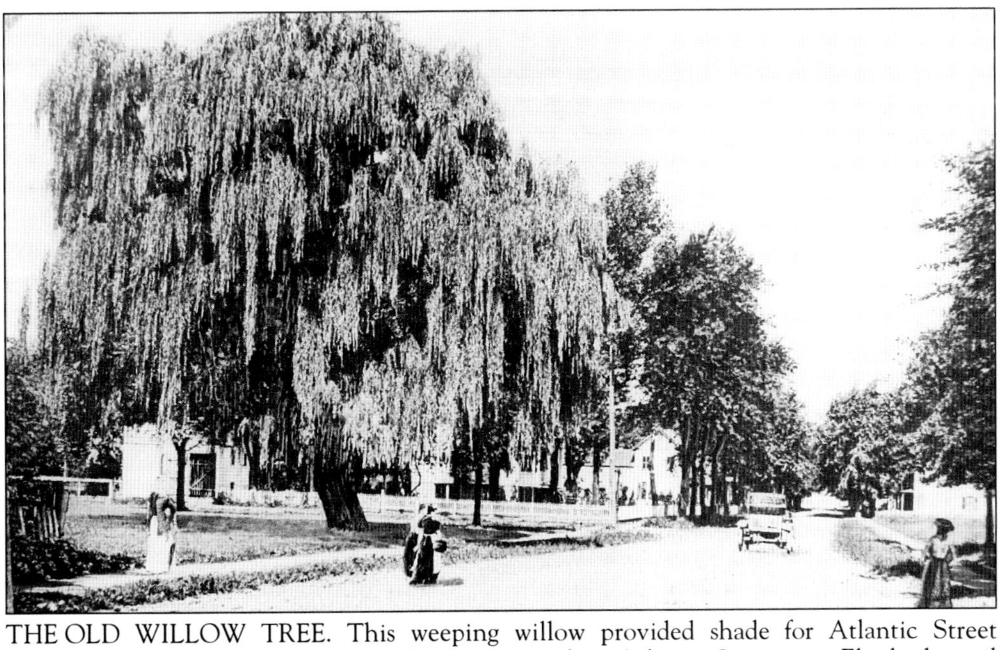

THE OLD WILLOW TREE. This weeping willow provided shade for Atlantic Street pedestrians for well over one hundred years. It stood on Atlantic Street near Elizabeth until around 1987, when it was removed due to the large amount of decay that had taken a toll on this great natural landmark.

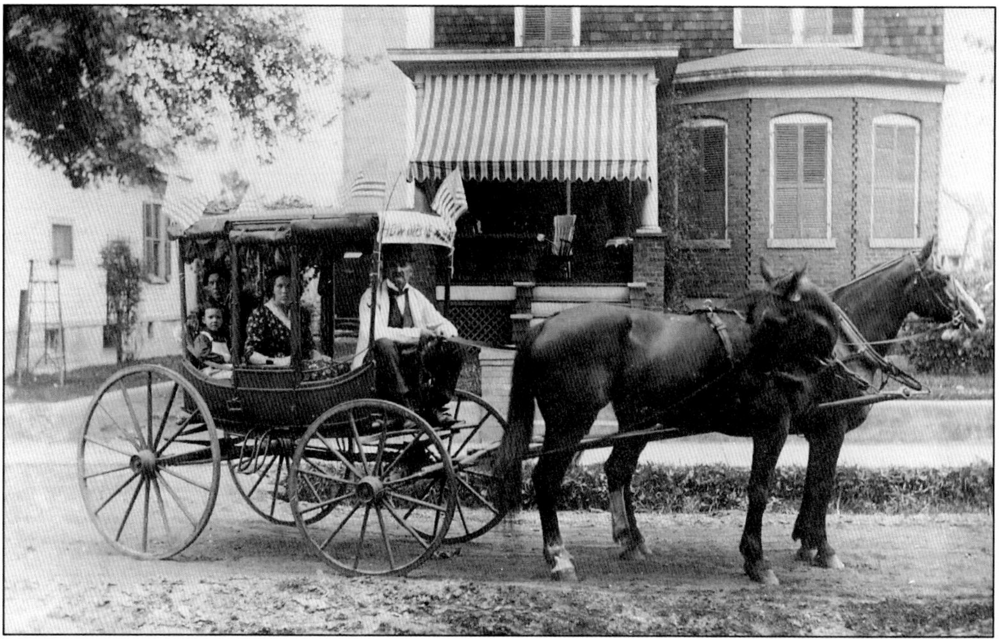

THE VAN DORN CARRIAGE, *c.* 1905. Mr. George Van Dorn was so proud of his old carriage that he hung a sign on the front that read "How old is this carriage?" Well, one may ask, just how old was that carriage? Records indicate that it was built in 1805 in New York City and had been in the family since it was new. Mr. Van Dorn and his family stopped for this photograph in front of the house that George built on Division Street in 1891.

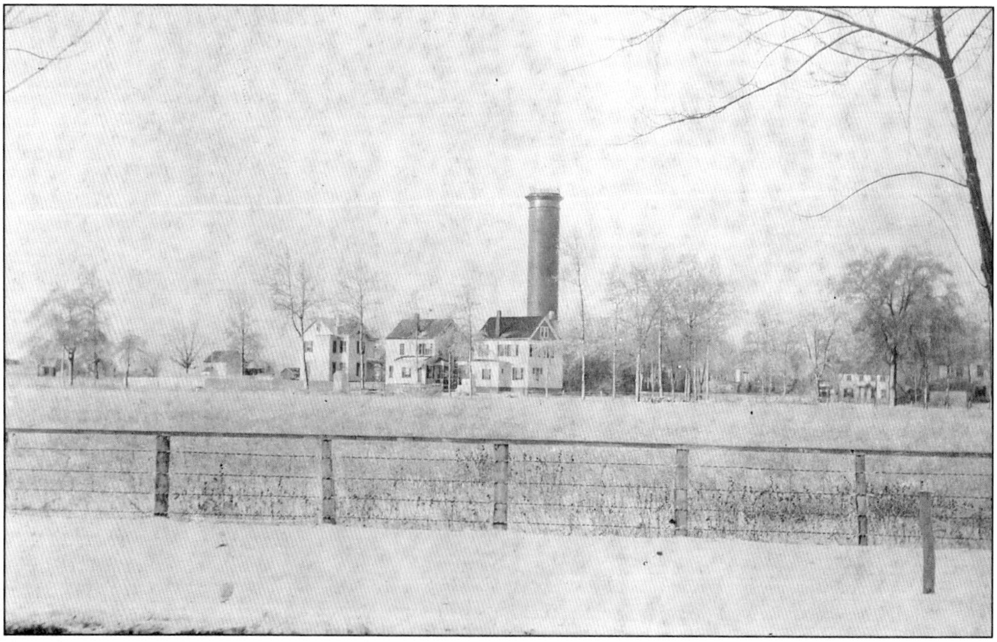

AN OLD STANDPIPE VIEW. Taken in the winter of 1900, this view clearly shows how rural parts of town were in the early twentieth century. The houses in the foreground had recently been completed while the house to the right was built around 1830. Today, this area is engulfed by single family homes.

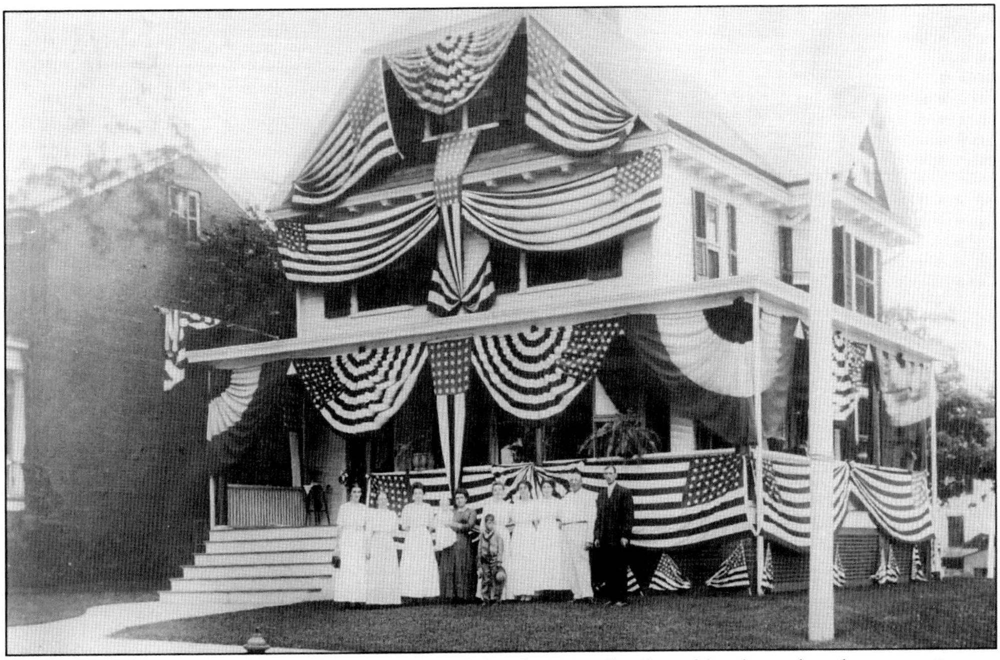

FOURTH OF JULY, *c.* 1902. OK, so some of the flags are displayed backwards, who cares, it sure looked great anyway. Here the whole family gathers for the celebration of Independence Day at their home on the southeast corner of Front and Beers Streets. This house was recently remodeled into professional offices after being a runner up in the most-broken-down-house-in-town contest. It is both a rare and fine example of late-nineteenth-century Shingle-style architecture.

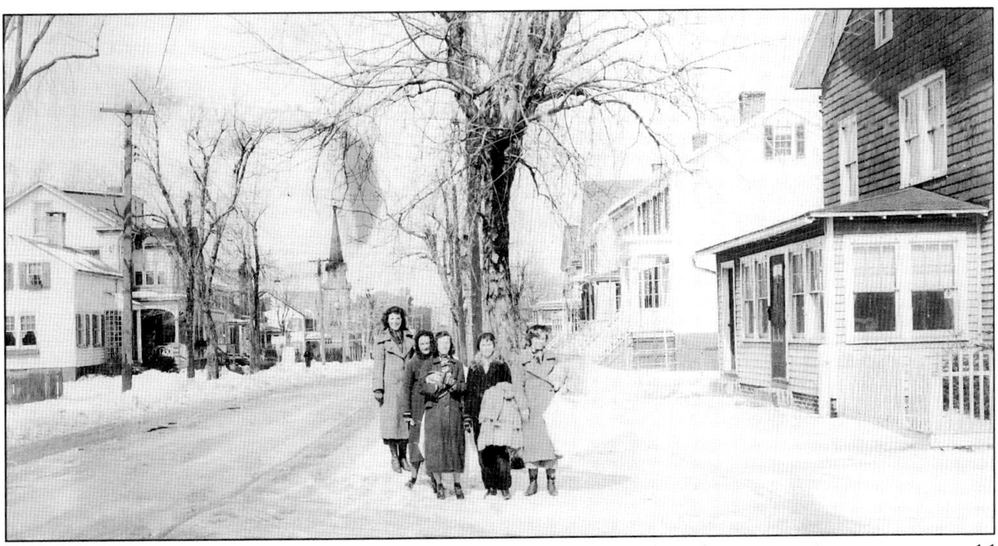

HIGH SCHOOL FRIENDS. Posed on the corner of Broad and Warren Streets on a cold February in 1936 are, from left to right, Marjorie Morley, Aileen Dolson Preston, Norrine Jones Schanck, Gerry Morley Lawlor, and Mildred Morley. Norrine Jones married J. Leon Schanck Jr. on January 26, 1941. After raising two children, Patricia Norrine (Doehler) and Martha Jean (Galloway), she helped organize the Keyport Historical Society in 1972, and retired as a teacher from the Keyport School District in the 1980s.

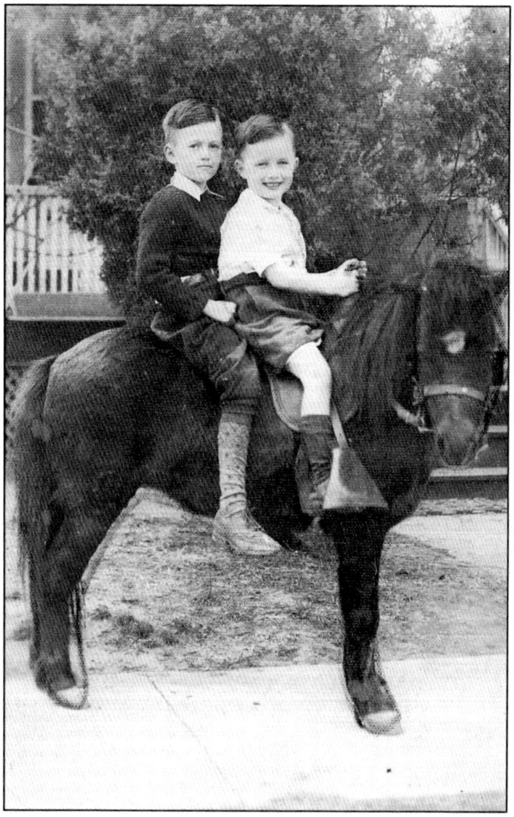

YOUNG BOYS ON A PONY, 1943. What could be better than playing cowboys and indians? How about a pint-size horse that could be delivered to your door? For 75¢ youngsters could ride for about thirty minutes. The boys are John and Gene Regan and the place is the boys' home at 2 Spring Street.

A COVERED WAGON, c. 1900. During the latter half of the nineteenth century, local wagon builders produced all types of one-of-a-kind jobs. This two-horse hitch is pulling what could be described as a pullman coach, which carried both people and cargo as well. Note the photographer's shadow in the foreground.

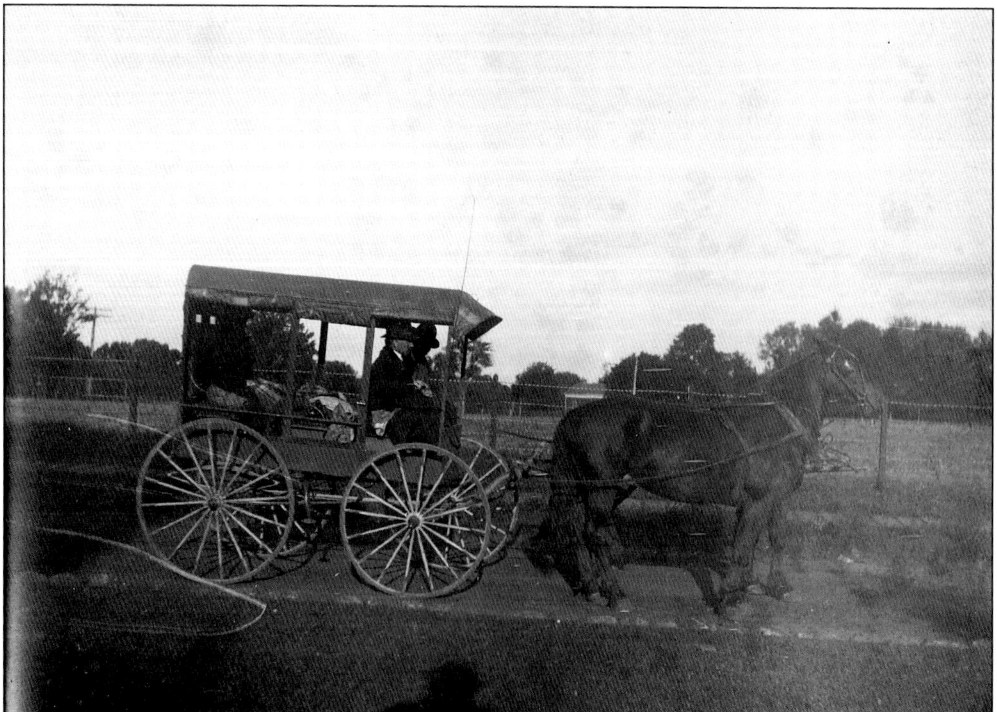

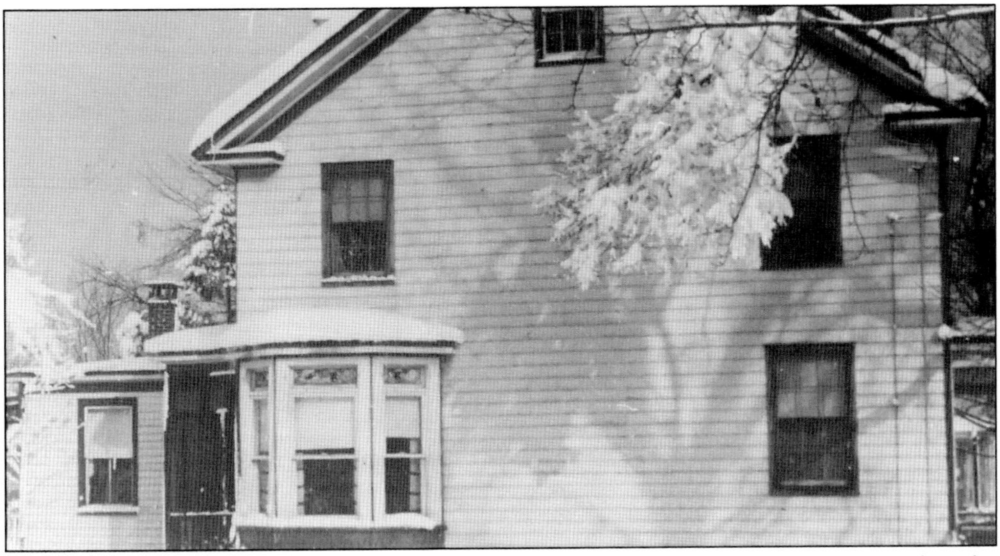

THE CUTTRELL HOUSE, *c.* 1940. Another of Keyport's oldest houses can be found in the Browns Point area at the foot of Broadway. Built sometime after the Revolution by ship captain and boat builder James Cuttrell, this structure remains much as it did when Mr. Cuttrell and his family moved in nearly two hundred years ago. The original detached kitchen, which was built around 1821, is located in the backyard of this house.

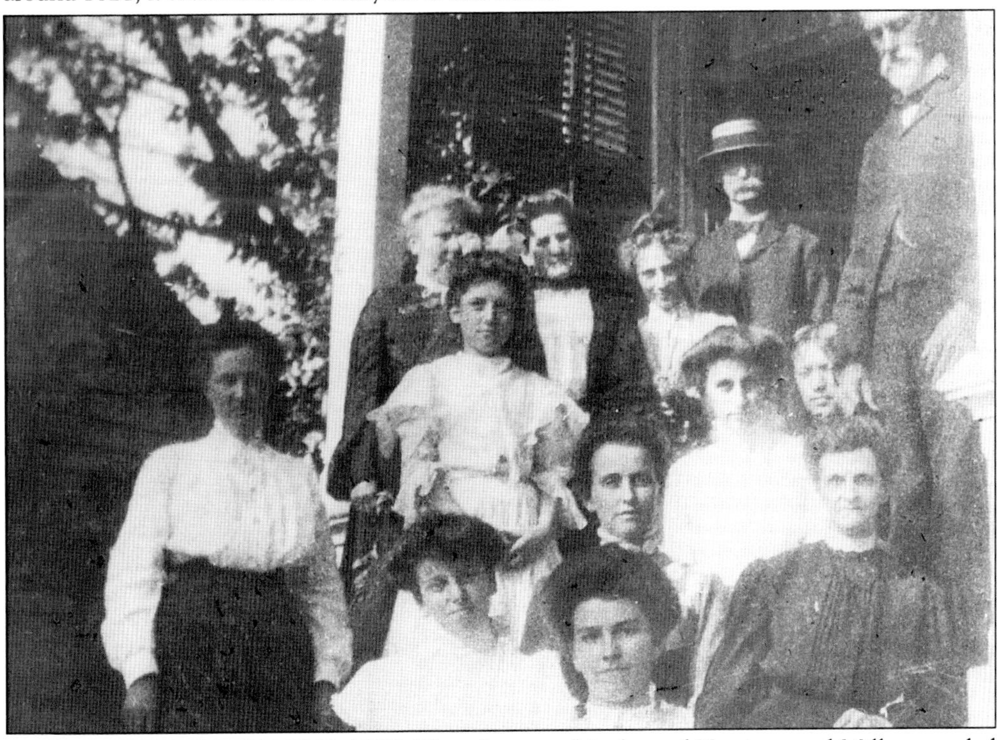

THE VANDERBILT FAMILY, 1897. The photographic firm of Hastings and Miller traveled from New York to Keyport to photograph the Vanderbilt family at their homestead at 25 Green Grove Avenue. One of the men in the view may be Albert Vanderbilt, who tragically took his own life in the backyard garage in 1935.

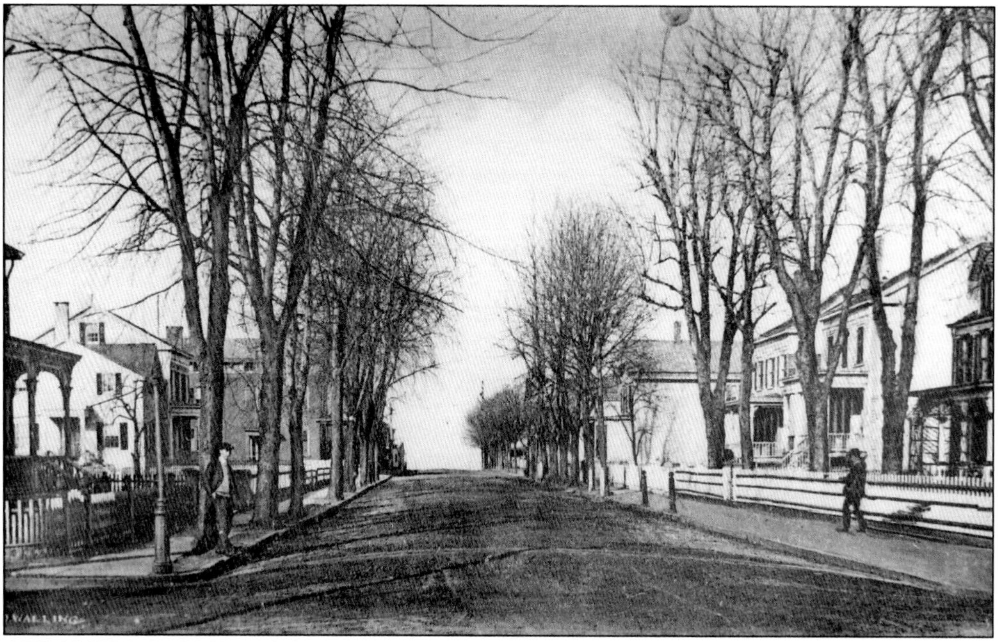

ATLANTIC STREET LOOKING NORTH, 1899. This view gives a good indication of the residential area along Atlantic Street during the late nineteenth century. The original builders of these houses are, from left to right, as follows: G.M. Tilton, Samuel Tilton, J. Storms, Mrs. Stevenson, J. Dorsett, C. Stout, and W. Collins.

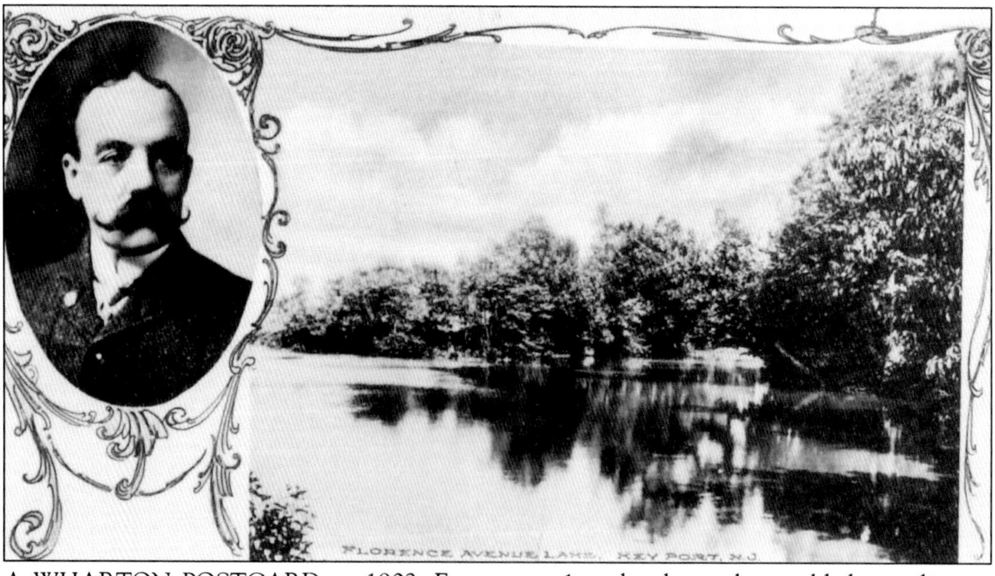

A WHARTON POSTCARD, *c.* 1902. For a mere 1¢ a local traveler could drop a line to a relative back home at the turn of the century. One of the many local photographers and postcard publishers was William C. Wharton. Wharton lived in Mechanicsville and when not using his camera and tripod he volunteered his time with the Liberty Hose Co., which he helped organize in 1893.

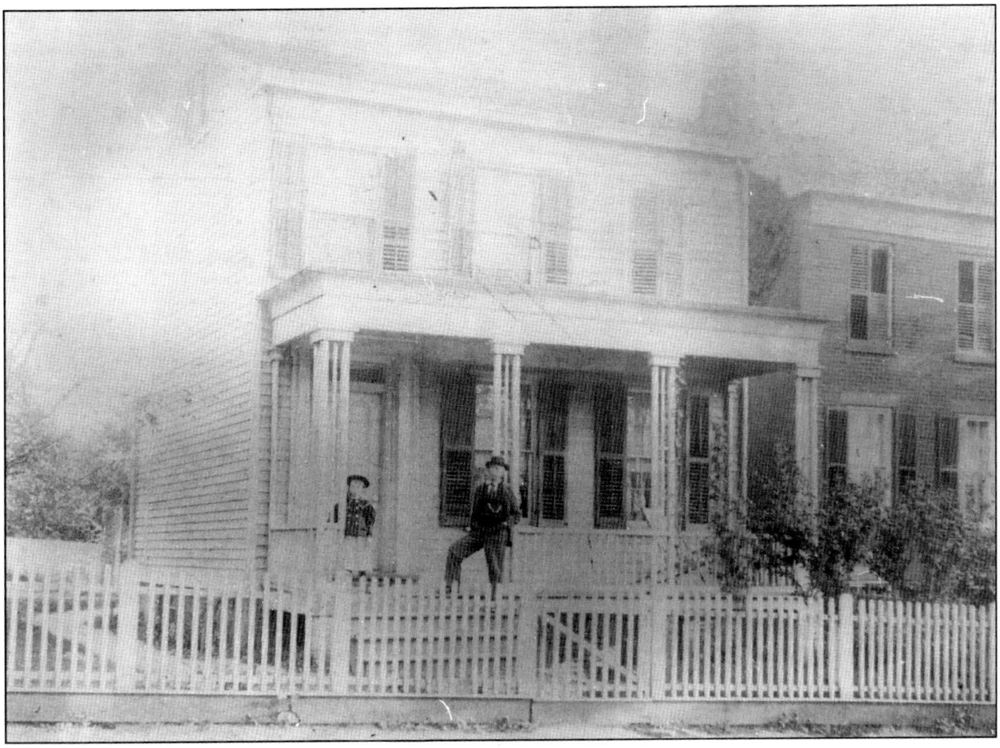

THE CAPTAIN LUFF HOUSE, 1874. During the mid-nineteenth century most of Keyport's ship captains built their houses overlooking the bay and its fleet. Captain G.W. Luff completed this house on the south side of Front Street in 1854, while the brick house next door was finished in 1838. This quaint frame home still retains the unique porch columns, while the fence was removed in the 1930s. The man on the porch just might be the ole' Captain himself.

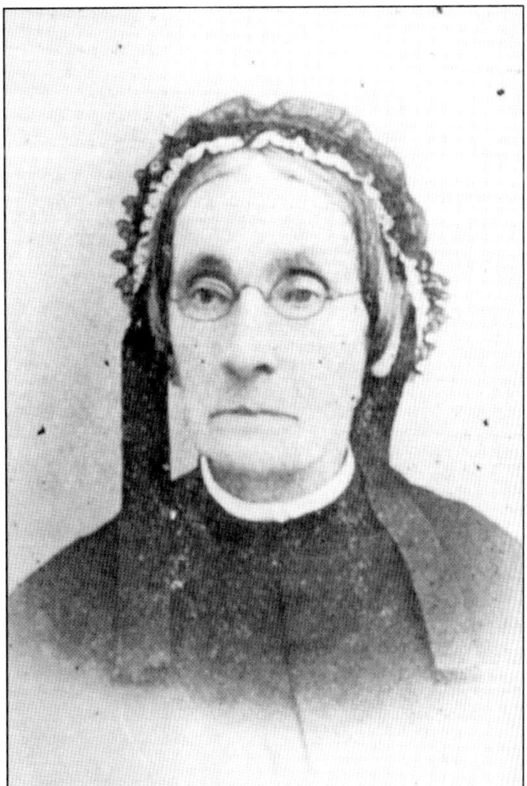

MRS. SUSAN B. WHARTON. Mrs. Wharton was an active member of the Methodist Episcopal Church during the early part of the twentieth century. She was responsible for organizing the first Sunday school in the village, which began in 1835. It is said that children of all ages and colors were welcome to learn in the house on First Street (see Volume I, p. 12). Mrs. Wharton lived into the late nineteenth century and will always be remembered for her pioneering teaching spirit.

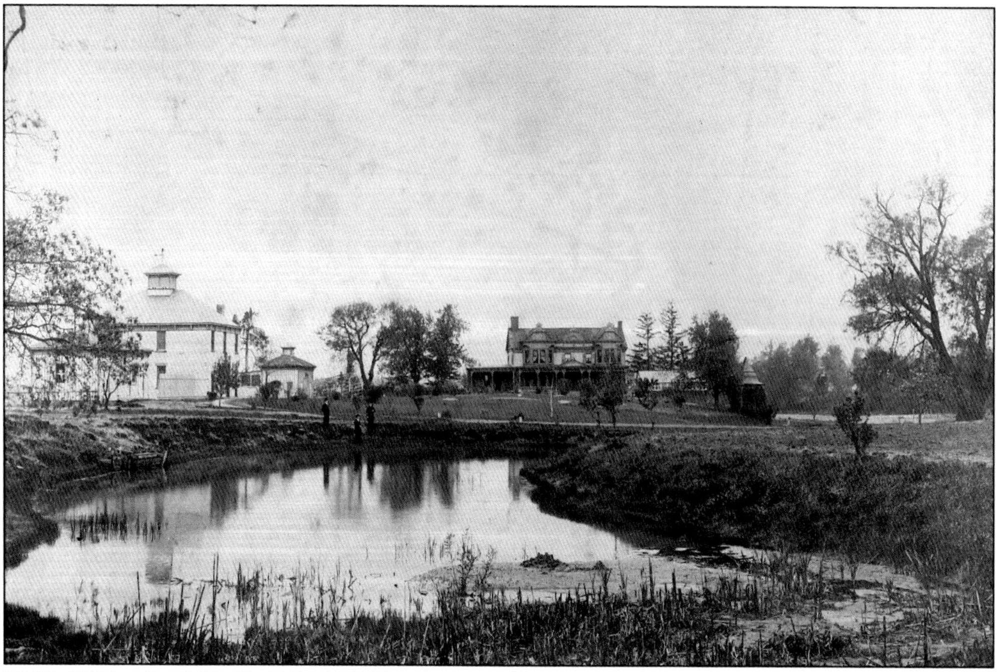

THE KEY GROVE PLANTATION, *c.* 1904/1996. One of the finest views of the Key Grove Manor house and outbuildings is the one above, taken in 1904. The house, which was approaching its 200th birthday in 1914, appeared as solid and stately as the day it was built. The building to the left served as the carriage house and stable, while the fine pagoda overlooking the creek can be seen to the right in the photograph (see Volume I for a complete history). During the winter all of Keyport's youngsters would skate and sleigh ride on the grounds of this forgotten landmark.

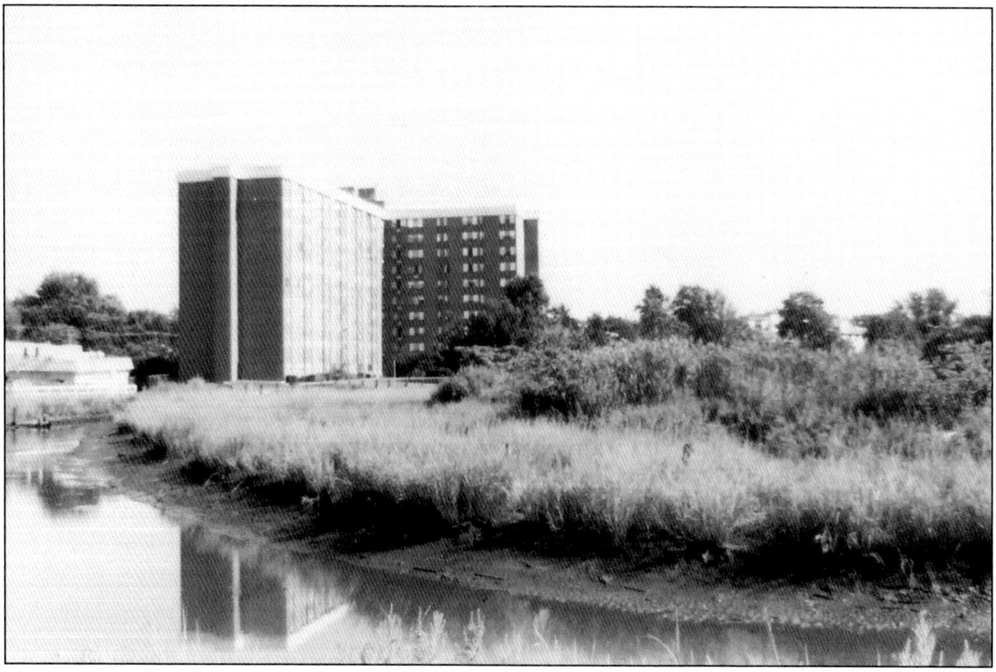

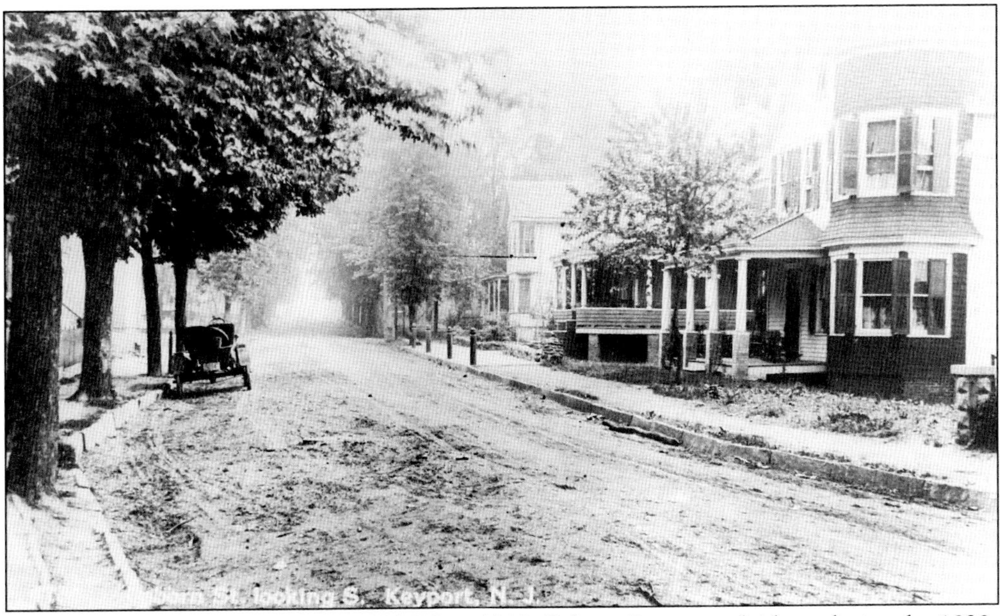

OSBORN STREET LOOKING SOUTH, *c.* 1909. Osborn Street was laid out during the 1830s and was named in honor of Squire Ezra Osborn, who was one of the first men to buy land in the new town. It runs from East Front Street to Maple Place, where it is intersected by the railroad; it then continues to Union Street, where it dead ends at the Keyport Central School.

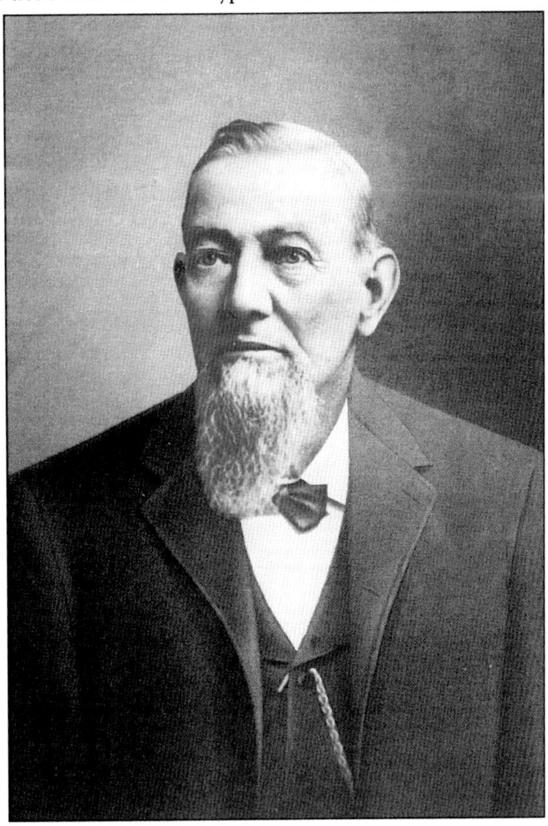

DAVID A. WALLING, *c.* 1910. Mr. Walling was born in Keyport on August 29, 1832, just two years after the town was created. He left Keyport in the 1850s for New York City, where he became a cabin boy on the high seas. During the Civil War he commanded a Union supply vessel, and at one time barely escaped from the hands of the Confederates. Captain Walling died, a most respected man, in Tinton Falls on April 7, 1914.

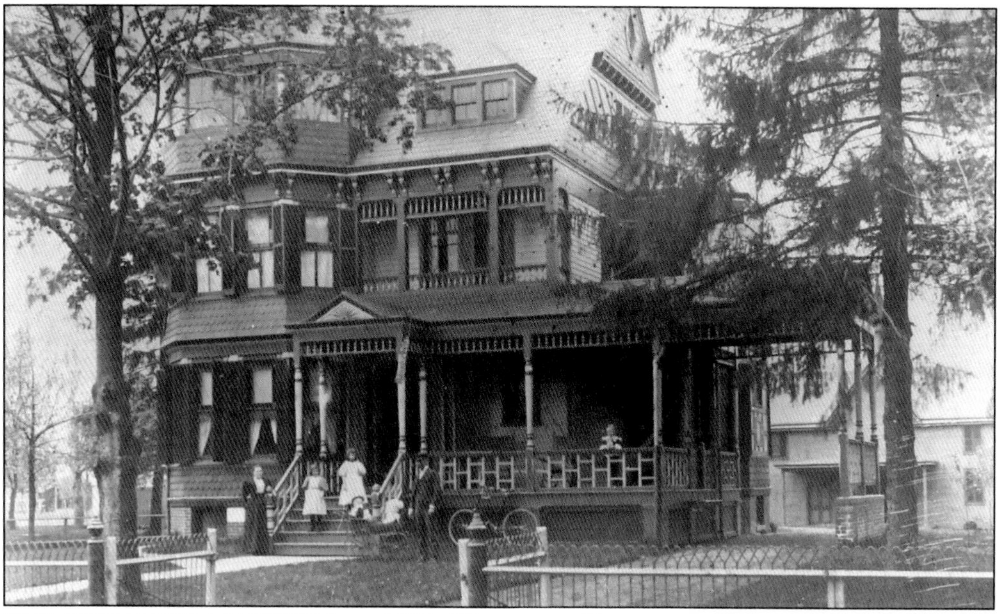

THE SCHANCK MANSION, *c.* 1888. Winters in Keyport could be cruel, and John G. Schanck knew what the people needed. By the close of the nineteenth century almost all houses burned coal for heat, either in pot-bellied stoves or those new things called "furnaces." J.G. Schanck opened his business at Broad and Mott Streets in 1880 and soon after built this beautiful Victorian, Shingle-style house on Main Street in 1886. It still stands, minus the fancy trim, as an apartment building.

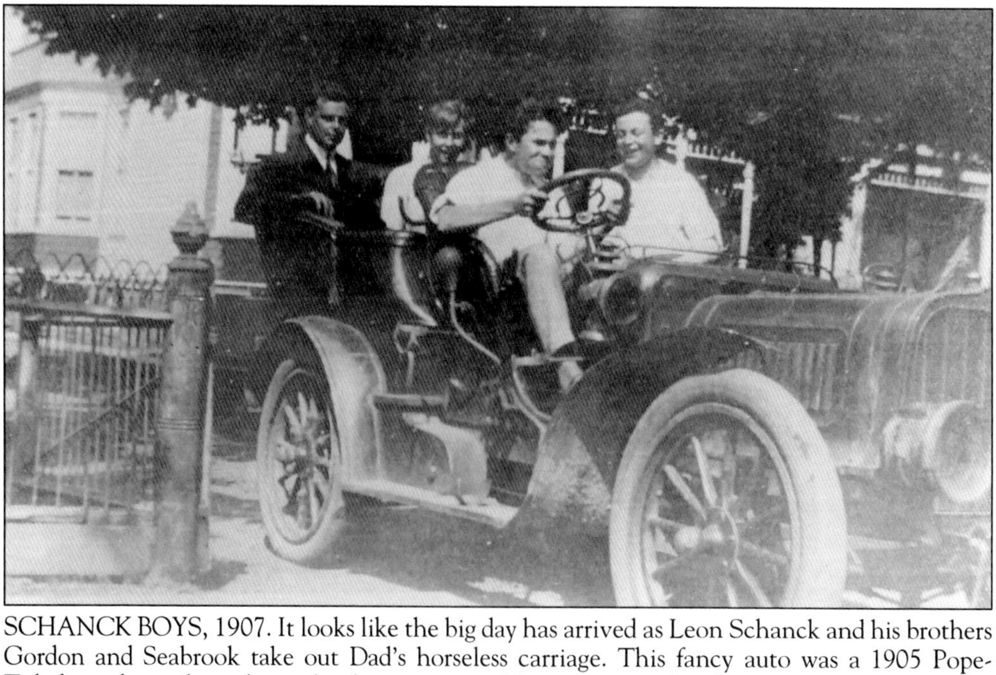

SCHANCK BOYS, 1907. It looks like the big day has arrived as Leon Schanck and his brothers Gordon and Seabrook take out Dad's horseless carriage. This fancy auto was a 1905 Pope-Toledo and may have been the first car owned by a Keyport family. The man in the suit is Percy Kingland. The car is pulling out the driveway of the house at the top of the page on Main Street.

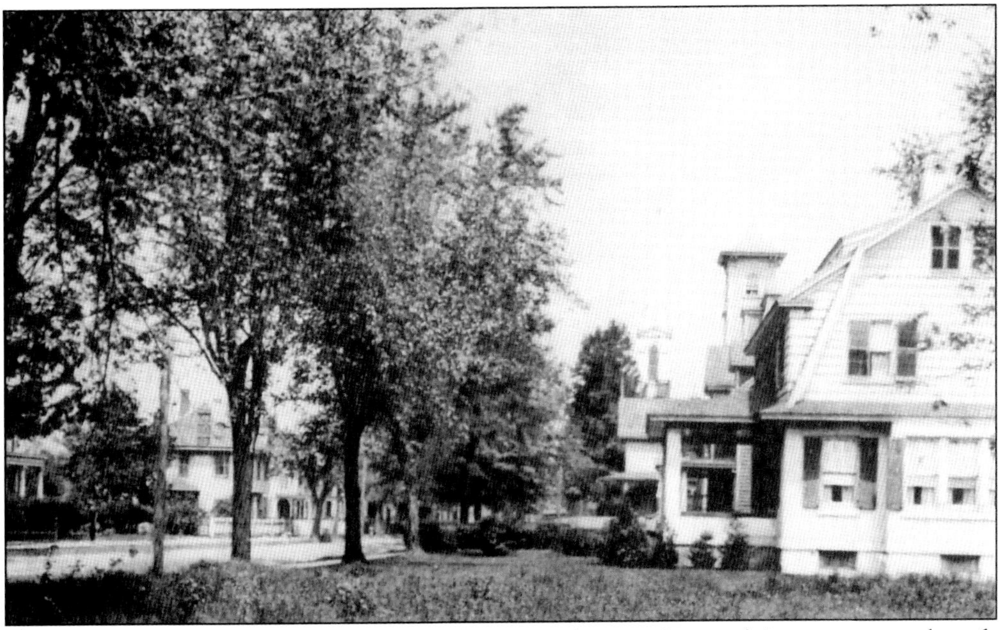

MAIN STREET LOOKING NORTH. After 1910 the popularity of American postal cards began to decline due in great part to the arrival of the telephone. One of the last black-and-white cards of Keyport was this one which shows Main Street, north from Warren Street.

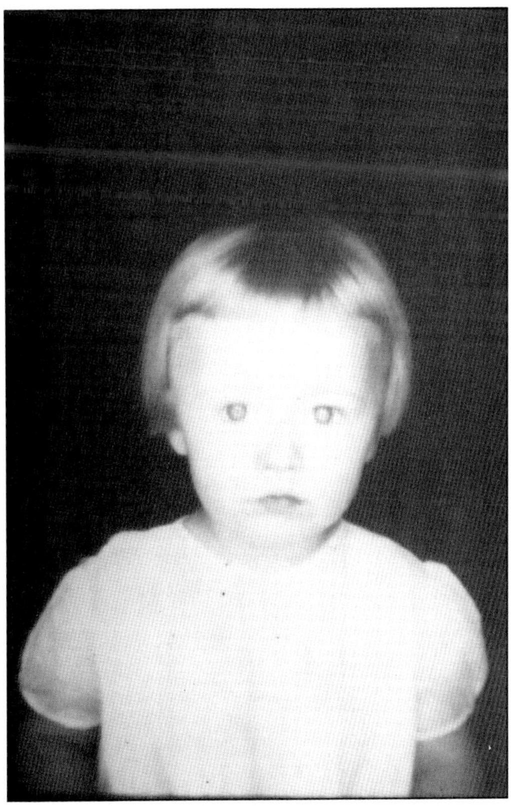

BETTY JEAN MEYERS. Little Miss Meyers appears a little scared in this view. Such experiences with a stranger (the photographer) have caused more than one tear to be shed by a shy child. The year was 1937, and little Betty was just about five years old.

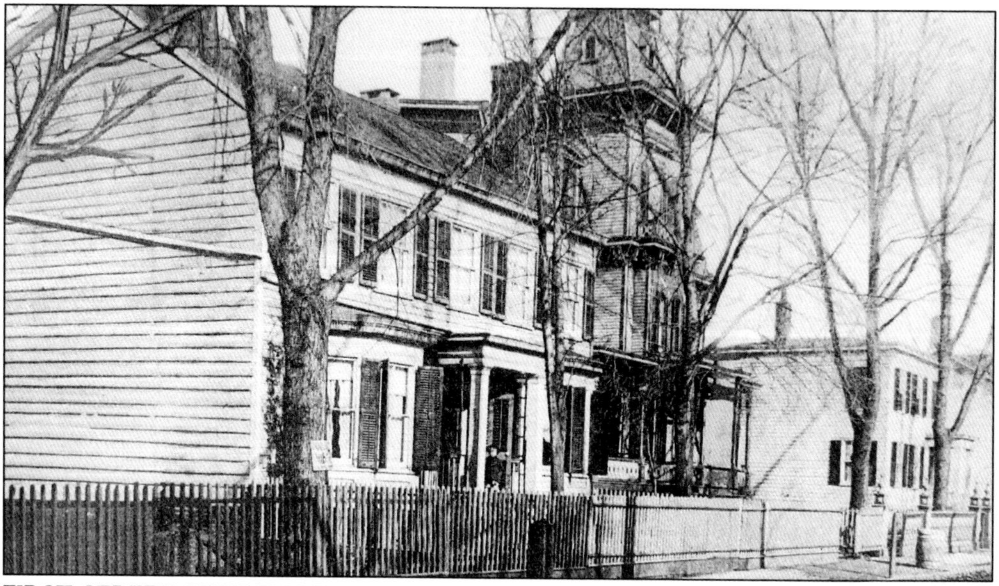

FIRST STREET RESIDENCES, *c.* 1900. Before 1835, First Street was nothing more than a small path that wandered along the shore front. By 1835 the street was laid out and in 1844 Keyport's second doctor, J. Edgar Arrowsmith, built the nice-looking frame house in the foreground on the north side of the street. Dr. Arrowsmith was elected village postmaster in 1856 and served until 1861. He died at his home on January 3, 1900, after fifty-six years of caring for the town's sick and injured.

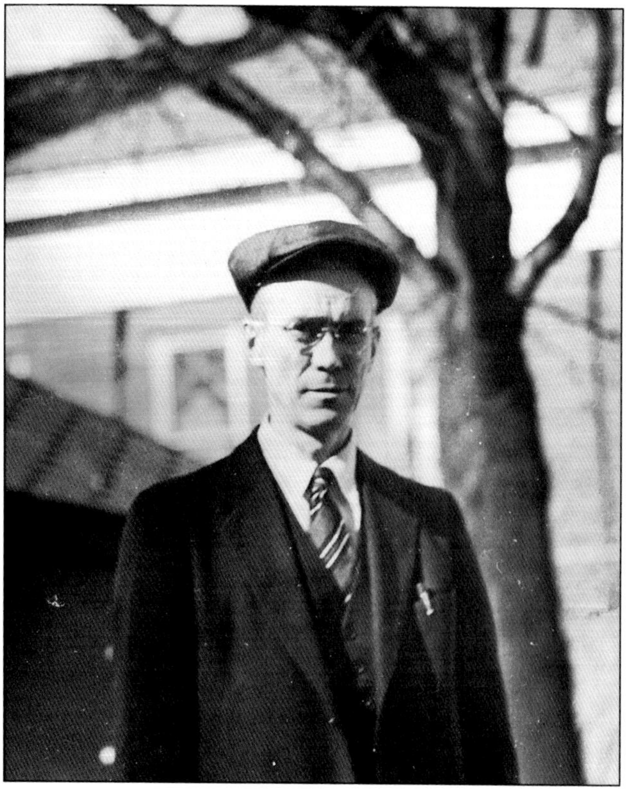

JAMES LEWIS, *c.* 1930. Many of the images from the early twentieth century in this book were taken by Mr. Lewis. He took to the air on several occasions for the first aerial views of the town during the 1930s.

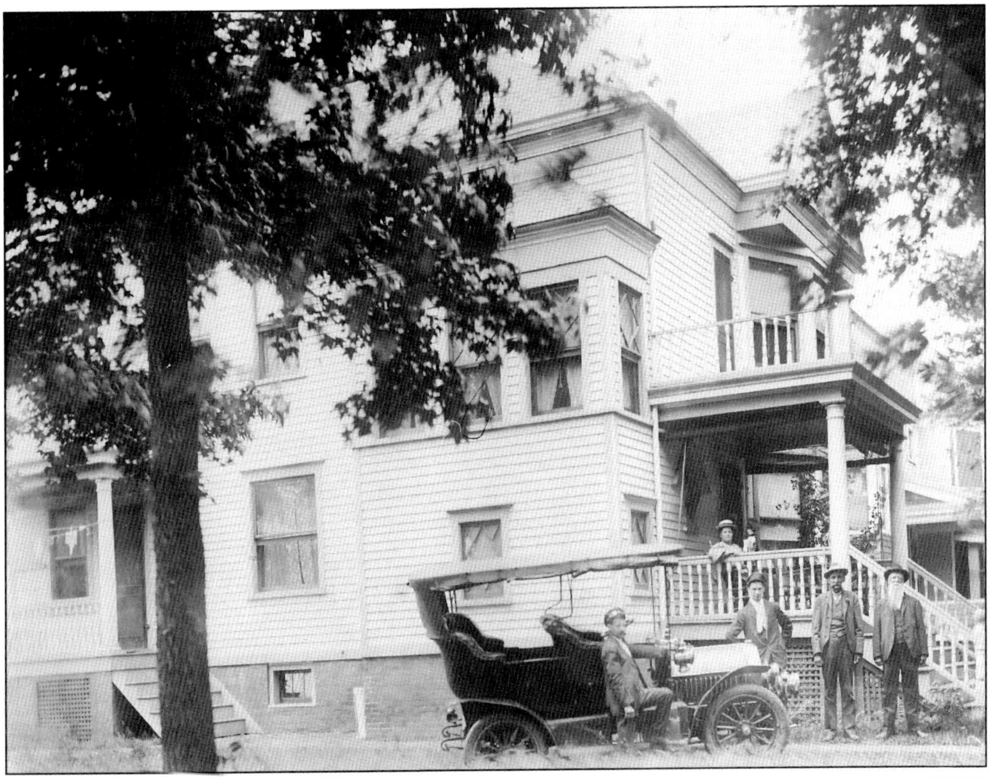

ATLANTIC STREET, 1910. This excited group of people gathered along one of Keyport's only multiple groups of identical houses which came much before the "great subdivisions" of the late 1950s. Four of the houses are identical; the last two face the opposite direction. They were built on the east side of Atlantic Street around 1903.

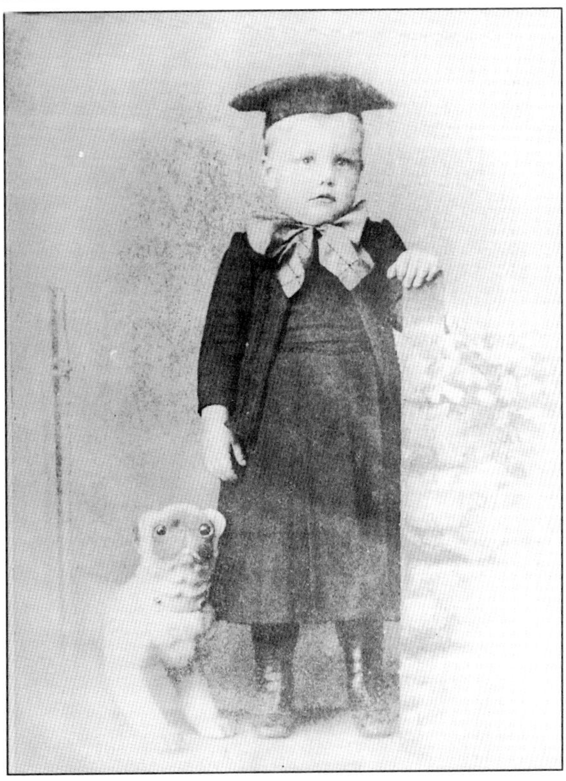

A YOUNG BOY WITH HIS DOG, c. 1890. It is hard to tell if the dog in this photograph is real or an early and accurate stuffed animal. The unidentified young man is either dressed for graduation or has just returned from a trip abroad.

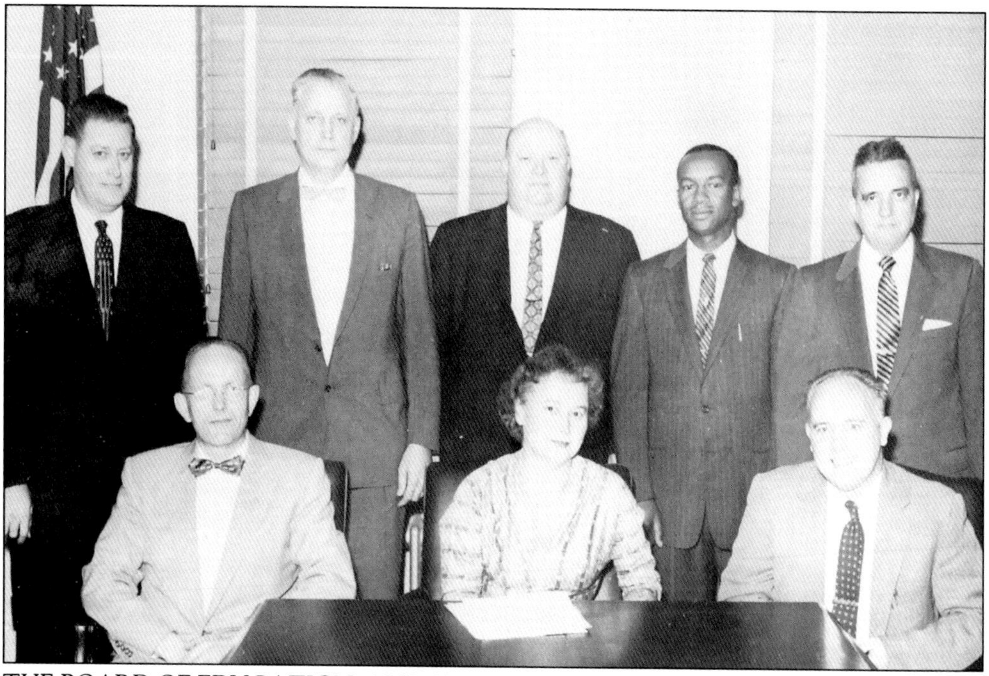

THE BOARD OF EDUCATION, 1958. Keyport schools were governed by a board of trustees until 1901, when it was voted upon to form a board of education. From left to right are as follows: (seated) H. Boggs, L. McAneny, and C. Hopla; (standing) L. Prager, H. Collard, W. Ormerod, P. Washington, and K. Wharton.

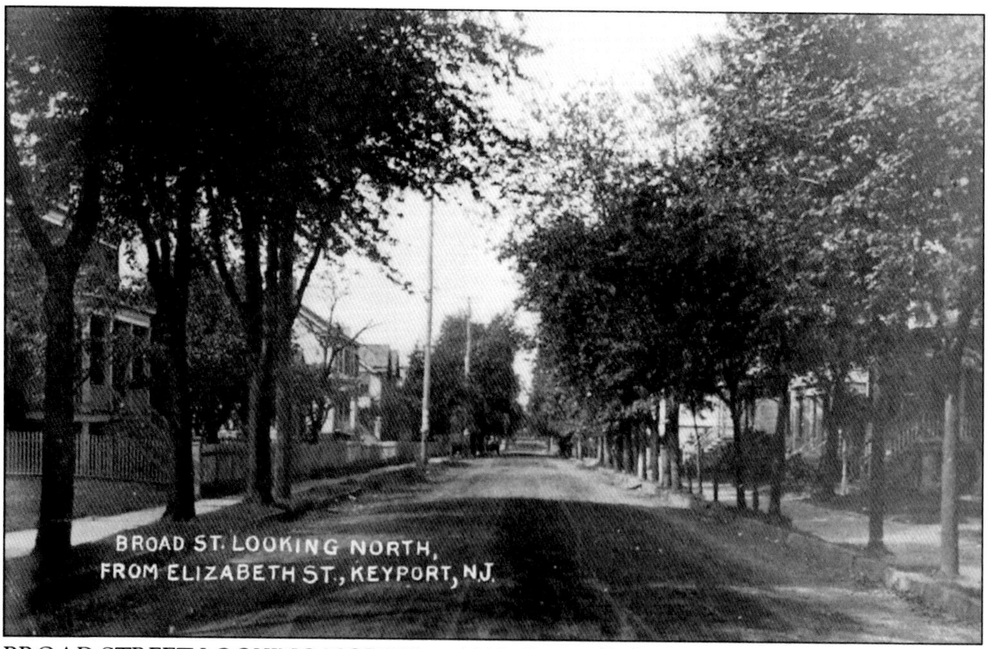

BROAD STREET LOOKING NORTH, *c.* 1910. Originally laid out in 1830, Broad Street was one of the finest residential streets in the village. Some of the first to build upon its lots were Asher Holmes (in 1840) and Henry Cherry (in 1854).

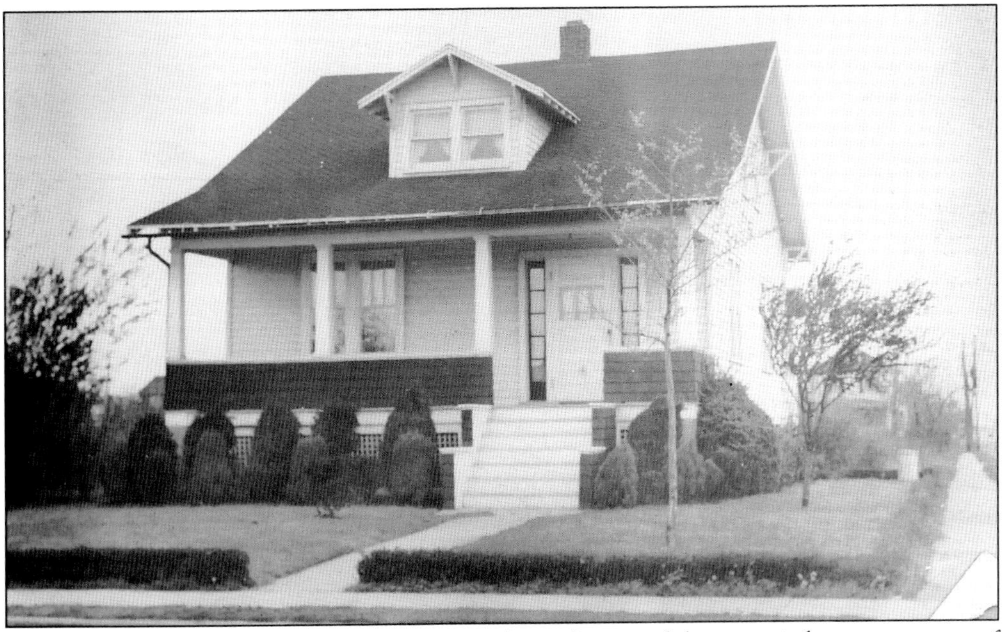

A HOUSE ON MAIN STREET, *c.* 1920. By the early part of the twentieth century, most of central Keyport had been built up, leaving the southern end to new development. During the 1910s Craftsmen-style or oversized bungalows, such as this one on the northeast corner of Main and Jackson Streets, began to appear.

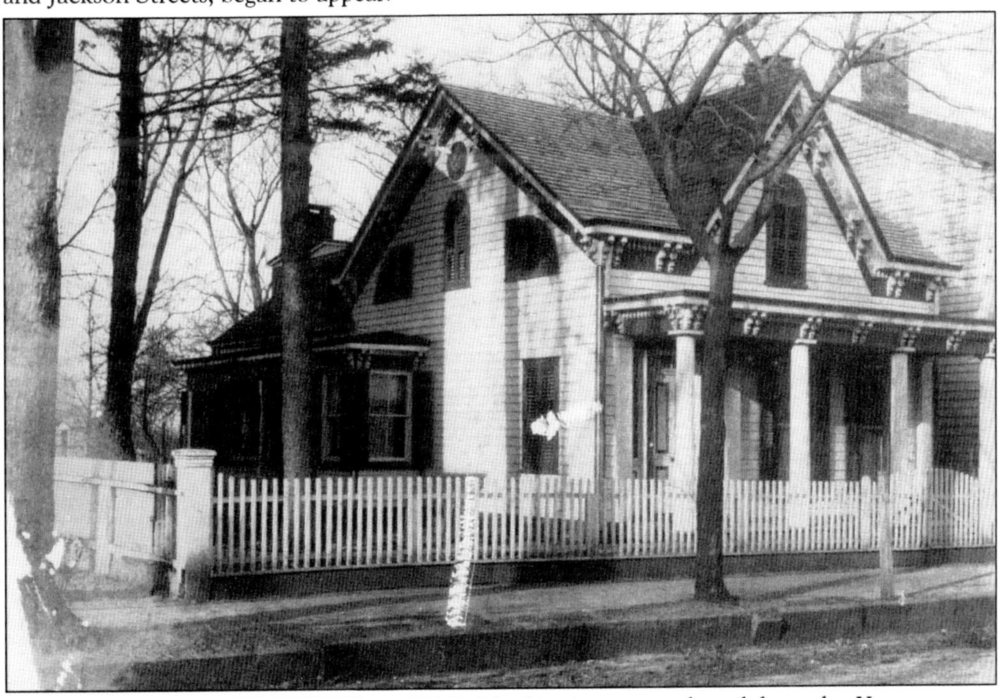

THE I.K. LIPPINCOTT HOUSE, *c.* 1835. Mr. Lippincott purchased from the Kearny estate lot numbers 1, 7, and 9 in November 1829. Soon after he erected this small cottage upon lot number 1, which eventually became 34 Main Street. In 1995 the house was restored to its former splendor by owner Bill Cerase. It is now operated as an antiques business.

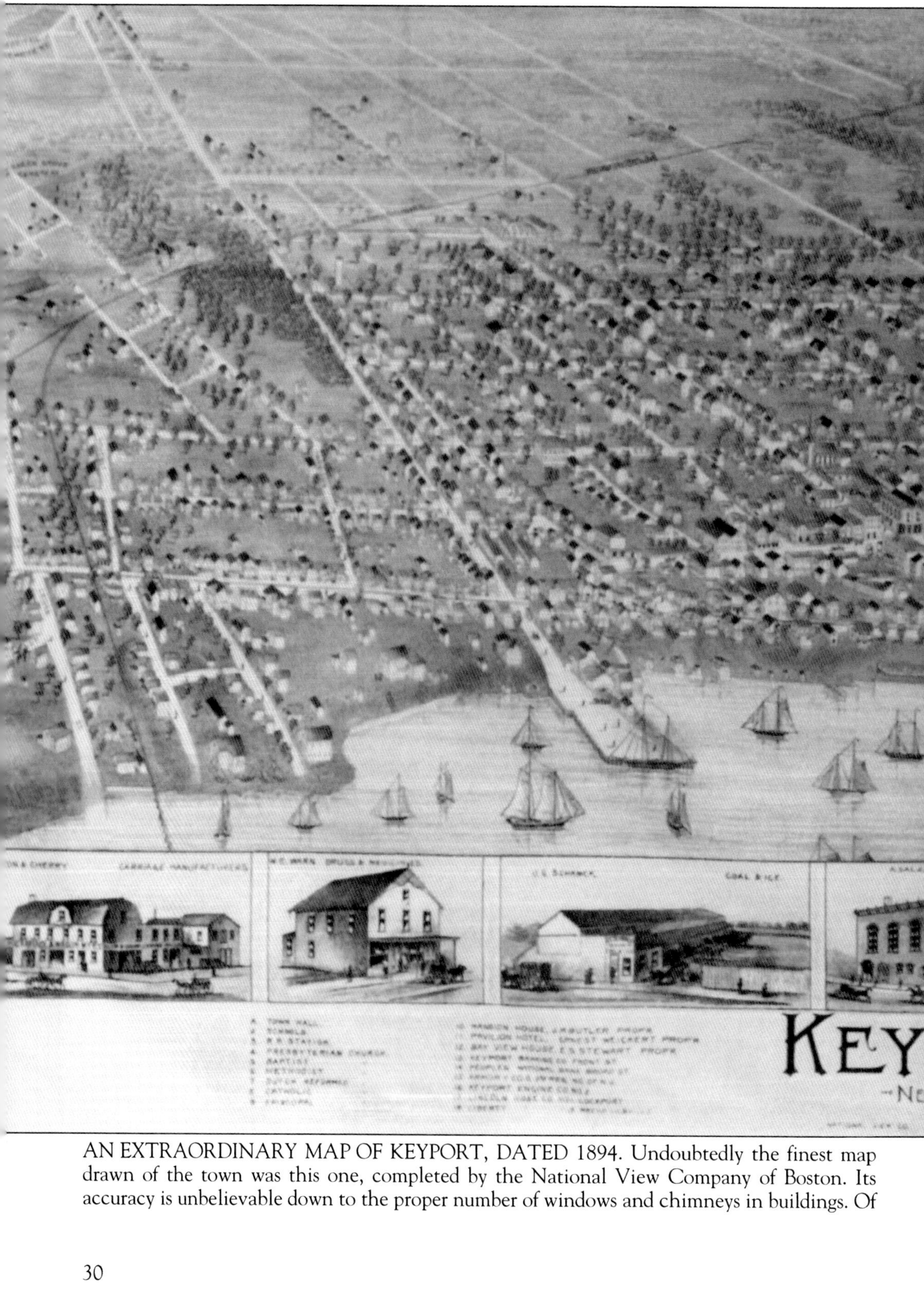

AN EXTRAORDINARY MAP OF KEYPORT, DATED 1894. Undoubtedly the finest map drawn of the town was this one, completed by the National View Company of Boston. Its accuracy is unbelievable down to the proper number of windows and chimneys in buildings. Of

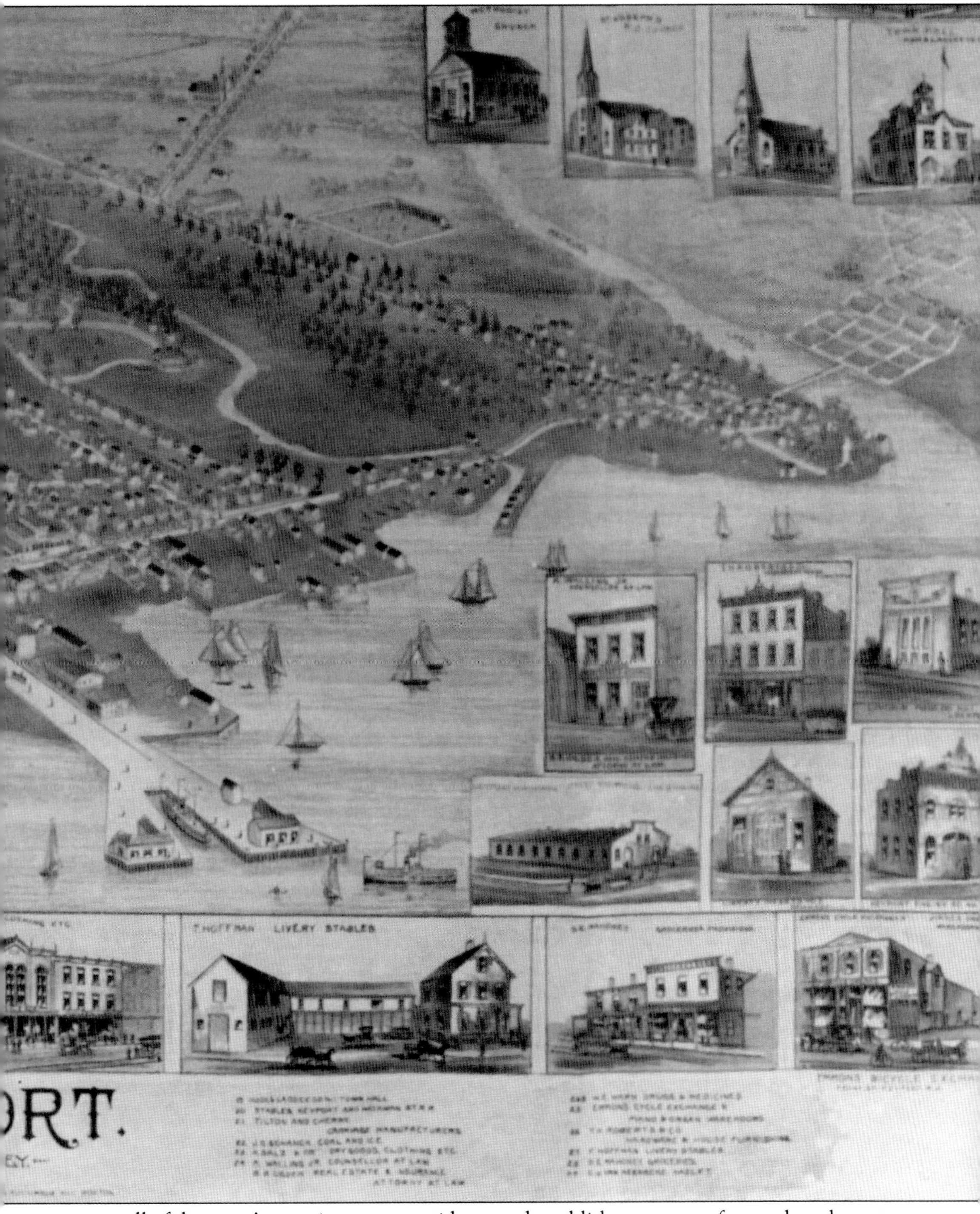

course, all of the town's most important residents and establishments were featured on the outer rim of the map. Note that all of the schooners are sailing into port while none are sailing out!

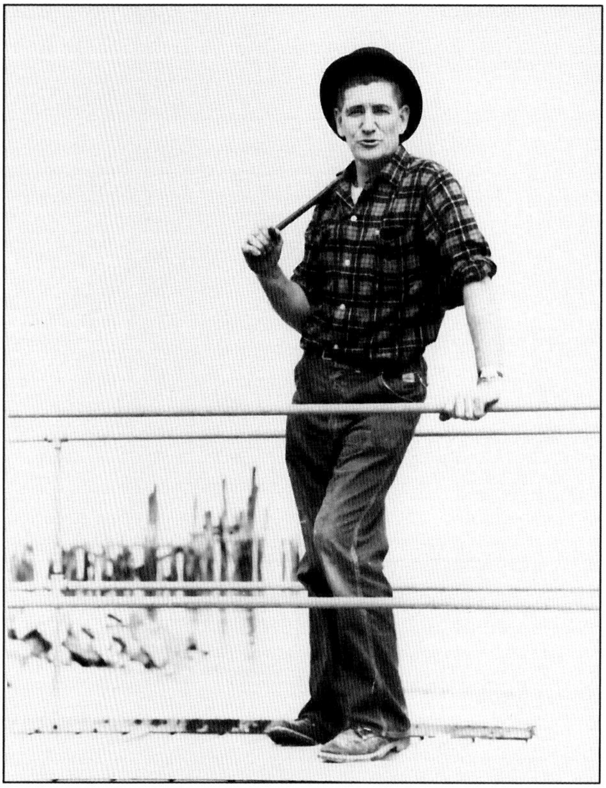

ALBERT BENNETT, *c.* 1961. One of the strongest advocates of forming the Keyport Historical Society in 1972 was Al Bennett. Al, who was born in Holmdel, moved to town in the 1930s and married Fay Fields. During his life he was a historian, a fireman with the Hook & Ladder Co, a plumber, and last, but certainly not least, a great photographer and friend to those who knew him.

FAY FIELDS, *c.* 1920. Long before she became Mrs. Bennett, this photograph was taken on the old bridge over the Luppattacong Creek. Fay graduated from high school in Keyport. She and Albert raised their children in their First Street home and later retired to California.

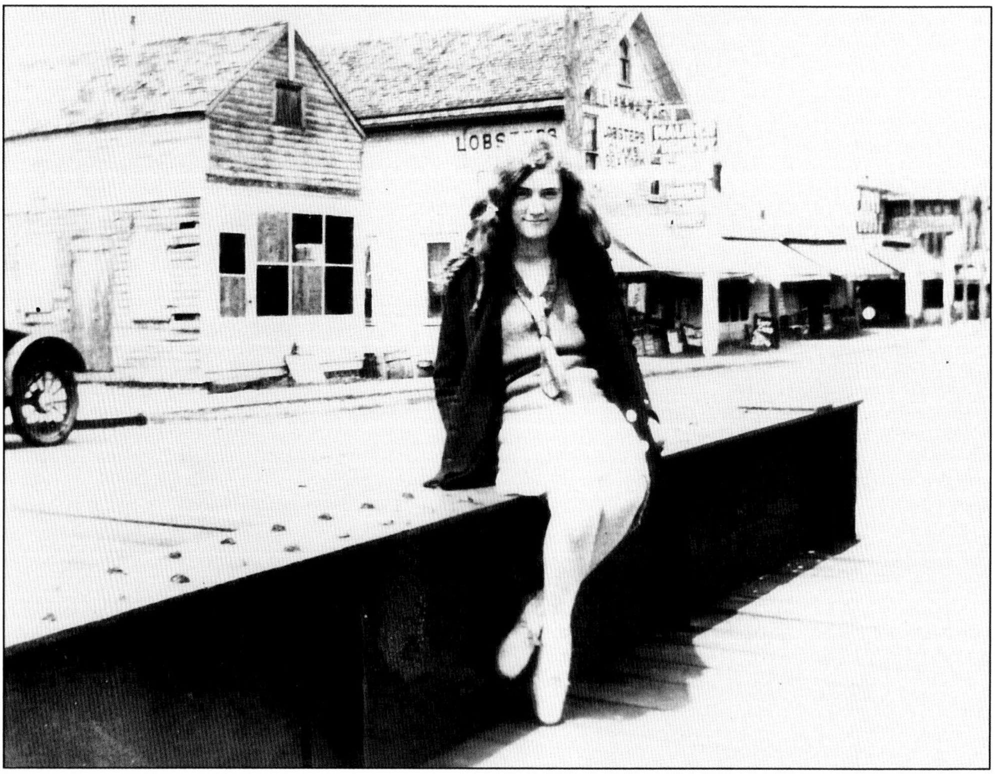

Two

Those Magnificent Flying Machines

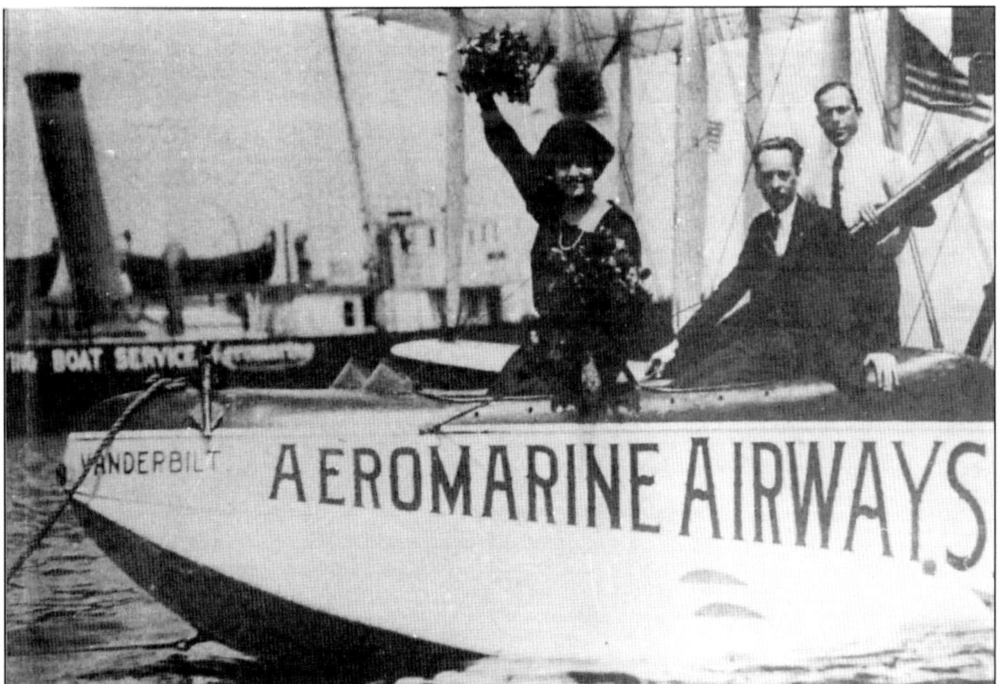

THE VANDERBILT, *c.* 1919. The term flying boat has all but disappeared from our language today, but during the first half of this century it was a great device, a boat that could fly or vice versa. Here some Aeromarine executives pose with a young woman out on Raritan Bay.

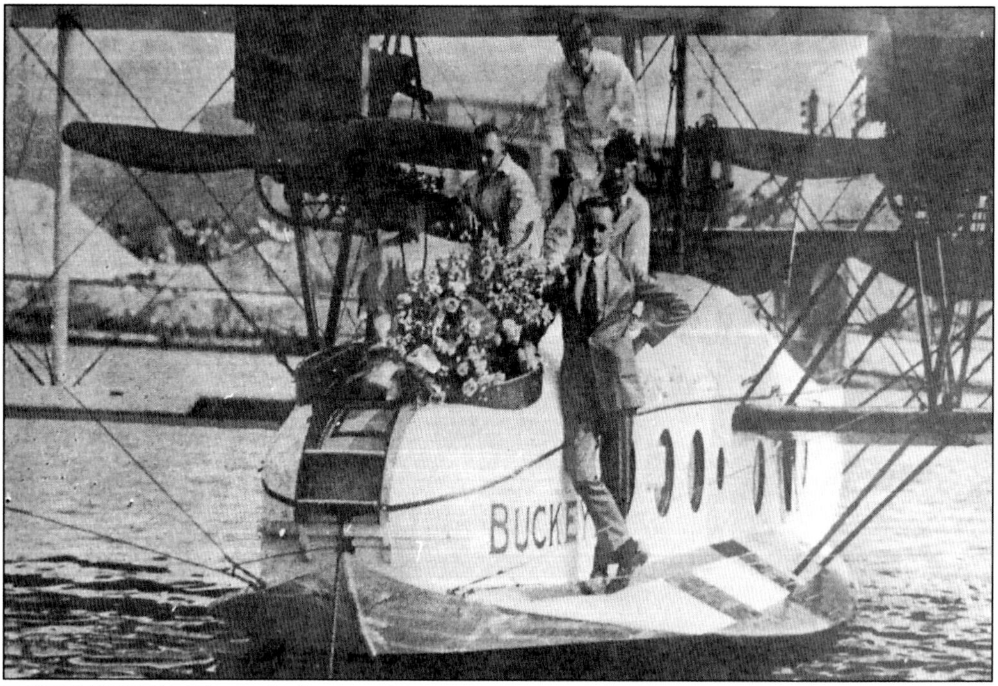

THE BUCKEYE. The early designs of American passenger planes were developed in Keyport at the Aeromarine complex. Although they looked a bit like Flash Gordon's spaceship, they did the job and did it well. This twin-engine plane could transport twelve to fourteen passengers to Havana, Cuba, in luxury never before known to airborne people.

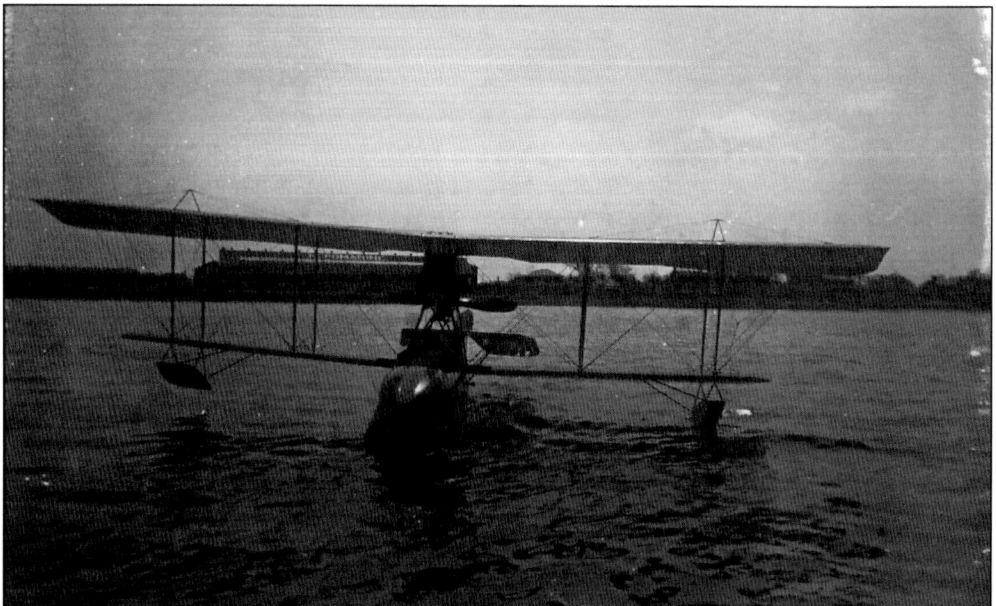

MODEL 50-S. The background of this photograph is composed of the factory buildings at the Locust Street plant and airport. It is interesting that when a plane like this one was photographed, the pilot, after landing the plane, would have to board a nearby boat so that he would not be in the picture.

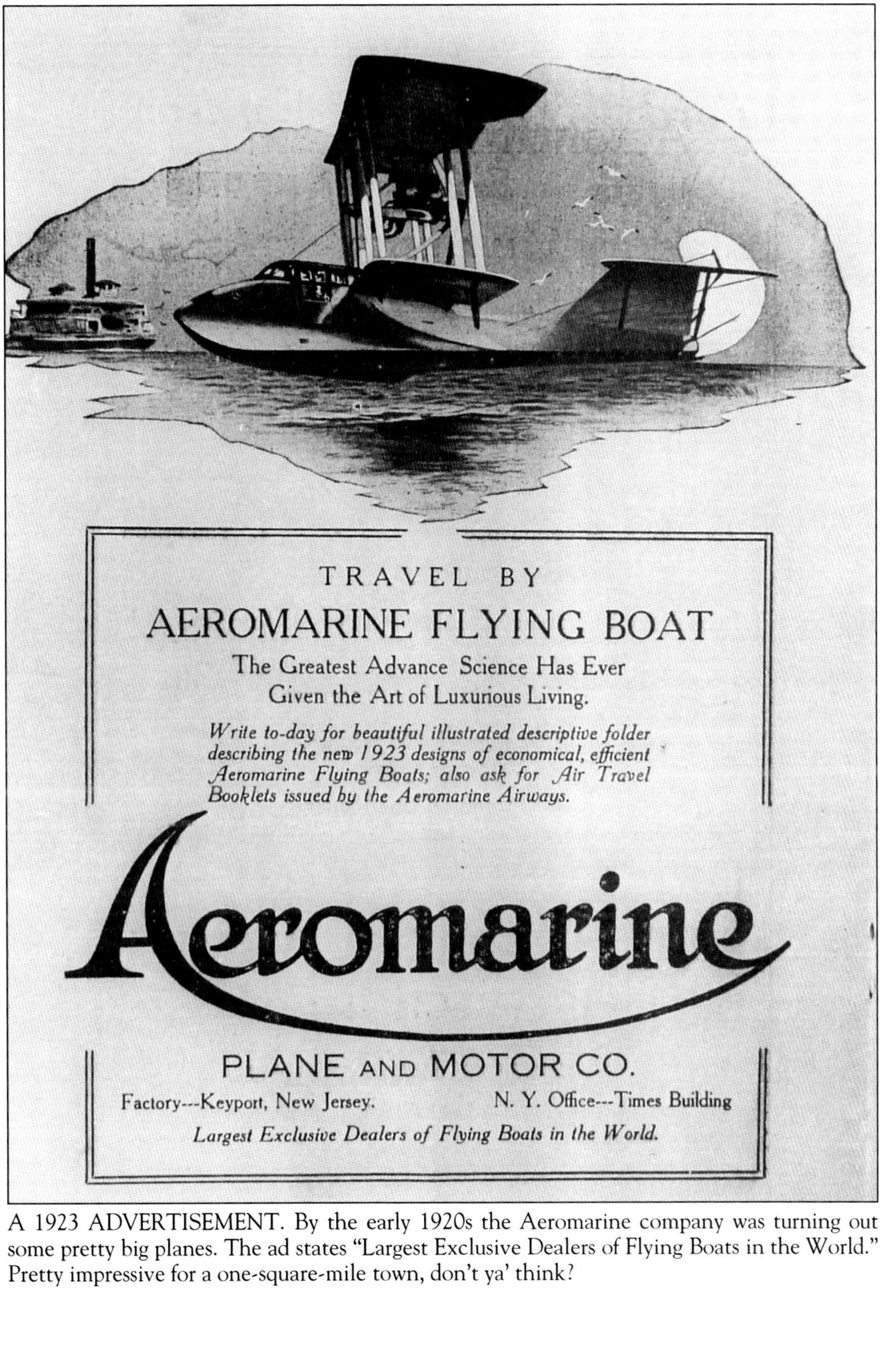

A 1923 ADVERTISEMENT. By the early 1920s the Aeromarine company was turning out some pretty big planes. The ad states "Largest Exclusive Dealers of Flying Boats in the World." Pretty impressive for a one-square-mile town, don't ya' think?

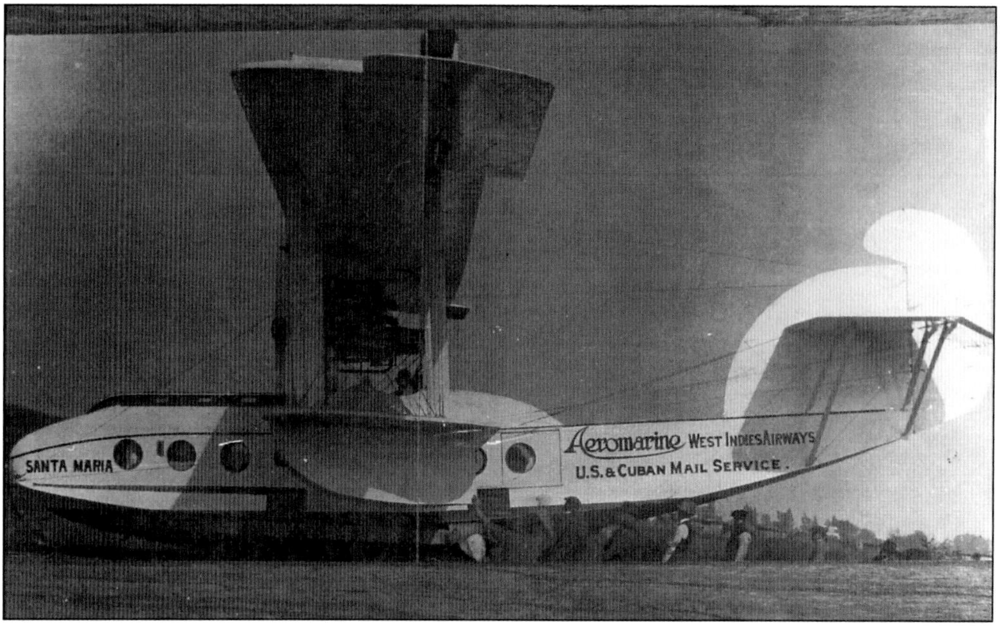

THE SANTA MARIA. Completed around 1924, the Santa Maria and her sister ships were the largest produced by the company. With a wingspan of nearly 90 feet, the twin-engine, wood-and-canvas-body plane was a true marvel of engineering. It is not known how long these planes were used or what became of them after their careers carrying passengers and mail ended.

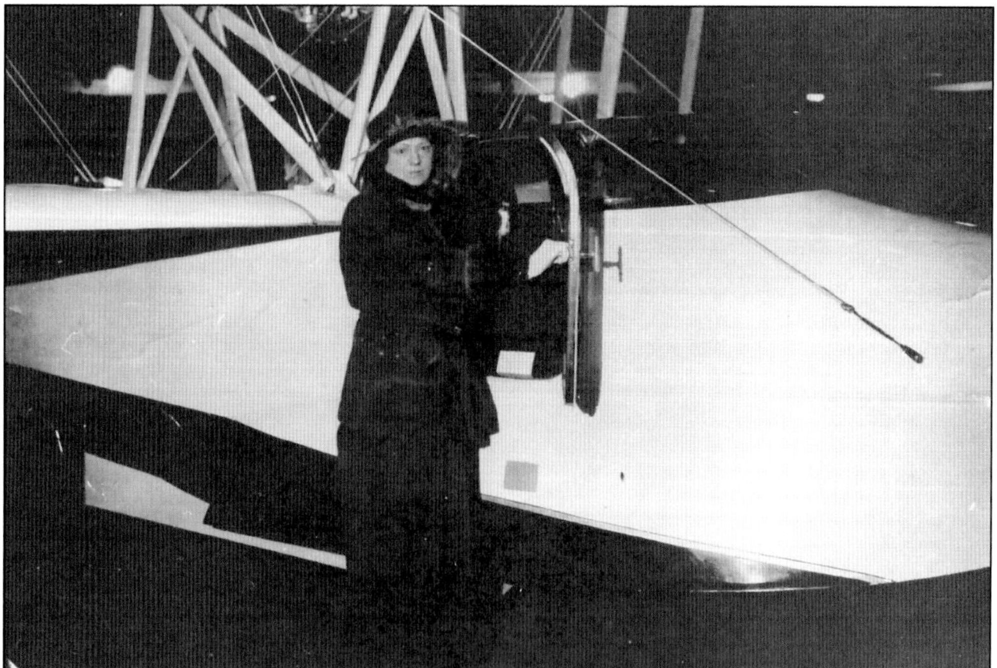

ETHEL BARRYMORE, *c.* 1925. Publicity shots have long been used to sell or boost a company's product, and the airplane business was no different. Famed motion picture actress Ethel Barrymore traveled to New York City for this photo shoot, which was being held at the New York Aeronautical Exposition. The plane is a model 50-B.

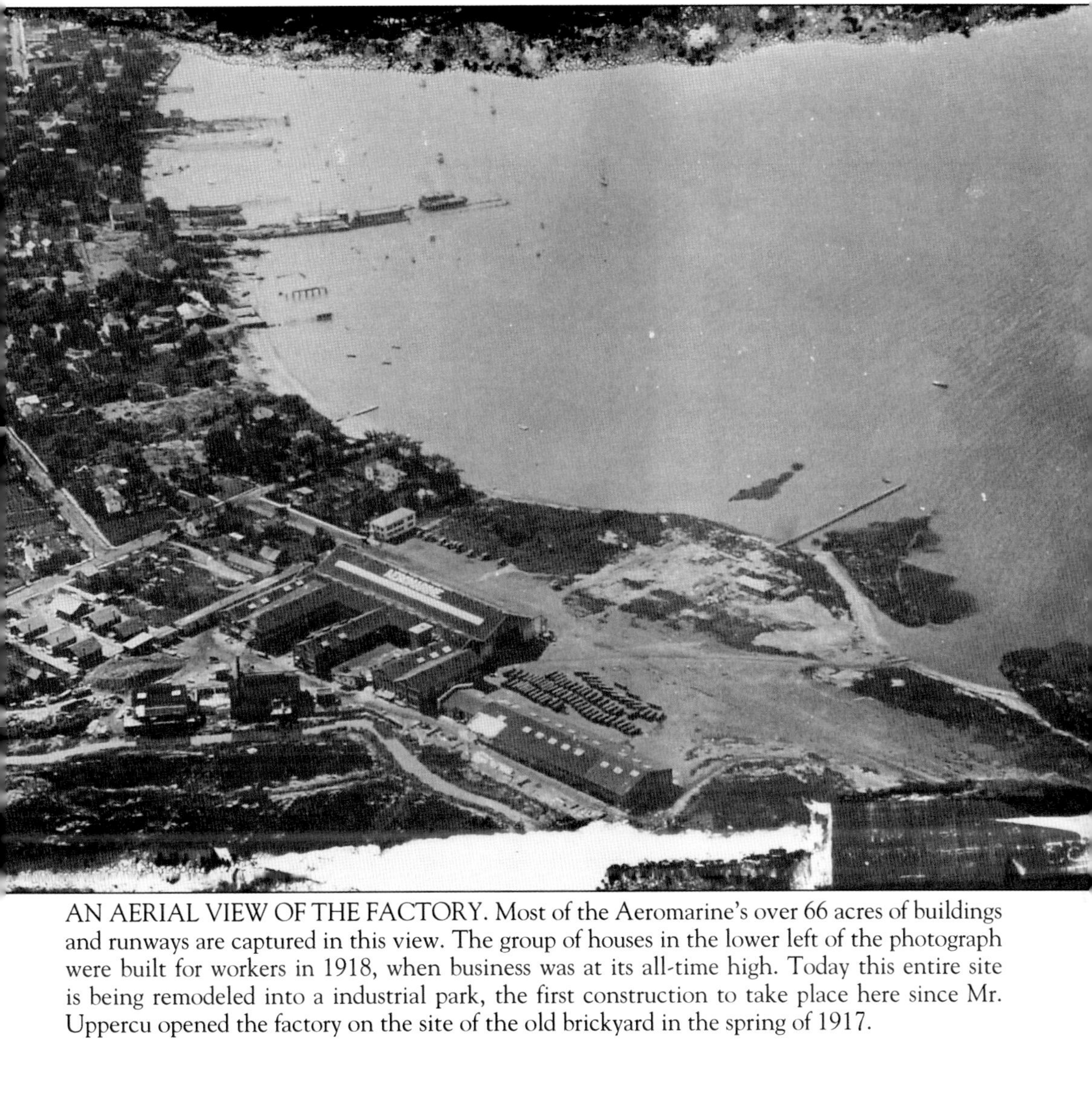

AN AERIAL VIEW OF THE FACTORY. Most of the Aeromarine's over 66 acres of buildings and runways are captured in this view. The group of houses in the lower left of the photograph were built for workers in 1918, when business was at its all-time high. Today this entire site is being remodeled into a industrial park, the first construction to take place here since Mr. Uppercu opened the factory on the site of the old brickyard in the spring of 1917.

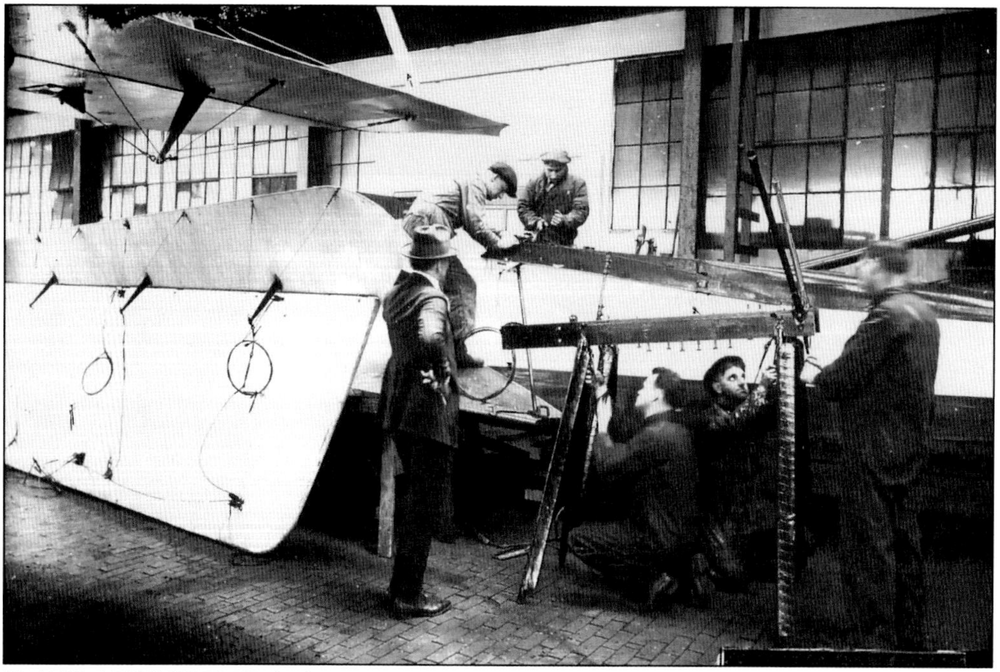

PLANE ASSEMBLY. With their supervisor close by, all of the men are on their best behavior. Five men pictured here are near the completion of another flying boat. The main assembly line was located in the large building with AEROMARINE painted on the roof (see preceding page).

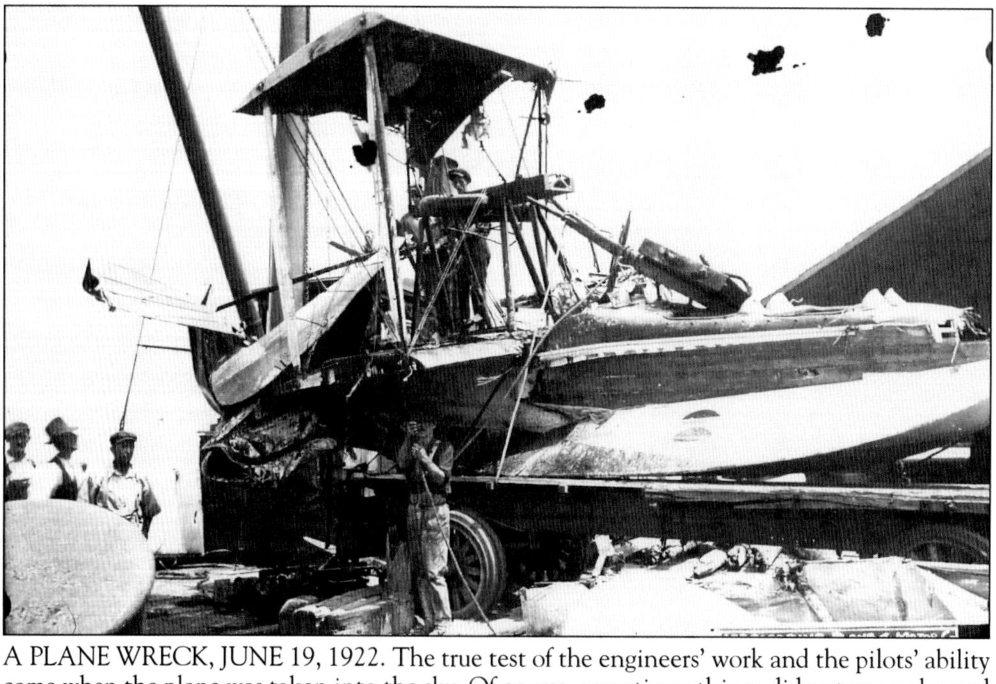

A PLANE WRECK, JUNE 19, 1922. The true test of the engineers' work and the pilots' ability came when the plane was taken into the sky. Of course, sometimes things did not go as planned and gravity did its thing, quickly pulling the ill-fated hulk to disaster. It is unknown how the pilot fared in this crash.

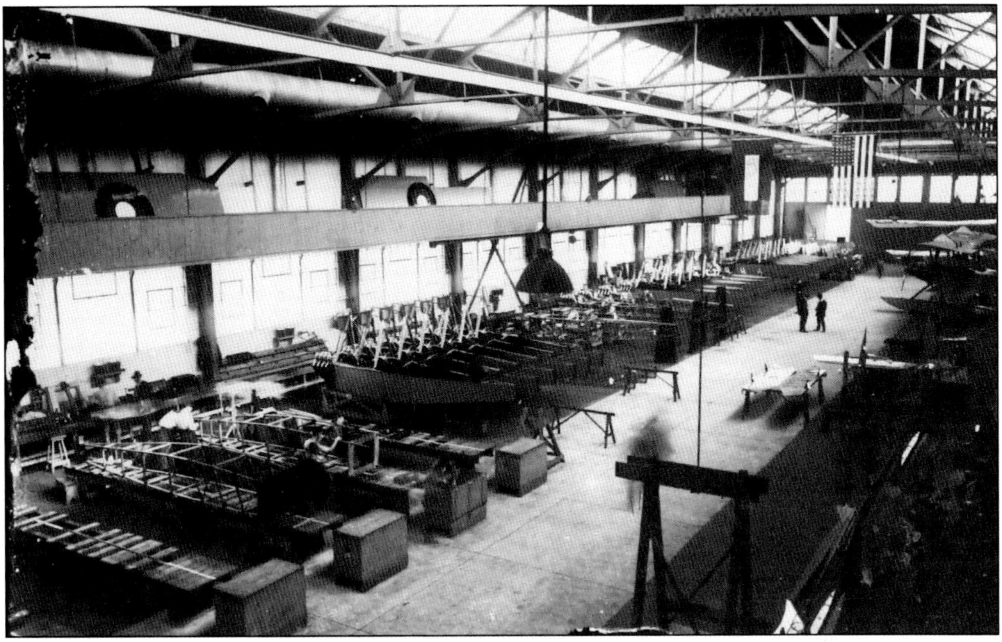

THE INTERIOR OF A FACTORY, *c*. 1918. Busy workers appear as blurs all over the floor of the assembly line at the plant. Many of the planes being constructed here would later be used by the United States Navy as training planes. World War I was responsible for much of the Aeromarine's innovations in the aeronautical field.

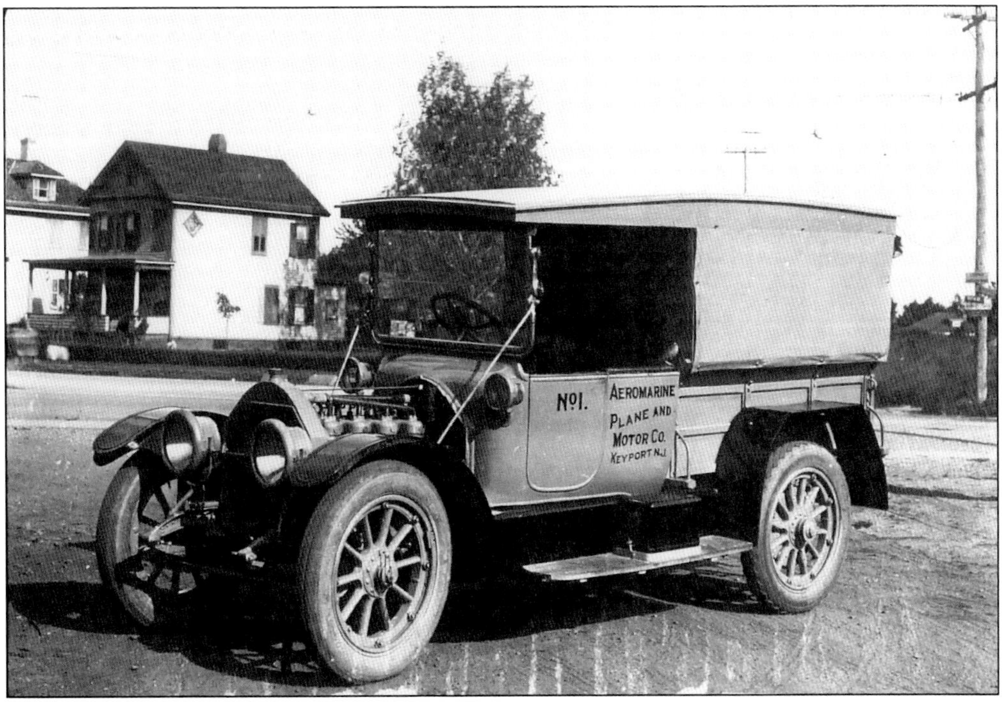

AN AEROMARINE TRUCK, 1919. This stylish delivery truck was another design created by the Aeromarine Company. The truck body was built on an unknown-type chassis, and with roll-down canvas flaps, four headlights, and solid rubber tires, this was one tough truck.

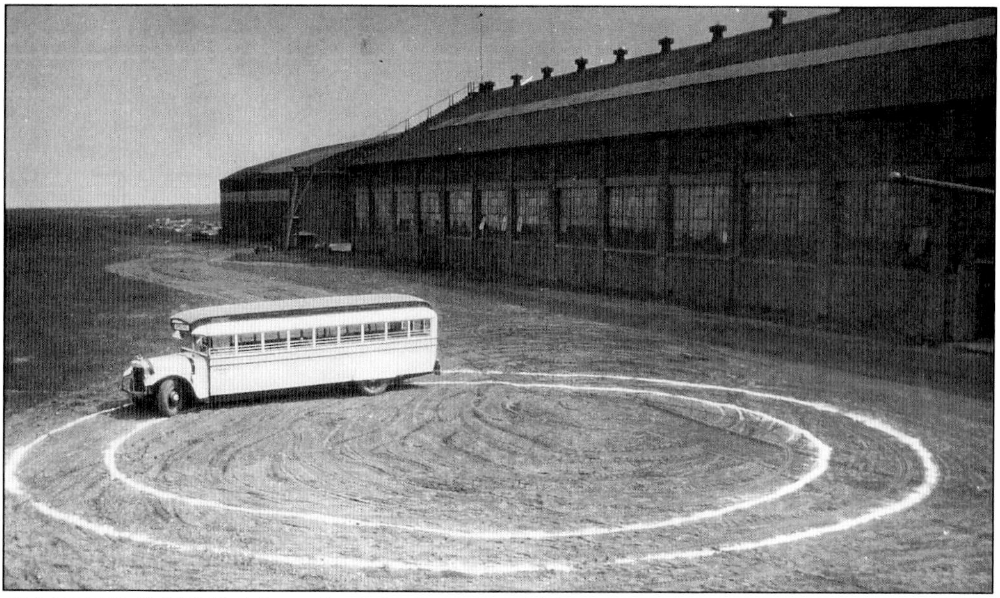

AN UPPERCU BUS. This vehicle had an incredible turning radius for its size, which made it ideally suited for passenger service on busy city streets. One of the single-deck coaches is shown here making its trials at the factory. The view is looking east from Walnut Street along the runway.

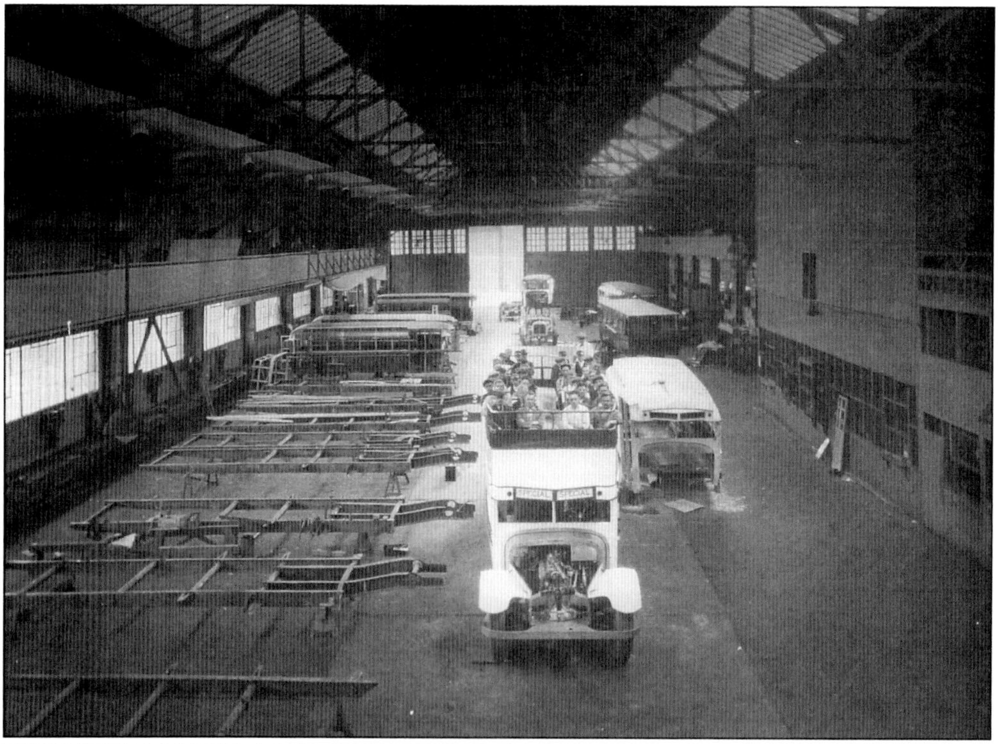

THE UPPERCU BUS ASSEMBLY LINE. No less than seventeen "special" coaches can be seen here at various stages of completion. The group of men (most likely workers) on the upper deck of this bus couldn't get very far—it looks like the engine is only partially installed.

Three

To the Rescue

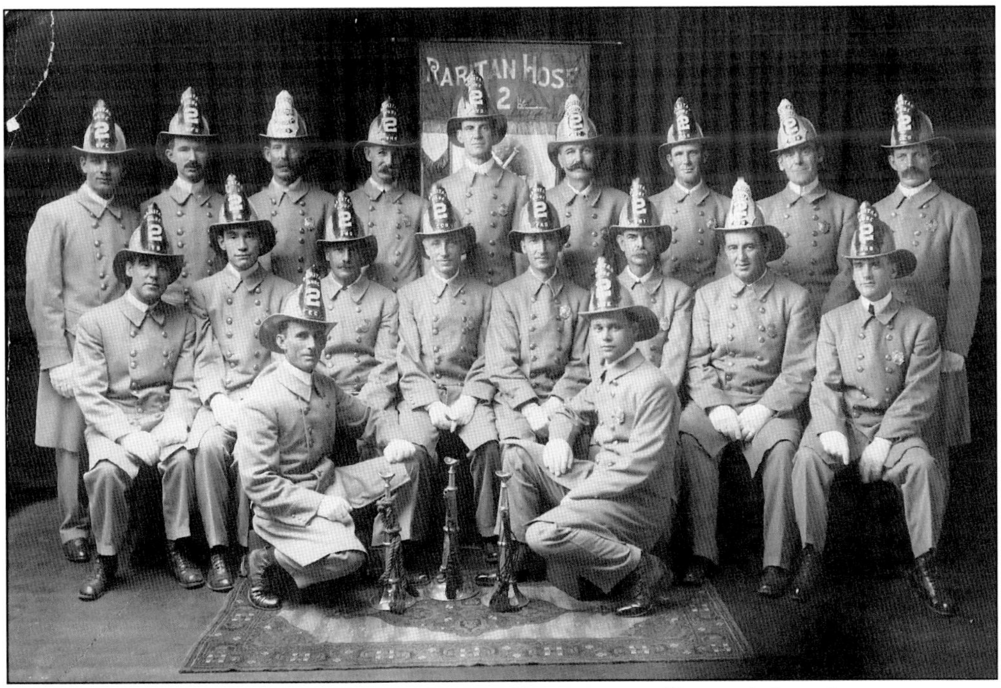

RARITAN HOSE CO. NO. 2., *c.* 1908. Raritan Hose is among Keyport's finest hose companies. Organized on May 29, 1893, for many years this company allowed only military men to become members. Each fireman can be identified by his initials on the bottom panel of his helmet.

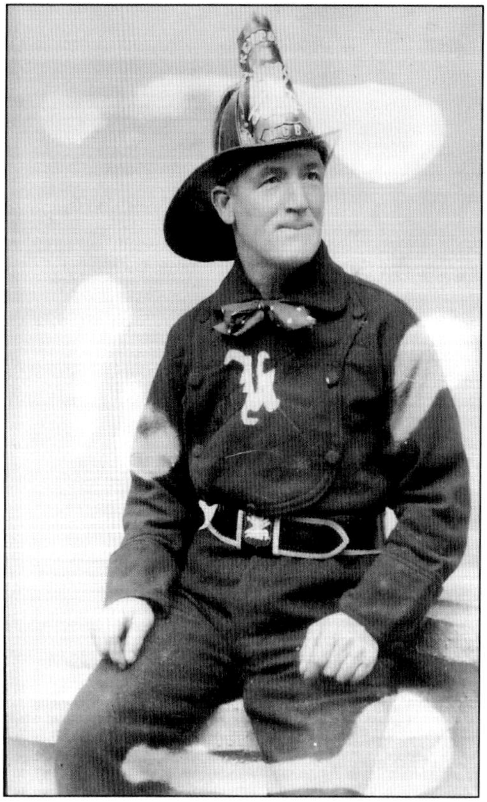

GEORGE W. BIRCH JR. In the early years, each fire company had distinctive uniforms. Around 1910, Mr. Birch posed with his father's 1879 Hook and Ladder uniform. During his fifty-six years of service to the village, Mr. Birch served as fire chief (from 1936 to 1937), mayor, tax collector, and fire commissioner. He passed away in 1963.

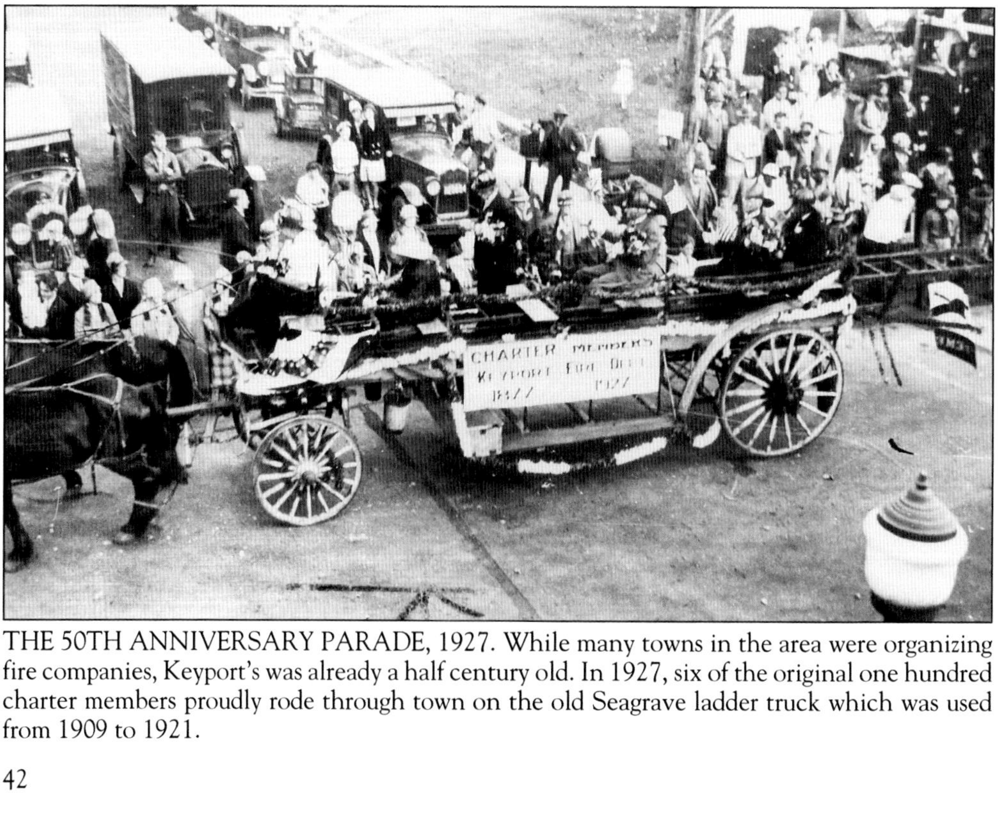

THE 50TH ANNIVERSARY PARADE, 1927. While many towns in the area were organizing fire companies, Keyport's was already a half century old. In 1927, six of the original one hundred charter members proudly rode through town on the old Seagrave ladder truck which was used from 1909 to 1921.

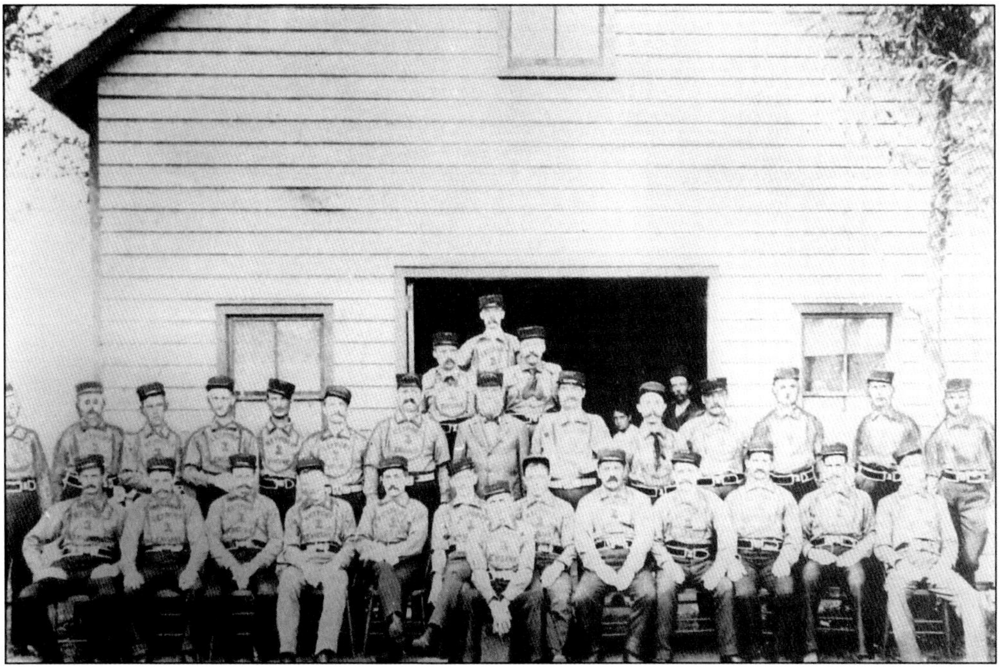

THE ENGINE CO., 1889. The engine men posed for their first portrait in front of the old house on the north side of First Street. At the time this photograph was taken they had no apparatus (they wouldn't get any until 1891) and had just received their uniforms.

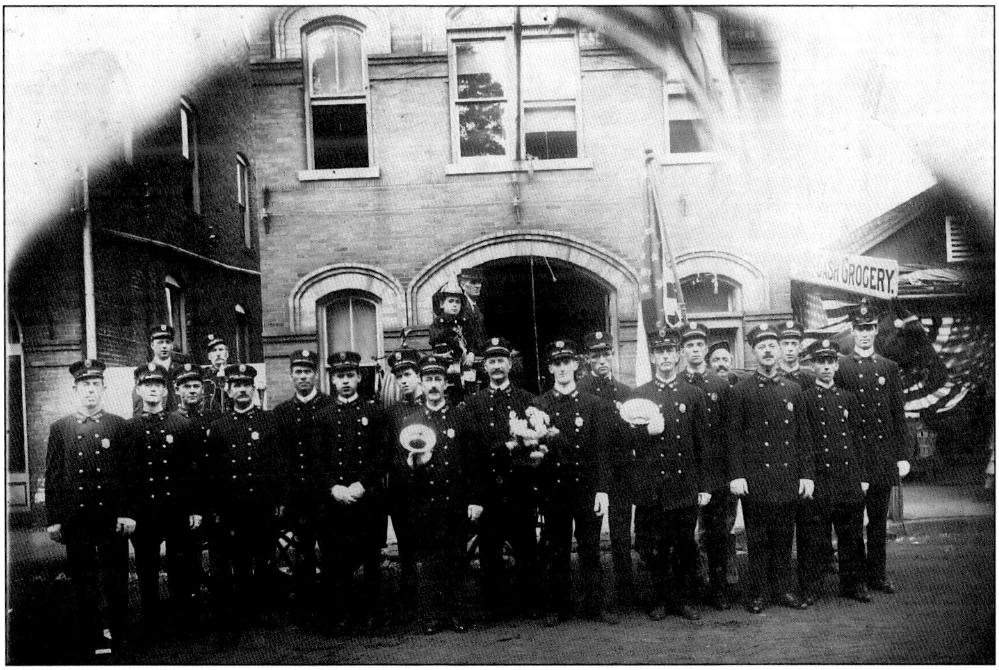

THE ENGINE CO., 1895. In less than six years the company had raised enough money for the construction of a new house (see Volume I) on Main Street. The new chemical engine also arrived in 1891, on a railroad flat car, and paraded through the streets of town by the commissioners, dressed as angels.

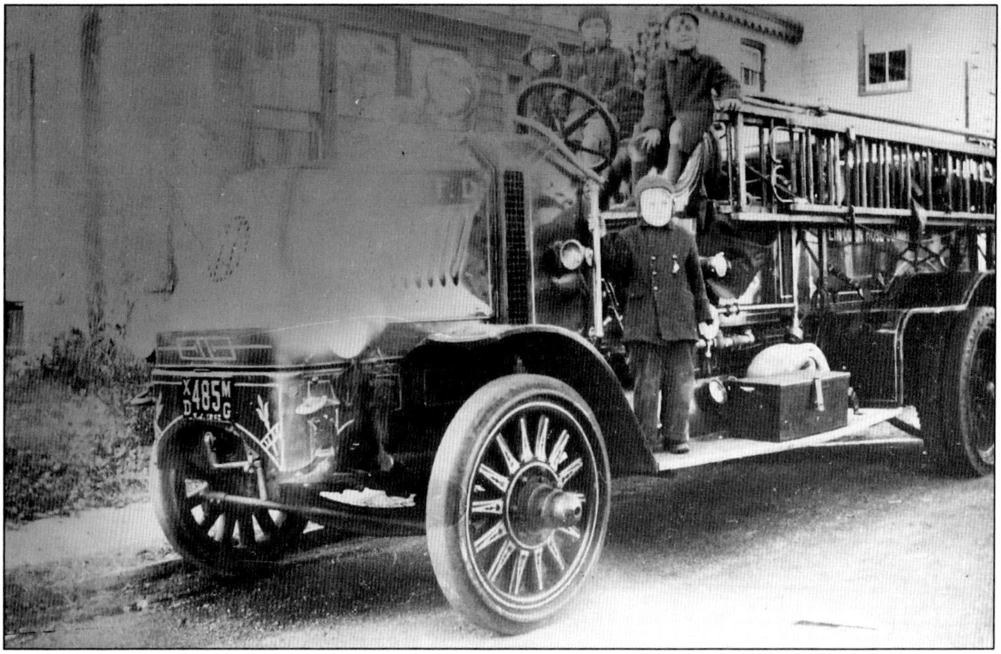

THE LINCOLN HOSE CO., 1940. Long before McDonald's, Keyport had their own Big Mack. Delivered at a cost of over $10,000, the 1920 Mack AC pumper was paid for by the men of Lincoln, some of whom mortgaged their own properties for the new engine. Standing on the running board is Jay Stout, while up in the cab are, from left to right, Richard Poling, David Raynor, and Thomas Poling. Ironically, all of them later joined this fire company.

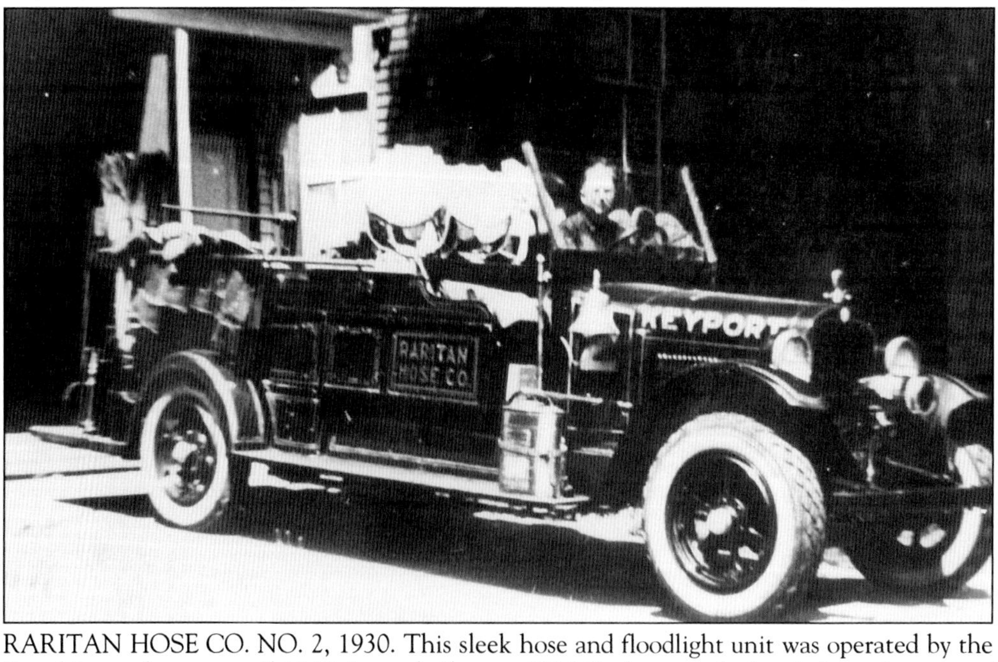

RARITAN HOSE CO. NO. 2, 1930. This sleek hose and floodlight unit was operated by the Broad Street firemen until 1946. It was built on a 1926 Graham truck chassis from the parts of the companies former 1917 Ranier, and is seen here pulling out of the old hose house on Broad Street, which was vacated in 1969.

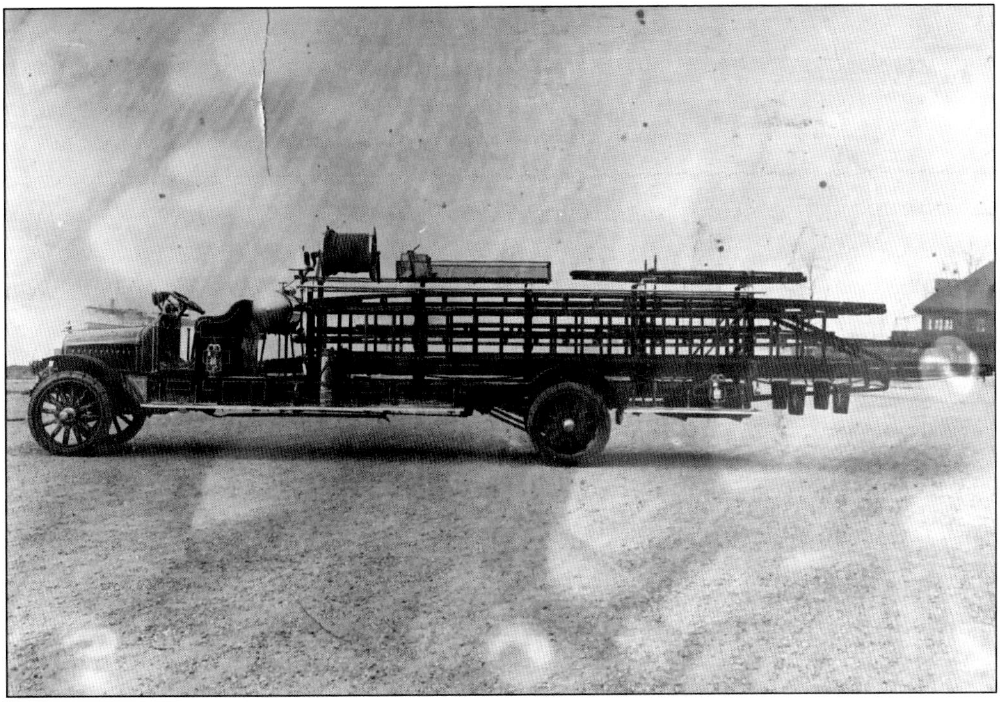

THE FIRST MOTORIZED LADDER TRUCK, 1921. After months of bitter arguments the town council finally gave in and decided to pay the principal on a motor-driven truck for the Hook and Ladder Co. So, after six years of fund-raising to pay the interest, the new Mack AB drove into town and was backed into the truck house with only an inch to spare on each side. It served until 1934.

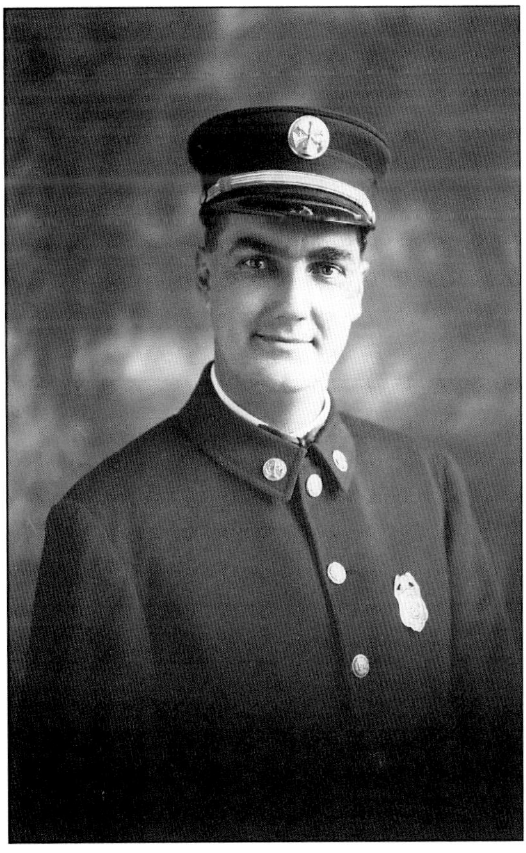

HARRY AUMACK, 1927. Mr. Aumack joined the borough's truck company around 1919, just in time to take part in pulling the old truck around town. At the 1927 department elections, he was chosen as second assistant chief, and he served in this capacity on several committees during the 50th anniversary celebration.

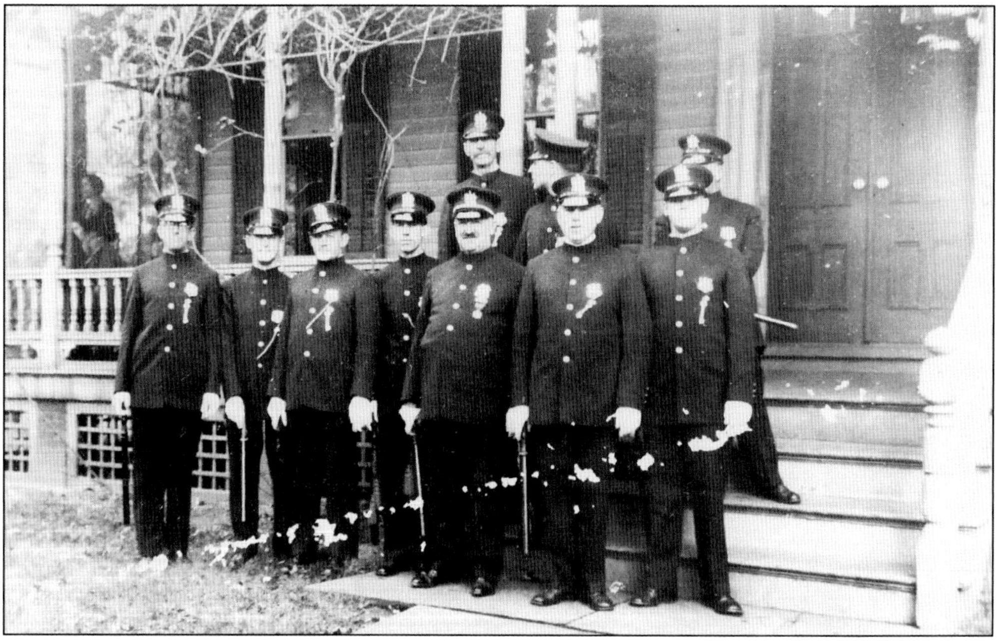

THE BOARD OF FIRE WARDENS, 1927. With nightsticks in hand, Keyport's fire police are shown ready for action during the fiftieth anniversary. Since 1952, the Fire Patrol has been located on Waverly Street, in the former Lincoln Hose house, which was built in 1893.

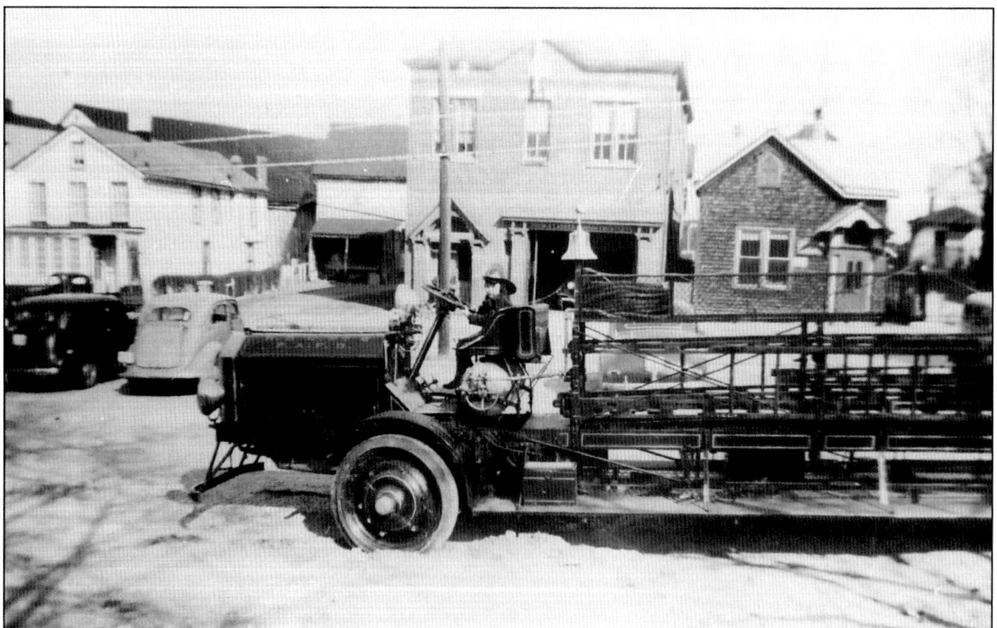

THE HOOK AND LADDER CO., *c.* 1949. As the old saying goes "A friend in need, is a friend indeed," and so the Perth Amboy Fire Department lent this old American LaFrance truck to Keyport while the Diamond T was being repaired. Keyport kindly repaid Perth Amboy by crashing the truck into a tree during a fire alarm.

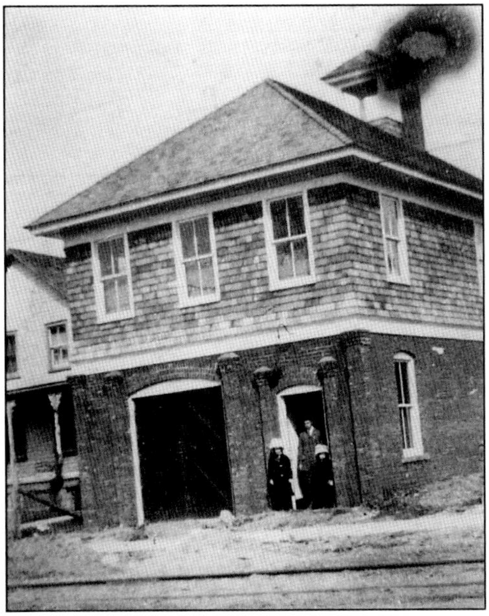

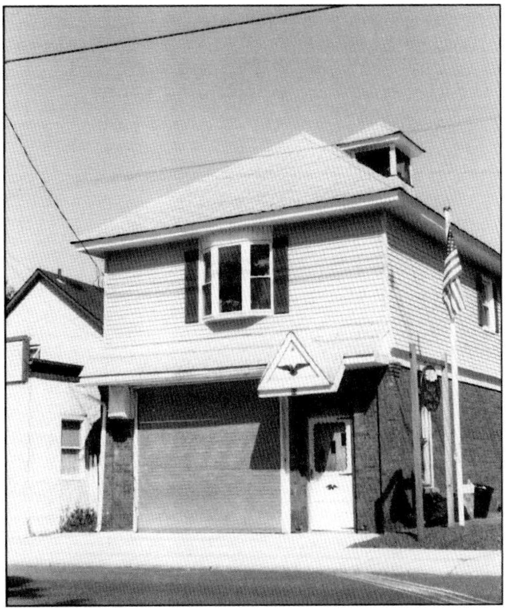

THE EAGLE HOSE HOUSE, *c.* 1915. This new station proved far more elaborate than the first, which was an old garage located further north on Broadway in someone's backyard. The building was built after three years of fund-raising through fairs and dinners, at places such as the Broadway Theater. After the building was dedicated on March 25, 1913, cake and coffee were served to both guests and visiting firemen. To the right is the firehouse in 1996.

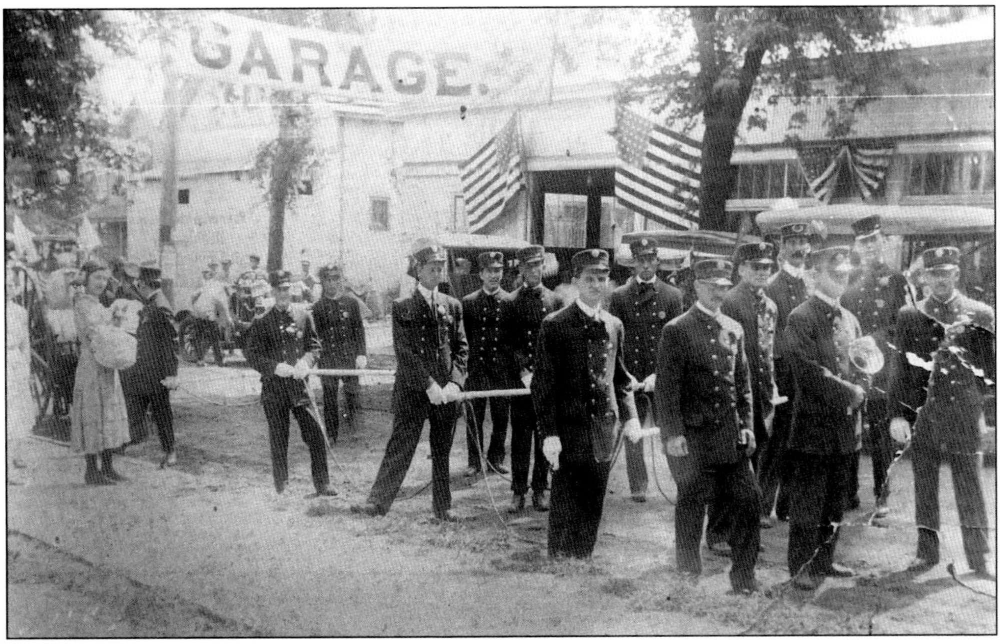

EAGLE HOSE MEN AND APPARATUS. Just where this photograph was taken is open to speculation, but it may be on lower Broadway. However, we do know that the men are not smiling for the simple fact that they were pulling their apparatus, while everyone else around them were cruising effortlessly in motor cars. This changed in 1916 when a Peerless touring car was converted into a hose wagon.

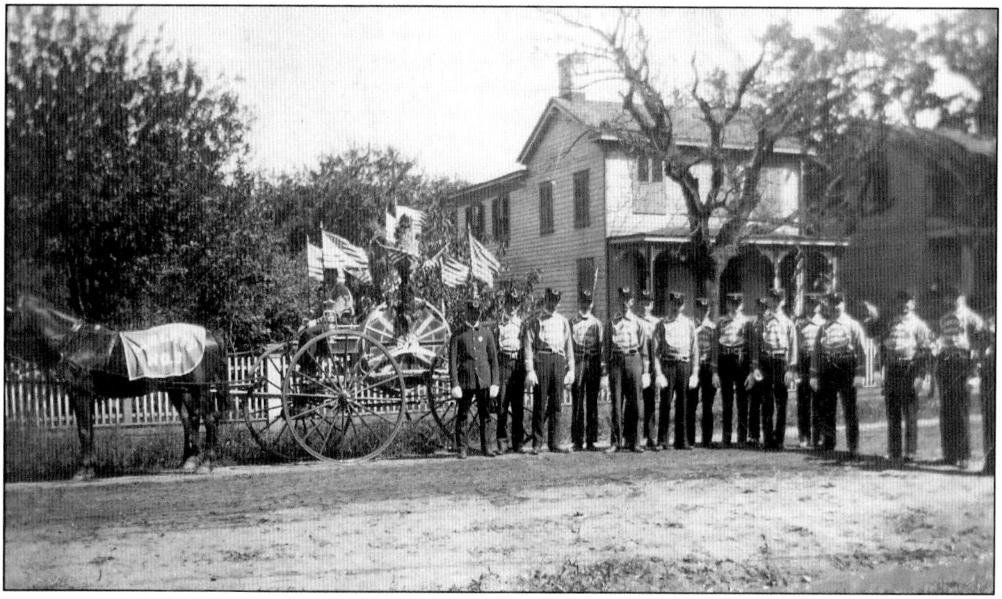

LIBERTY HOSE, 1899. All decked out for a parade, this view is looking from the firehouse entrance, across Atlantic Street. Seventeen of the eighteen active members were present this day along with the borrowed horse, who also had a personalized blanket.

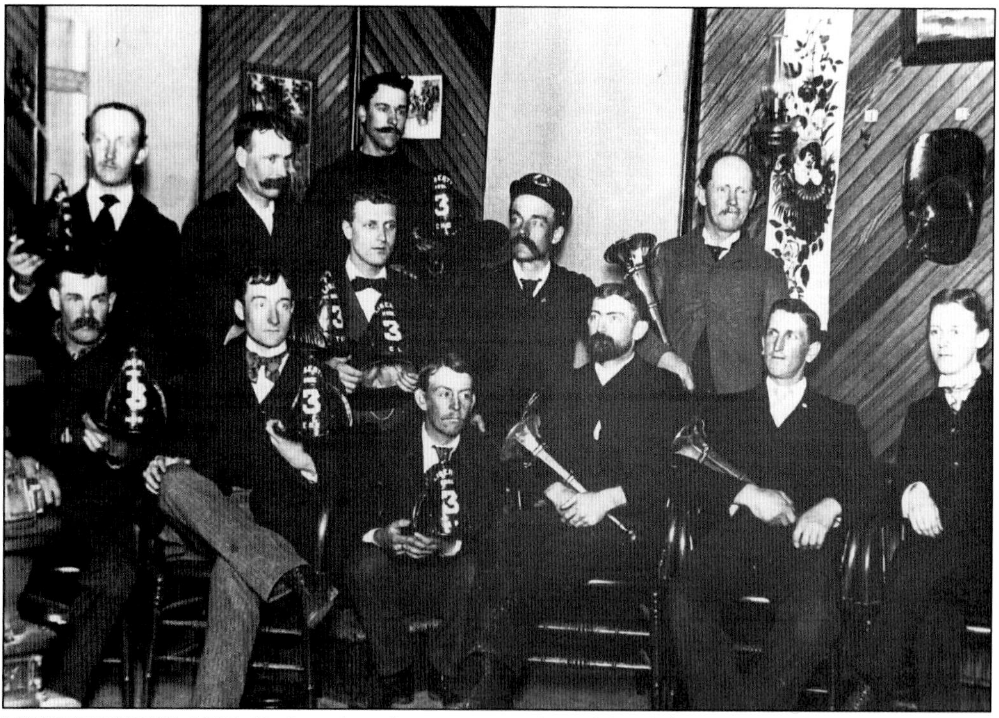

LIBERTY BOYS, 1895. Gathered in the upstairs parlor of the Atlantic Street hose house, this is a glimpse into a nineteenth-century Keyport firehouse, one of only a few images known to exist. The parlor walls were adorned with wood paneling, oil lamps, tapestries and, of course, the member's leather helmets. What could be better than sitting around the pot-belly stove playing cards with the guys on a cold winter night?

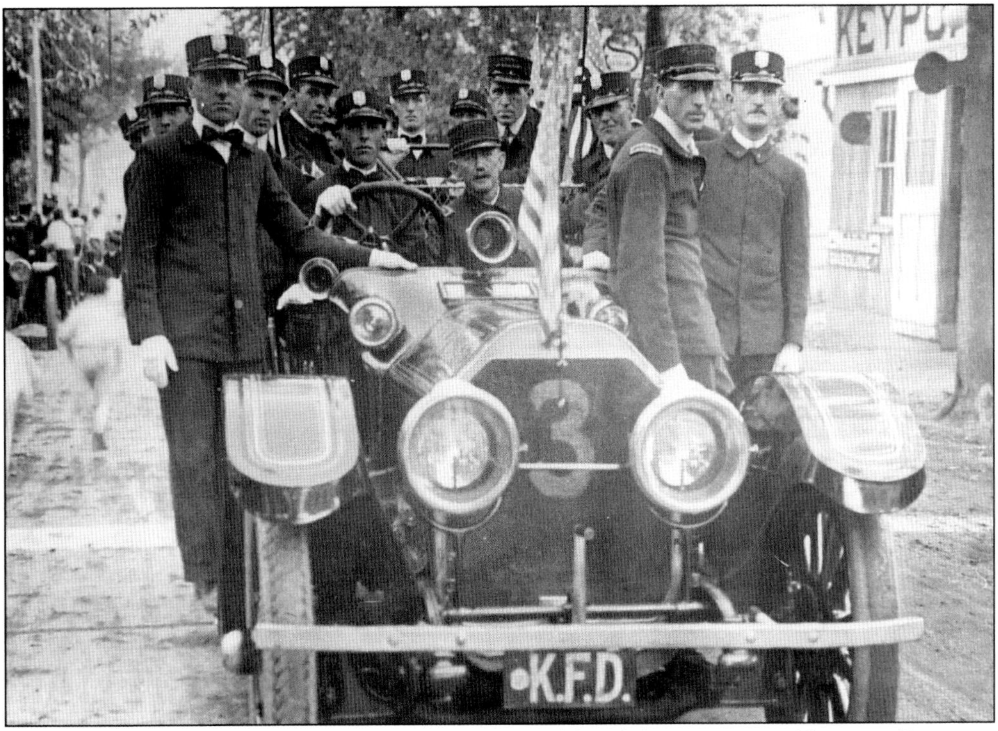

LIBERTY HOSE CO. NO. 3, 1925. The old 1915 Oldsmobile was powered by a small engine, but because of its strength and gearing it was able to provide great duty as a hose wagon. At least sixteen members piled on the Oldsmobile for this parade.

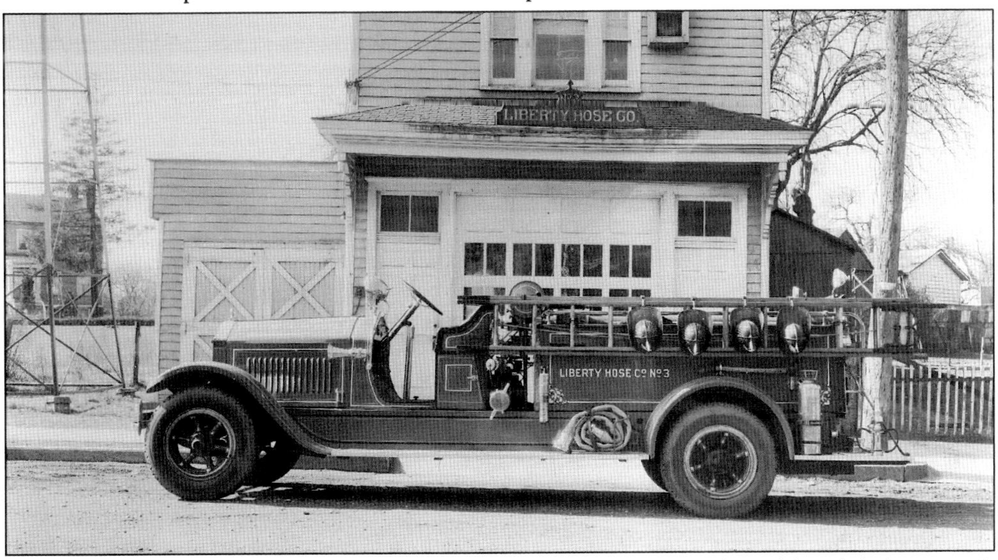

LIBERTY HOSE'S AMERICAN LAFRANCE, *c.* 1936. By 1928 the Oldsmobile hose truck was showing its age, so it was decided to replace it with a new pumping engine—the first one in South Keyport. Built in Elmira, NY, the new American LaFrance type 100 was officially delivered to the town in 1929. After it was replaced and sold in 1952, it disappeared for nearly forty-four years. In 1996 the old LaFrance was found in Somerset County, and was repurchased by the company.

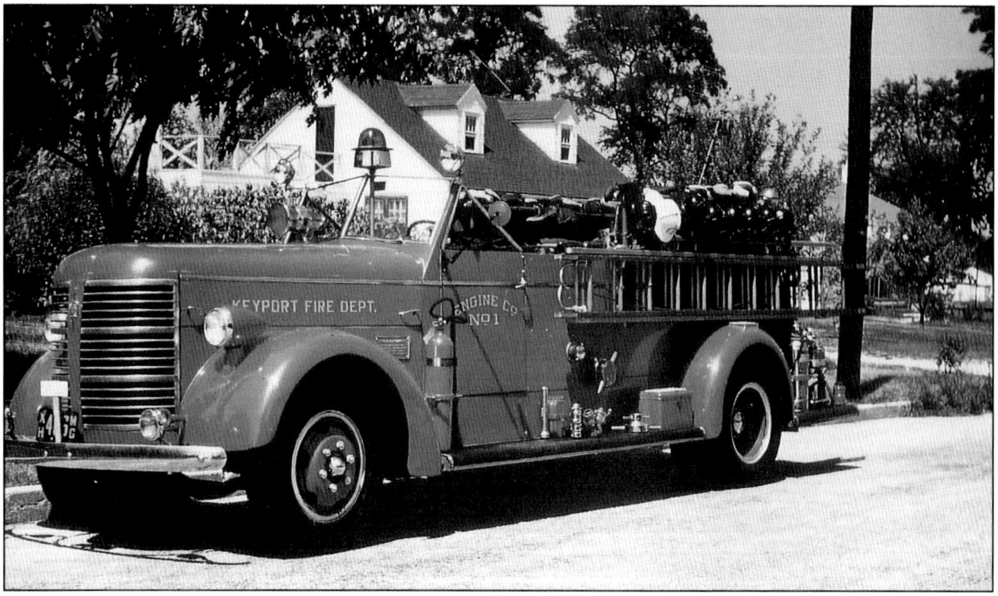

THE ENGINE'S ENGINE, 1965. Keyport's second fire company received their third piece of apparatus in 1942. It is said that if too many big men stood on the rear of the 1942 American LaFrance, the chassis would bend, and the cab doors would swing open. This series 600 was sold in 1967 to the Monmouth Park racetrack, and was last seen heading down the highway to a horse ranch in Missouri in 1973.

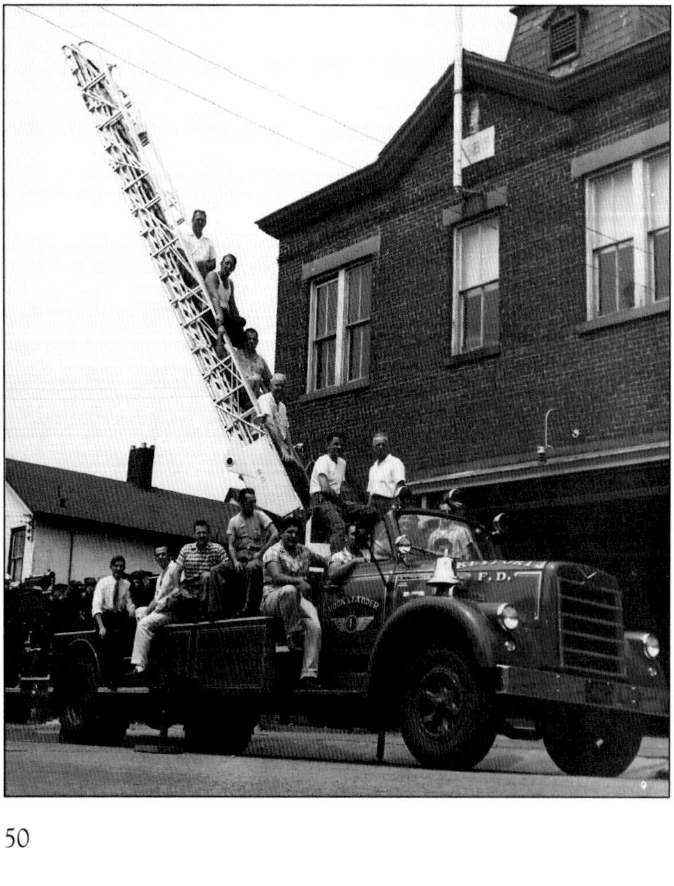

THE HOOK AND LADDER CO., 1962. Northern Monmouth County's first aerial ladder truck was delivered to the Hookies in 1958. Built on an International chassis, the apparatus was completed by the Seagrave Corporation in Ohio. After exactly thirty years of faithful service, many of the men in this photograph, such as Bob Rose and Harry Aumack, bid farewell to their old friend, as a new 100-foot Seagrave aerial ladder took the 58's place in the truckroom.

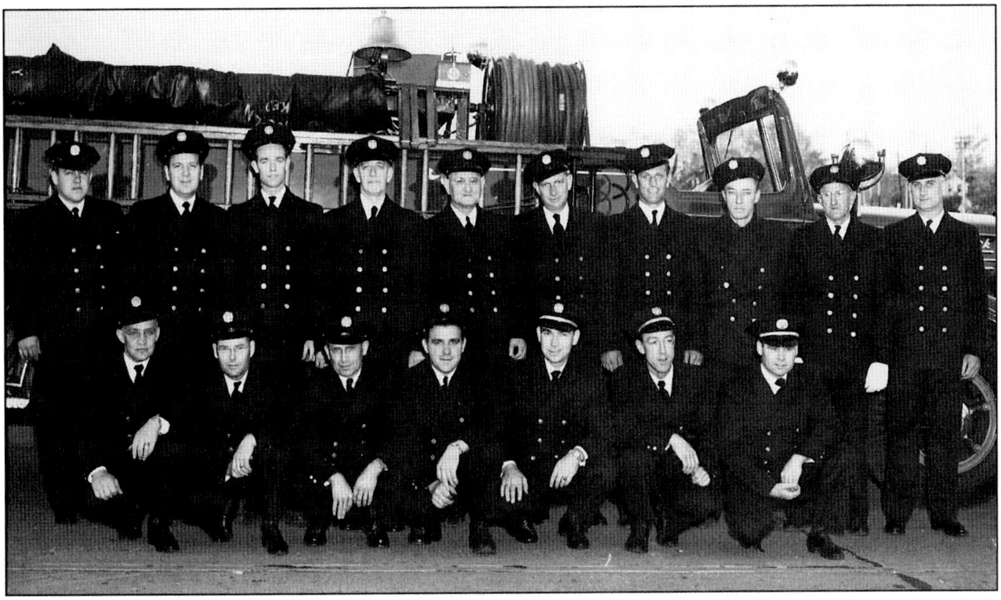

LINCOLN HOSE CO. NO. 1. The members shown here at the 1947 inspection are, from left to right, as follows: (front row) J. Pedersen, Dave Britton, Vernon Sullivan, Bob Walsh, Joseph "Pete" Collins, George Kipp, and Charley Stryker; (back row) Leon Lambertson, Earl Huber, Don Hill, Earnest Bailey, John Wilson, Ray Wallace, Leo Brown, Alan Lee, Danny "Axeman" Harris, and Leroy Huylar.

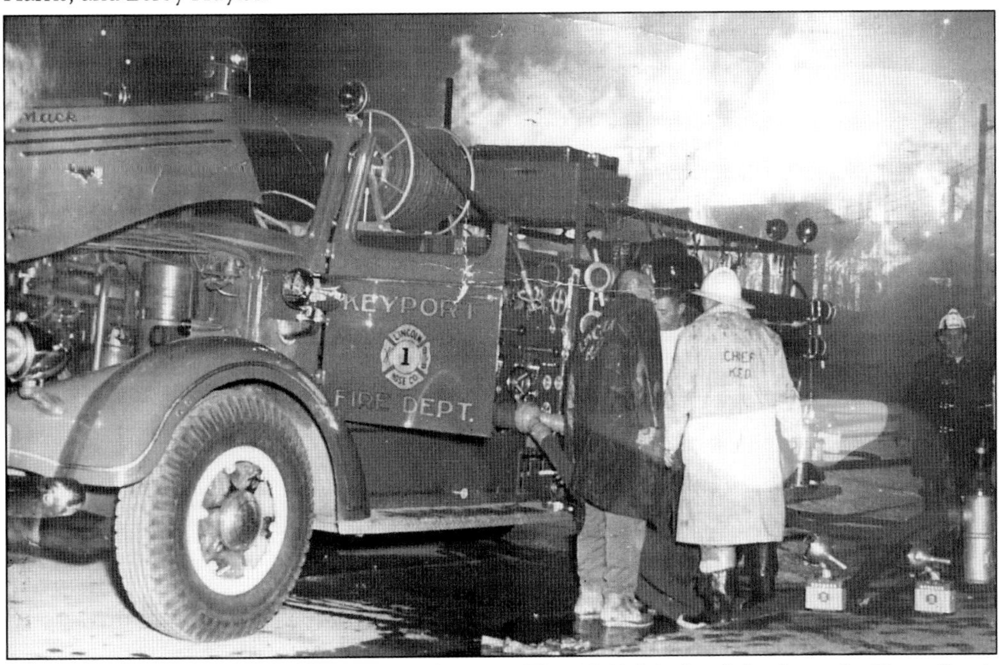

THE RARITAN INN FIRE, APRIL 25, 1962. The 1941 Mack of the Lincoln Hose Co. is giving all she's got to save the business district, while Chief Pete Collins confers with Alan Lee and Leo Brown. It was a stroke of luck, combined with an excellent fire department, that prevented a reoccurrence of what happened in the 1877 fire. Ironically, the Raritan Inn was the only building to survive while the business district was consumed by the flames.

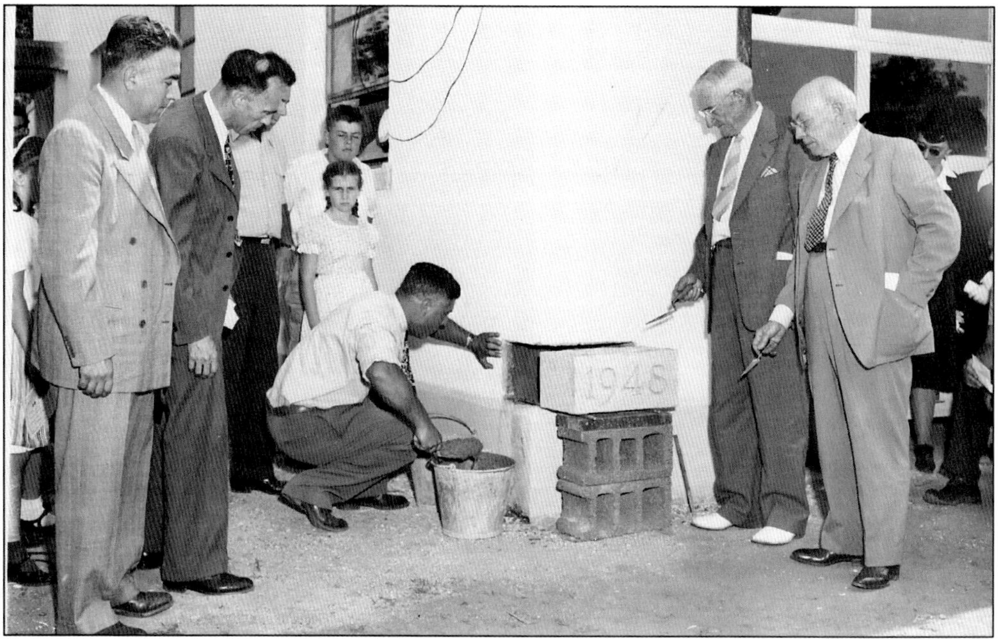

A CORNERSTONE LAYING, 1948. When the Liberty Hose Company completed its new firehouse on the corner of Route 36 and Atlantic Street it was heralded by many as one of the most modern in the state. Here, at the cornerstone laying, two of the company's charter members prepare to place the finishing cement upon it.

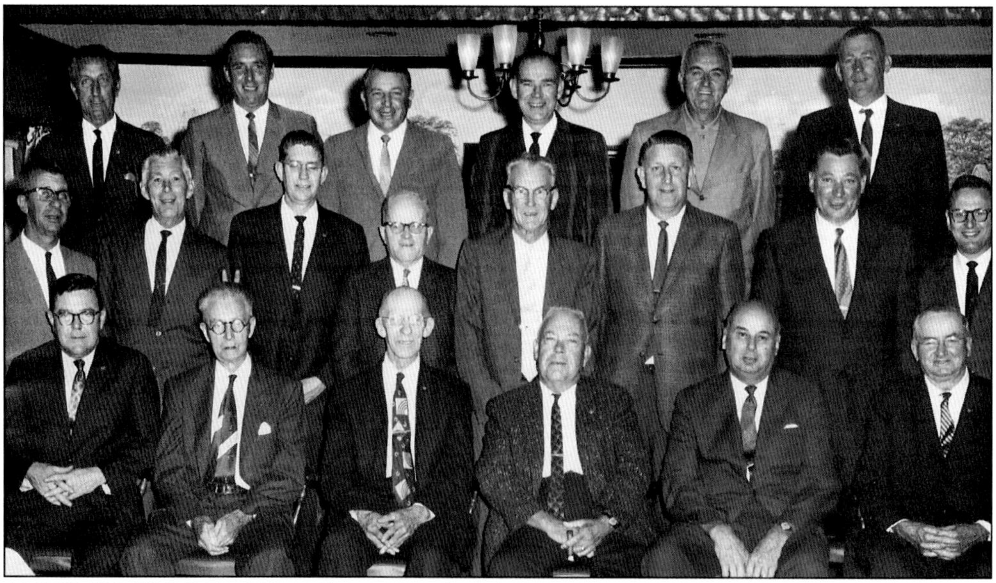

AN EX-CHIEF'S DINNER, MAY 1969. This photograph was taken by 1990 Chief Jim Atkins. From left to right are the following ex-chiefs and the year they were elected: (front row) H. Creed (1969), H. Poling (1945), D. Clark (1922–1924), E. Walling (1943), K. Conklin (1942), and W. Walling (1937); (middle row) G. Leone (1961), J.L. Schanck (1957), D. Redmond (1968), H. Currie (1954), C. Hopla (1952), B. Rose (1970), Inspector G. Ellison, and Commissioner J. Rosato; (back row) T. Tice (1958), W. Newman (1966), J. Collins (1962), E. Walker (1963), and F. VanPelt (1967).

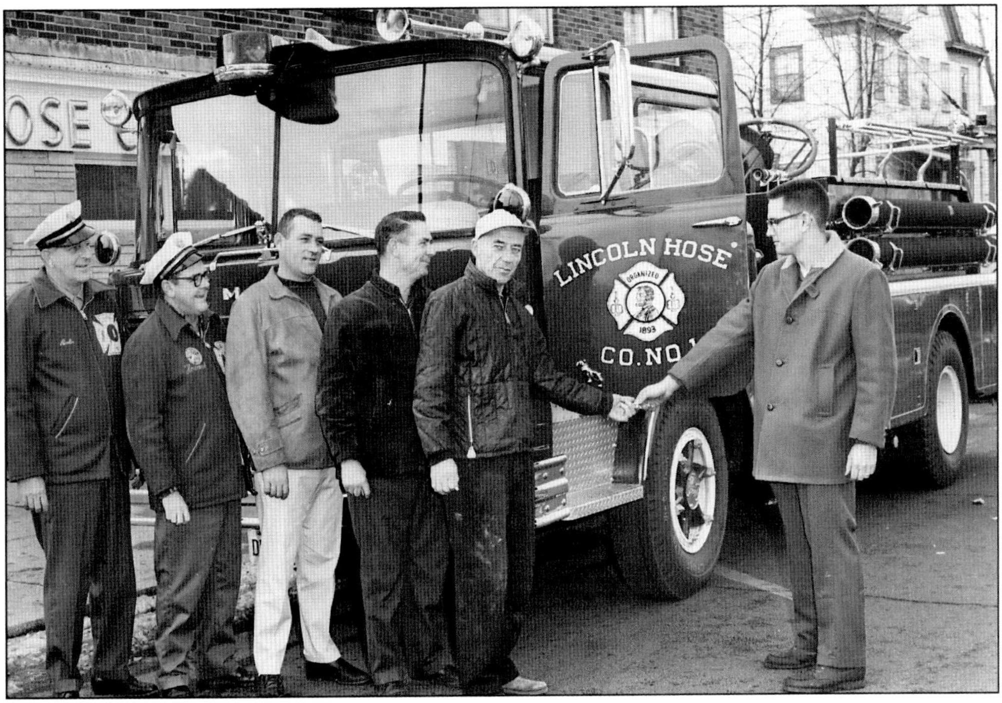

THE NEW LINCOLN HOSE CO. ENGINE, DECEMBER 21, 1968. Christmas came early for the Lockport boys when the borough took delivery of a new Mack CF pumper. The new apparatus was capable of pumping over 1,250 gallons of water per minute and was the third Mack operated by the company. Here, Bill Russell of Glasofer Mack hands the keys over to Alan Lee, with Leroy Hicks, Frank "Junior" VanPelt, and fire Chiefs Howard Creed and Bob Rose looking on.

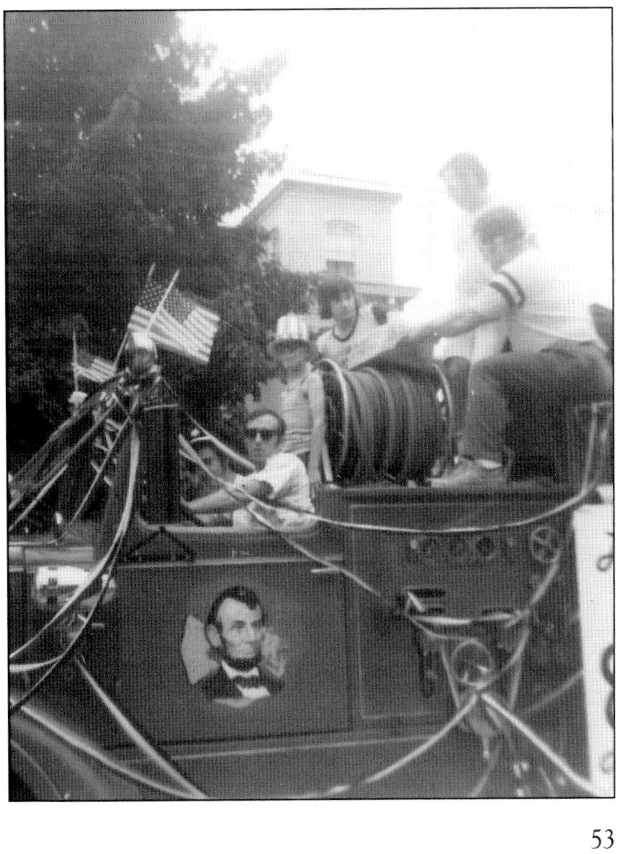

KEYPORT DAY, 1973. Though it had been sold almost five years before, several members borrowed the old 1941 Mack for a parade in 1973. It was decorated and a large portrait of Lincoln was put on the doors for the day. This old war wagon made its final appearance in the town on this day and hasn't been seen since.

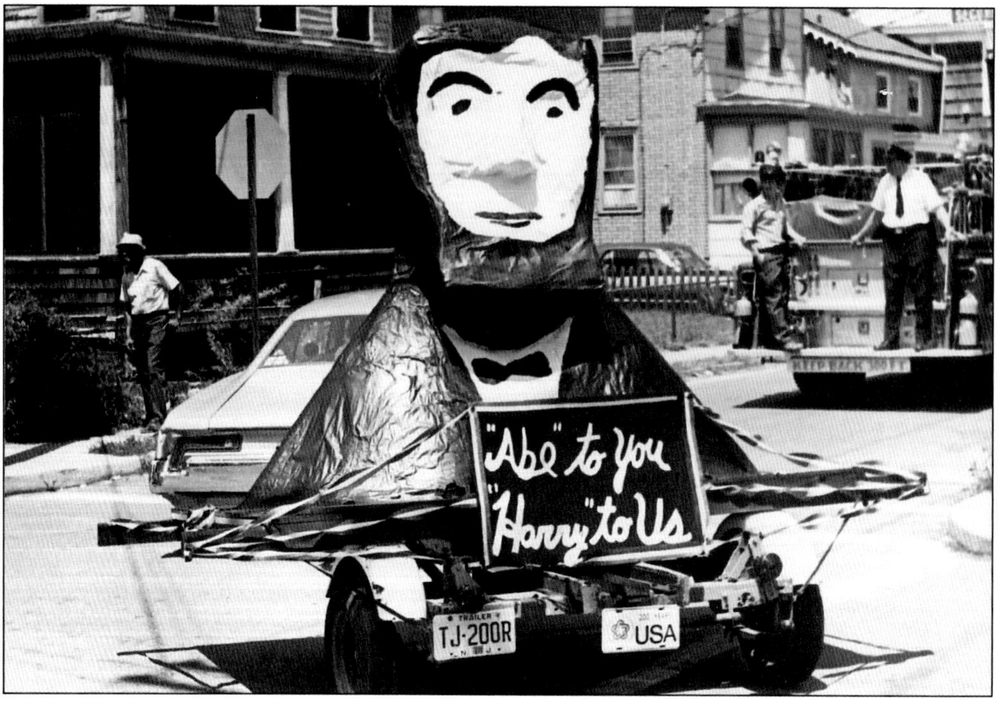

A KEYPORT DAY FLOAT, 1973. Let's see. Some paper machete, a little wire, and a trailer to built it on and, voila—an Abe Lincoln head and torso fit for any parade. The float was built by members of the Lincoln Hose Co. and won first prize in the 1973 Keyport Day Parade.

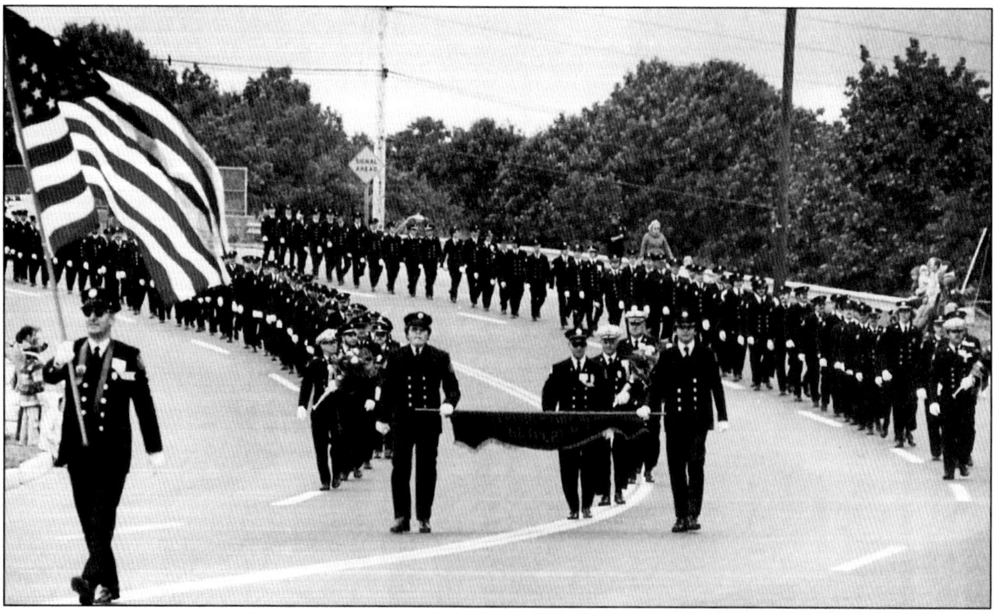

THE 100TH ANNIVERSARY PARADE. On October 8, 1977, over two hundred fire departments from across the state traveled to town to help celebrate Monmouth County's seventh oldest fire department. In the lead of the parade was Jules Rosato with the flag, and George Sappah and Mark Silva with the banner, followed by over 146 members of the Keyport Fire Department.

THE FIREMEN'S MONUMENT, 1970. The old fire bell was taken down in 1957 with plans that it would one day be used as a centerpiece for a monument. That dream came true in 1962 as the monument and the small park along Front Street were dedicated to all of the past and present Keyport firemen. In 1996 a additional tablet was erected honoring Jacob Leyrer Jr., the only firefighter to die in the line of duty since 1877.

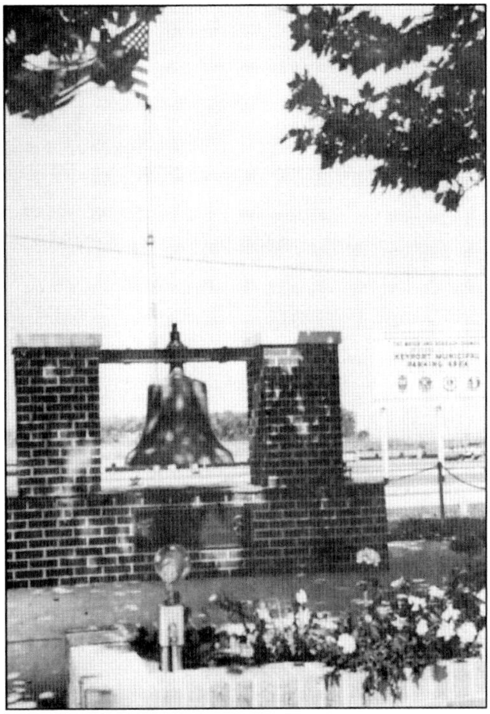

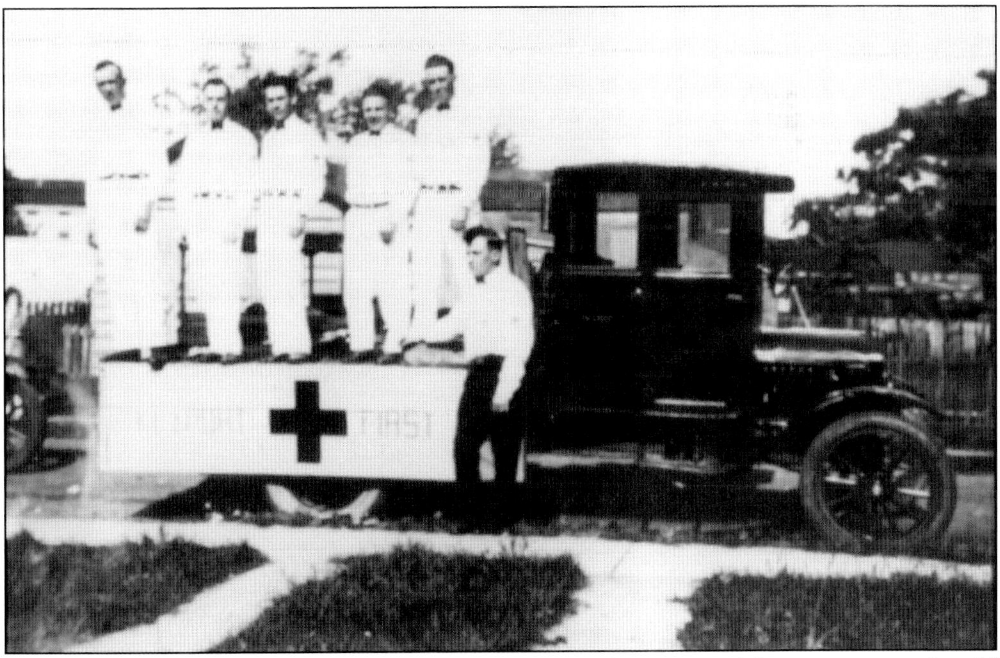

THE KEYPORT FIRST AID SQUAD, *c.* 1930. In 1927 a group of firemen met in the old Main Street engine house to begin taking first aid lessons. In the first year the squad answered thirty-three calls and saved four lives using a resuscitator and the Engine Company's 1919 American LaFrance. In 1928 the unit officially organized as the First Aid Squad of the Keyport Fire Department. This squad is on record as the first unofficial squad in the state and the second squad formed in Monmouth County.

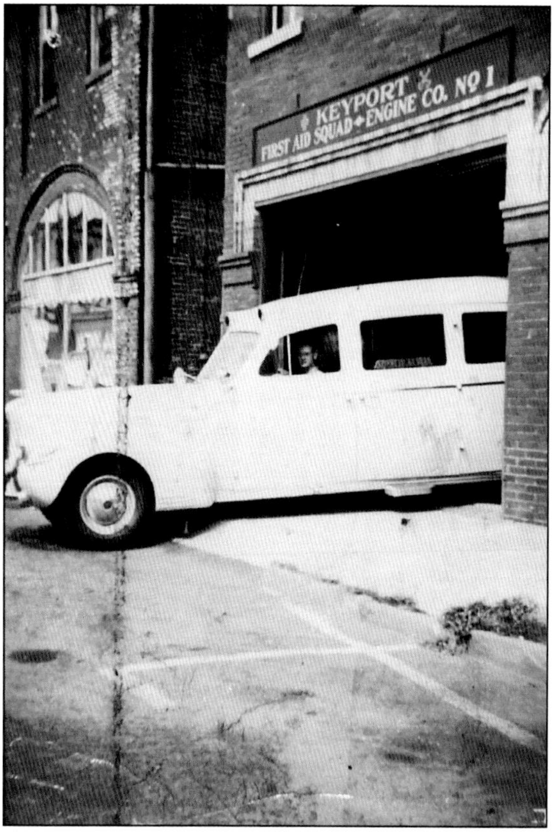

THE FIRST AID SQUAD'S LASALLE. The squad's second ambulance was this late 1930s LaSalle, with an unknown-type bodywork, shown here in front of headquarters on Main Street. The squad remained here until around 1942, when they purchased a building at 118 Broad Street; after rebuilding it into the new headquarters, they remained there until 1967. In 1968, over 950 calls were answered and in 1995 that number had more than doubled.

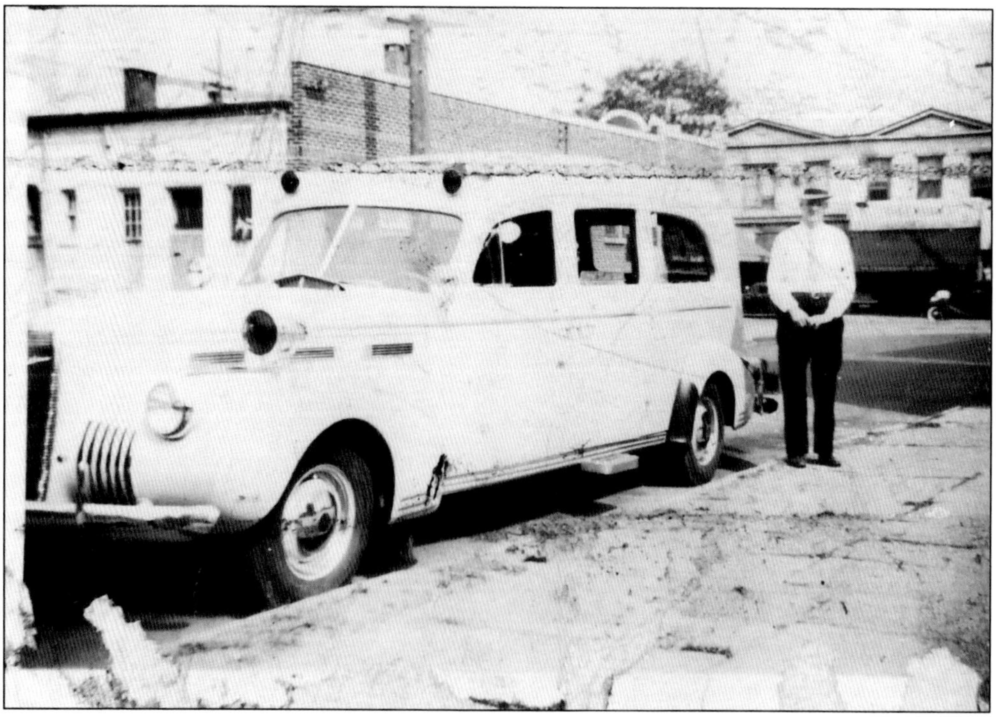

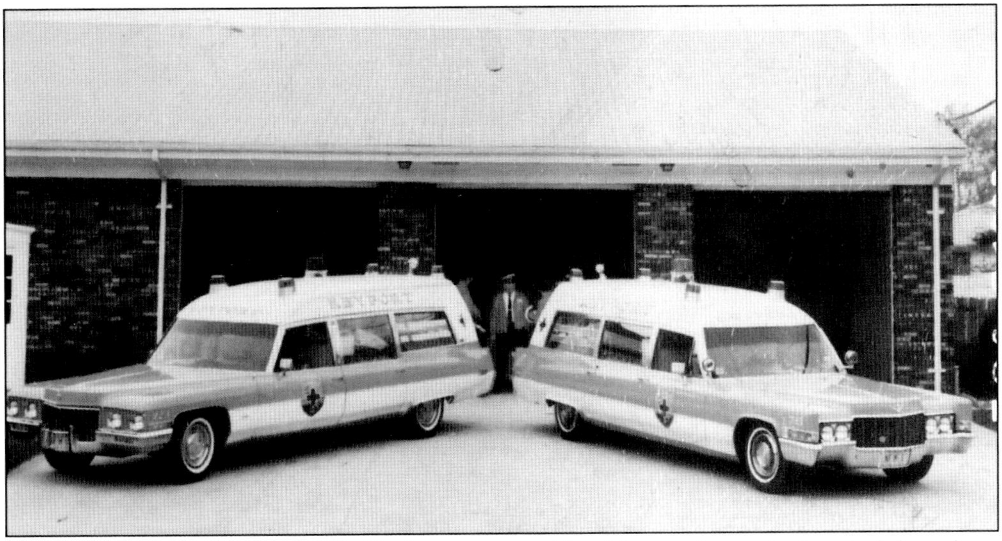

THE FIRST AID SQUAD, 1971. Nothing was capable of faster trips to the hospital than these two Cadillac Fleetwoods with big V-8 power. The Caddy to the left of the photograph was delivered in 1971 in the new orange and white color scheme with teal lettering and a large blue light. The 1969 Caddy was repainted to match and since that time all ambulances have been painted in this extremely pretty color scheme. These two units were also the first to feature the squad's new emblem.

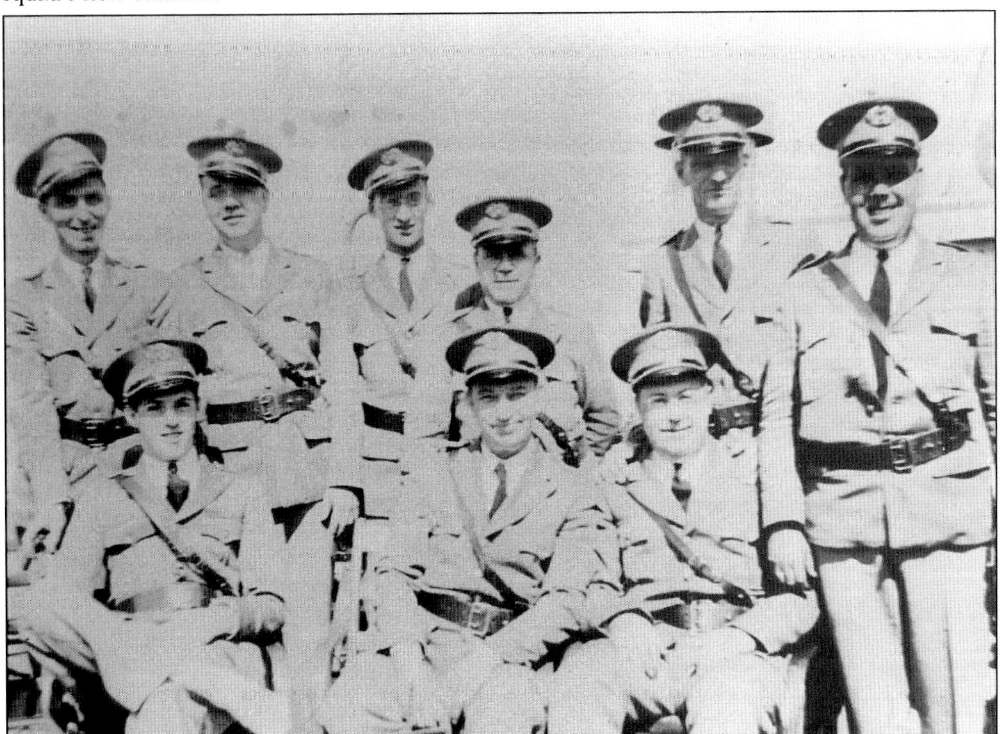

THE POLICE DEPARTMENT, 1935. No, these men are not storm troopers, they are Keyport's "finest" in a photograph taken sometime before World War II. To the extreme right is Maitland Walling, who later served as chief of the department.

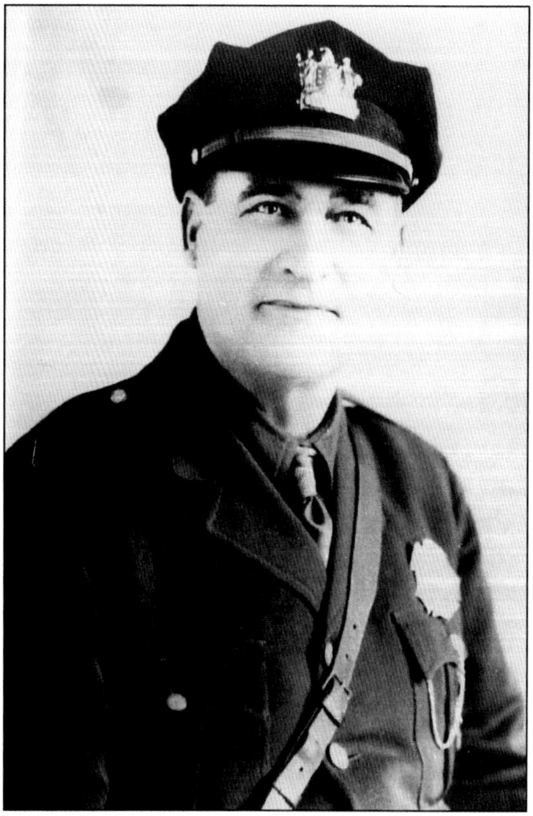

AN UNKNOWN POLICE CAPTAIN, c. 1937. Keyport's police department was officially begun around 1905, when the first full-time officer was hired to patrol the entire town on foot. Since that time the police department has grown to nearly twenty officers who patrol twenty-four hours a day, utilizing six cars and two bicycles.

A NEW POLICE CAR. Here, Chief Sproul and Police Commissioner Harvey Hartmen pose with the borough's new patrol car, a fine 1949 Pontiac. This six-cylinder Silver Streak model cost about $1,700 when new and was painted all black with lots of chrome. One thing could be sure—if you heard this car with its siren screaming through town on a Friday night, you just knew something "big" had to be going on somewhere.

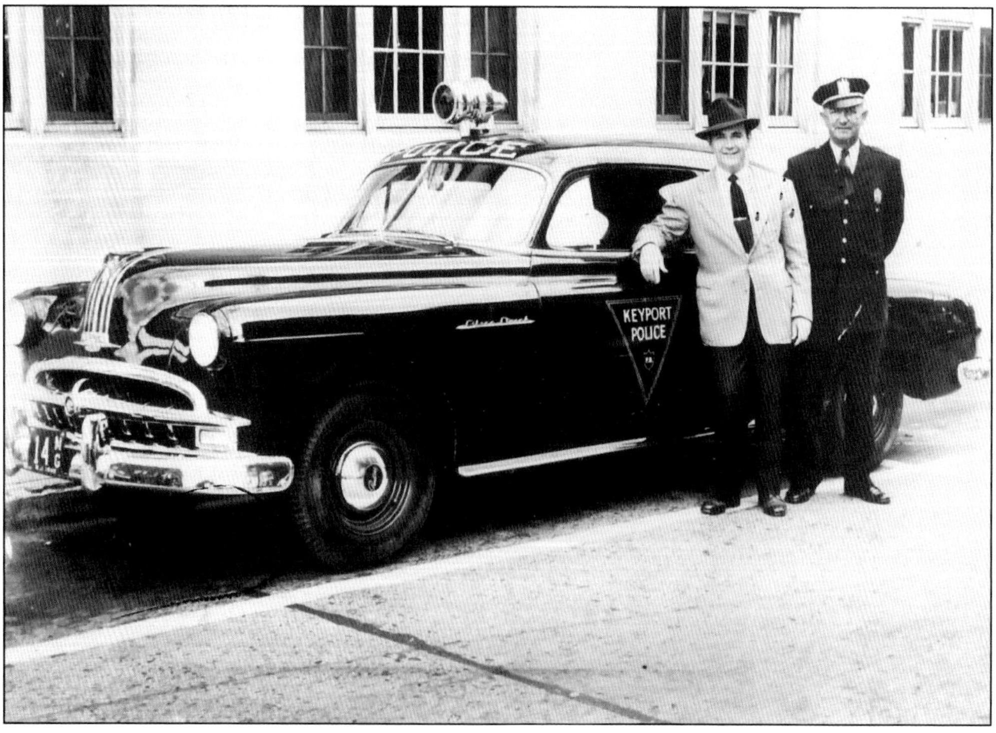

Four

Down by the Docks

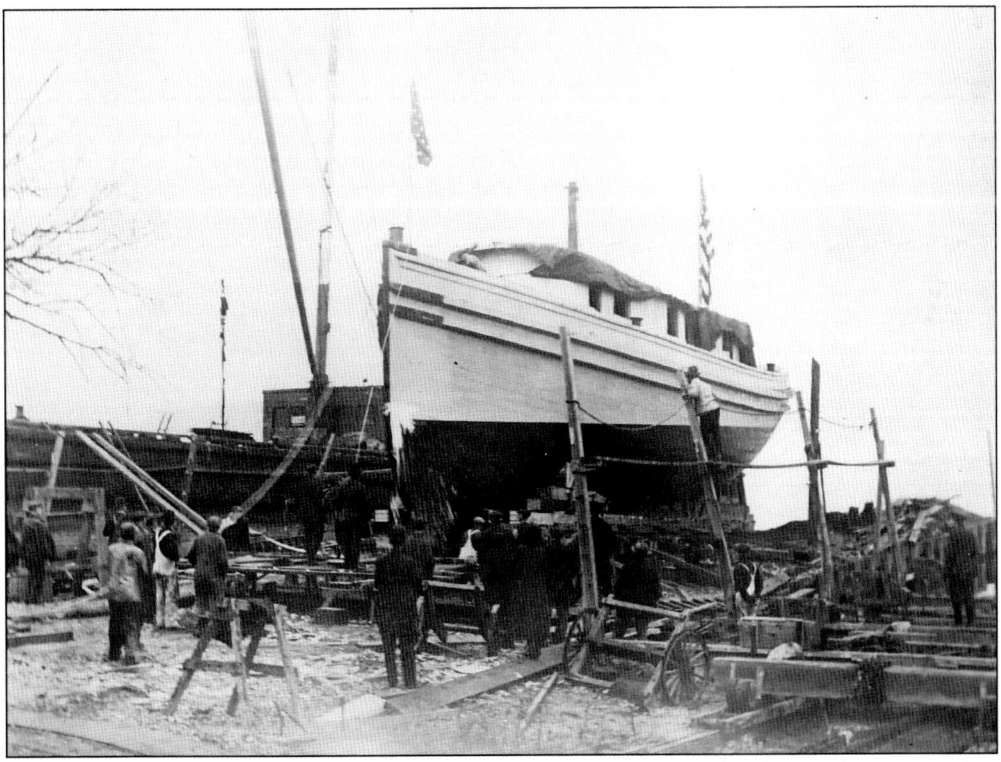

THE LAUNCHING OF A LAUNCH, 1920. As the champagne bottle smashes against her keel, a cheer from the men who built her can be heard from the blocks. The *Victor T. Kelly* was launched at Keyport, NJ, on November 27, 1920, by the Keyport Dry Dock Co. It was later modified with a diesel engine and its name changed to the *Terry Buchanan*.

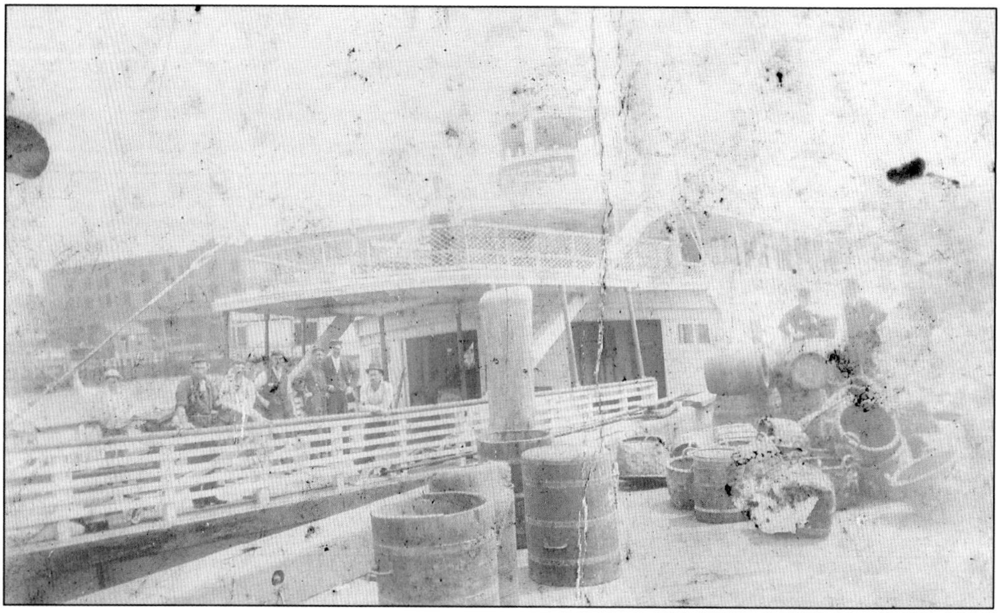

THE *MAGENTA*, c. 1870. Without the great steamboat trade the village of Keyport would have never flourished into the nineteenth century as a port. The *Magenta* played a big part in shaping the town, hauling freight and passengers on her 197-foot hull. Built in 1864, she was scrapped in 1905.

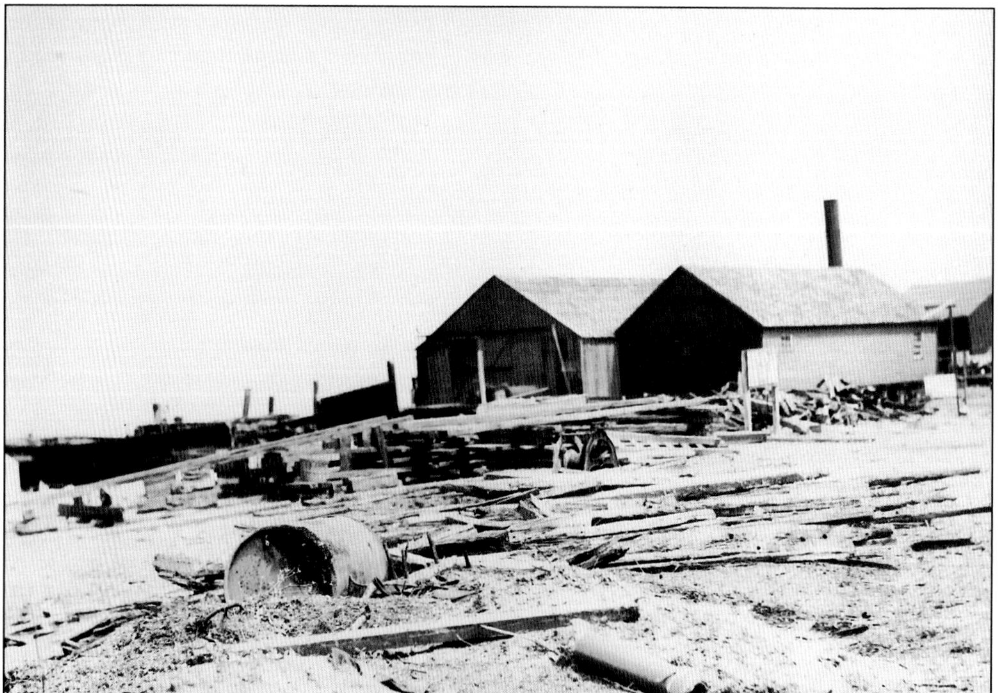

THE OLD BOATYARD, 1910. All along the shores of Raritan Bay and its creeks boat building has flourished since before the Revolution. One spot that has been in continuous operation as a shipyard is the property off Front Street, running northwest along the Luppattacong Creek.

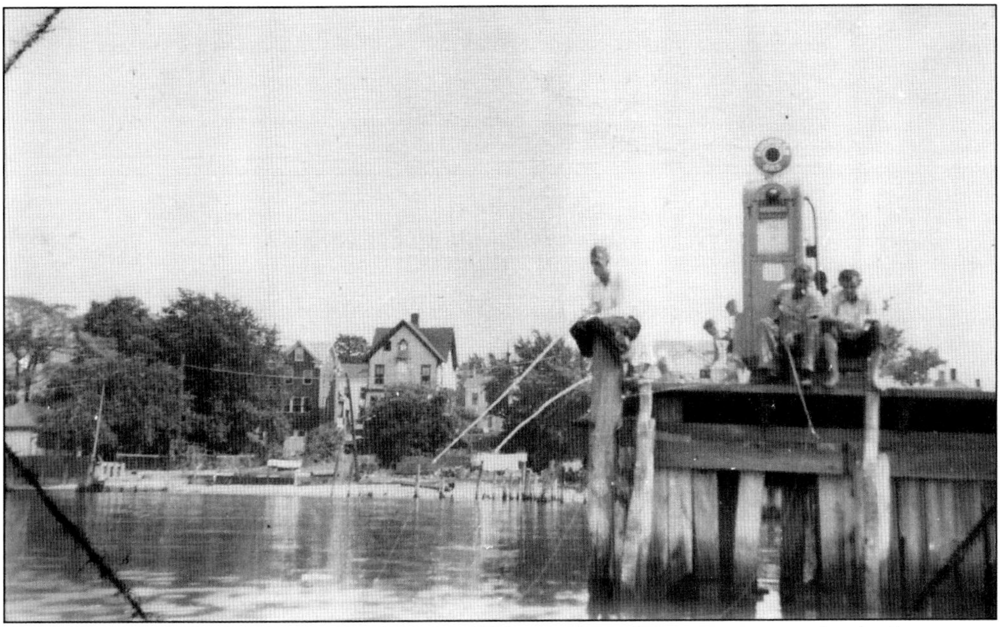

ERICKSON'S DOCK, *c.* 1960. Nothing could beat a lazy afternoon waiting for the big one in and around Keyport Harbor. For boaters and fisherman alike the old dock served as refueling station, jetty, and focal point for many "fishy" stories. It was replaced by the new fishing pier in 1976, which was later named in honor of former mayor William Ralph.

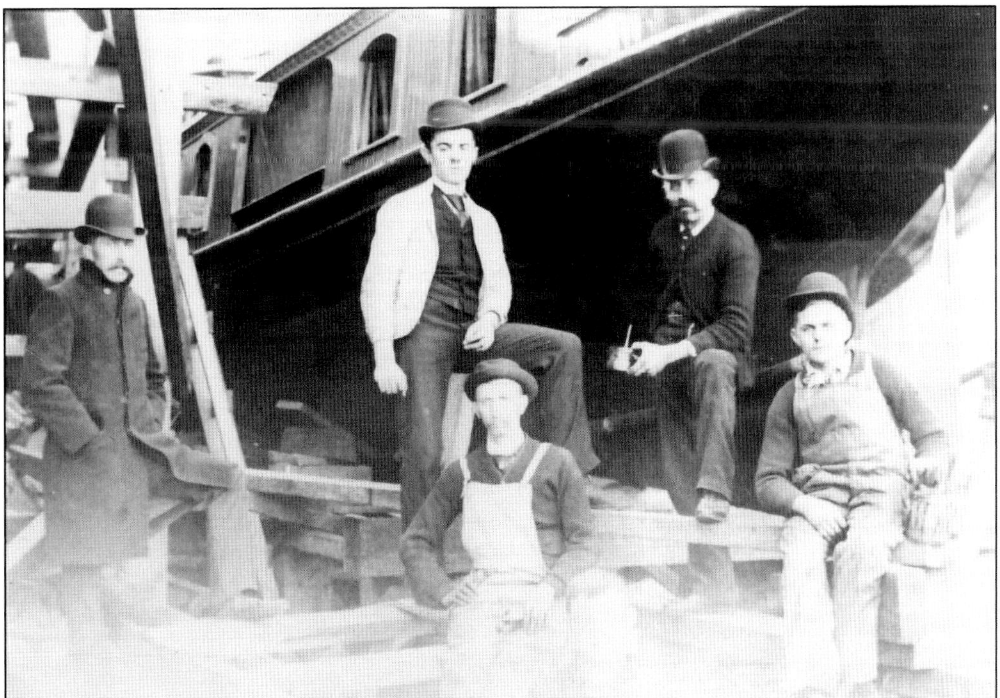

BOAT PAINTERS, *c.* 1887. Look into the faces of these men, none of whom appear very happy at the task at hand. Scraping and painting a boat's hull has always been essential in increasing the life span of sea craft, no matter how big or small.

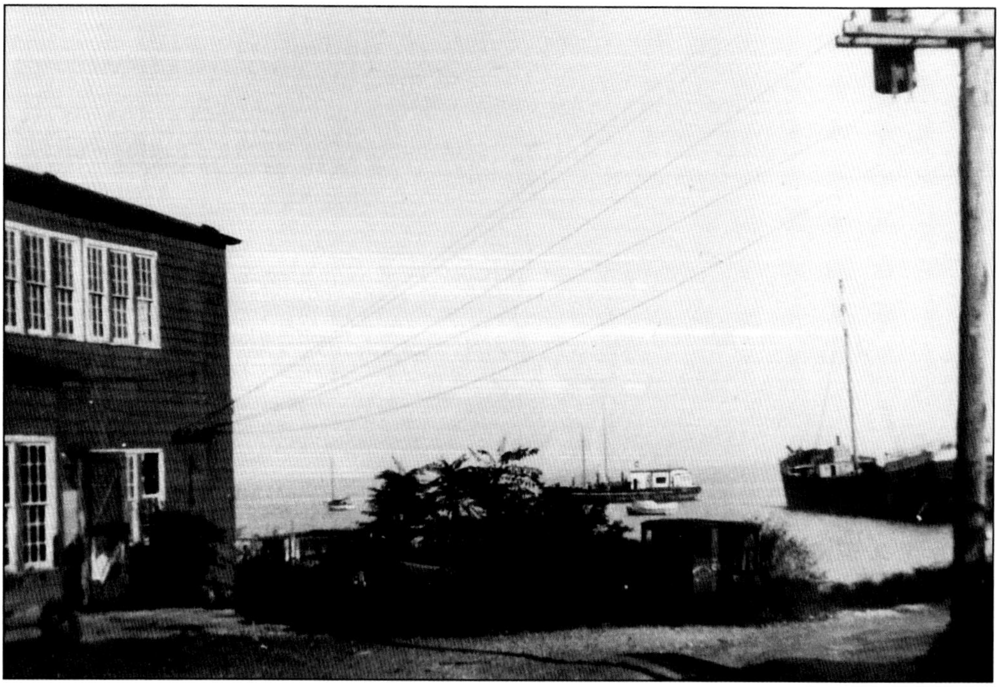

THE LOCKPORT BOATYARD, *c.* 1919. If you take Prospect Street down to the bay, you'll come to a fine boatyard where they'll fix your engine, mend your sails, or perhaps run a little moonshine for ya'. Rum running was a major vice in the 1930s, so much so that boatbuilders such as Holger Kofoed built boats for the government as well as the "Rum Runners" themselves.

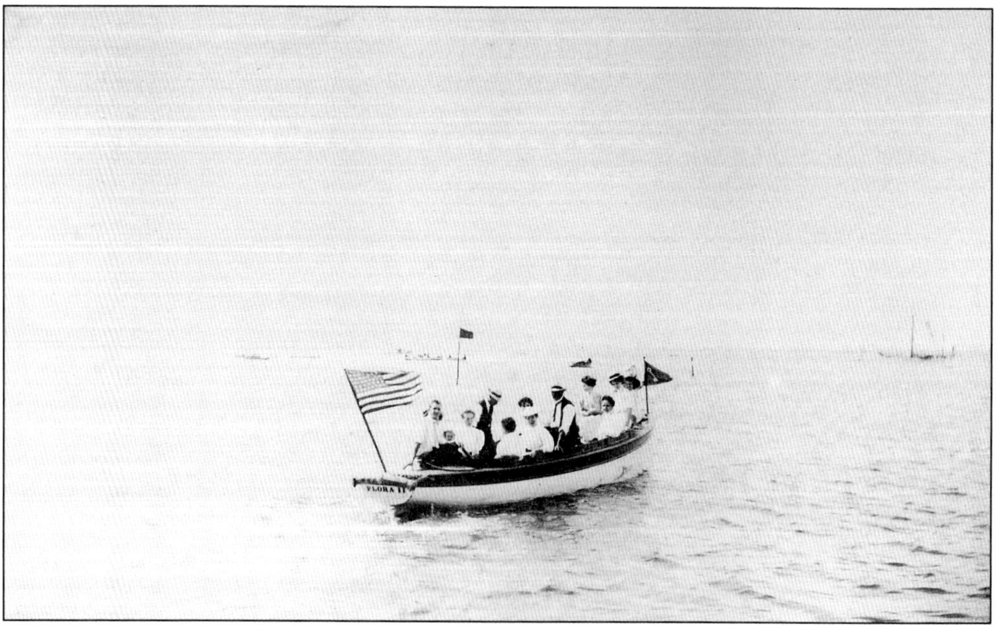

A LAUNCH, THE *FLORA II*, *c.* 1915. It is thought that this launch was operated by the yacht club to transport sailors to their boats when they were moored out into the channel. Of course, when not being used for its true purpose it was all right to go out for a ride in the bay with some friends.

AN ADVERTISEMENT, *c*. 1920. The Keyport Boat Works was located in West Keyport, and was owned by H. Martin Kofoed. This yard competed with the scores of other village boatbuilders into the 1950s. Like so many ads of today, the area for prices has been left blank!

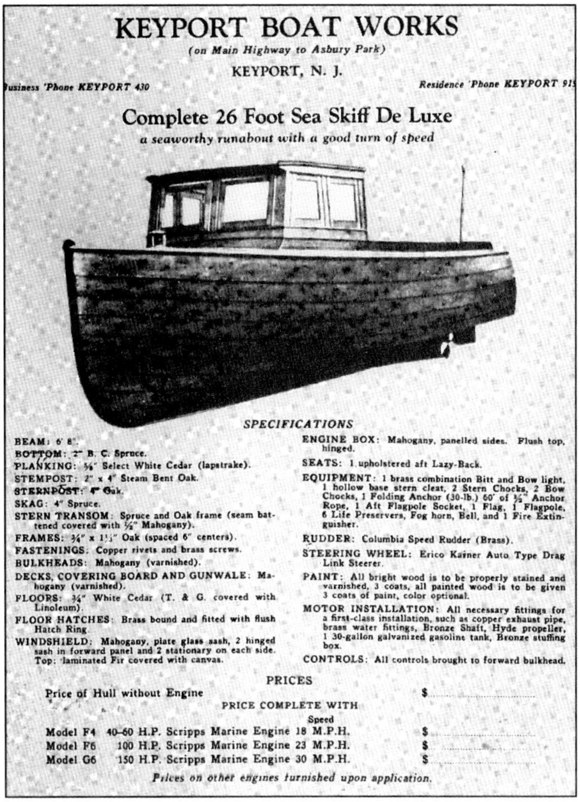

BURROWES' LUMBERYARD DOCKS, *c*. 1900. Thomas Burrowes purchased the lumber and coal business from David Warner around 1867. Mr. Burrowes went about rebuilding the dock and lumber sheds. The business prospered well into the twentieth century before it finally closed. The dock was later cleared of the buildings and became part of Erickson's Dock. The area was filled in around 1969 to create American Legion Drive.

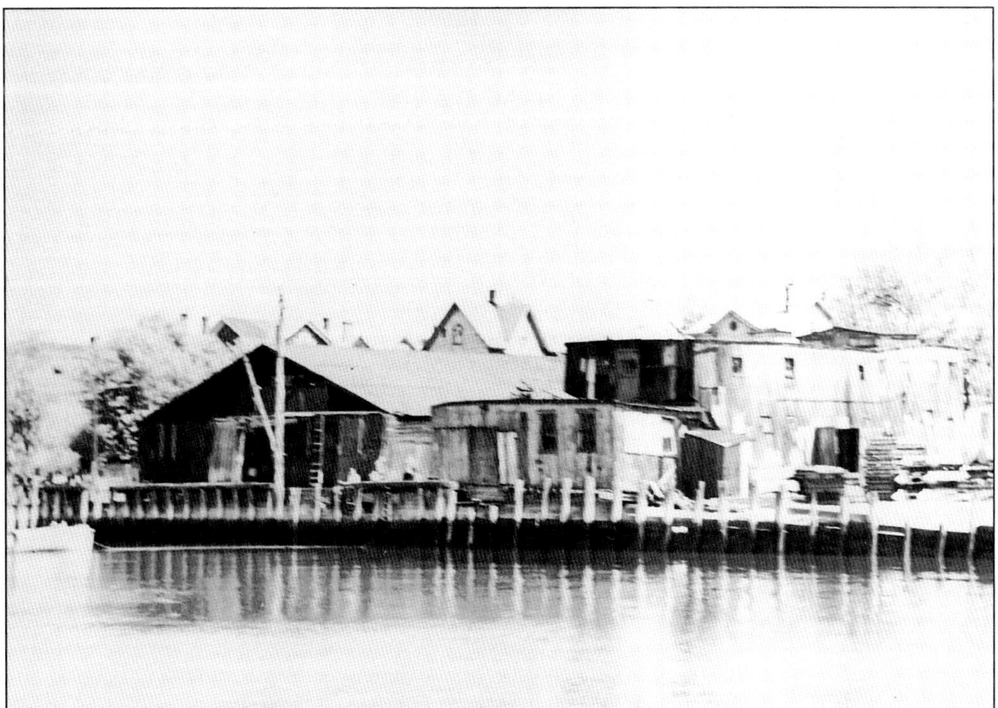

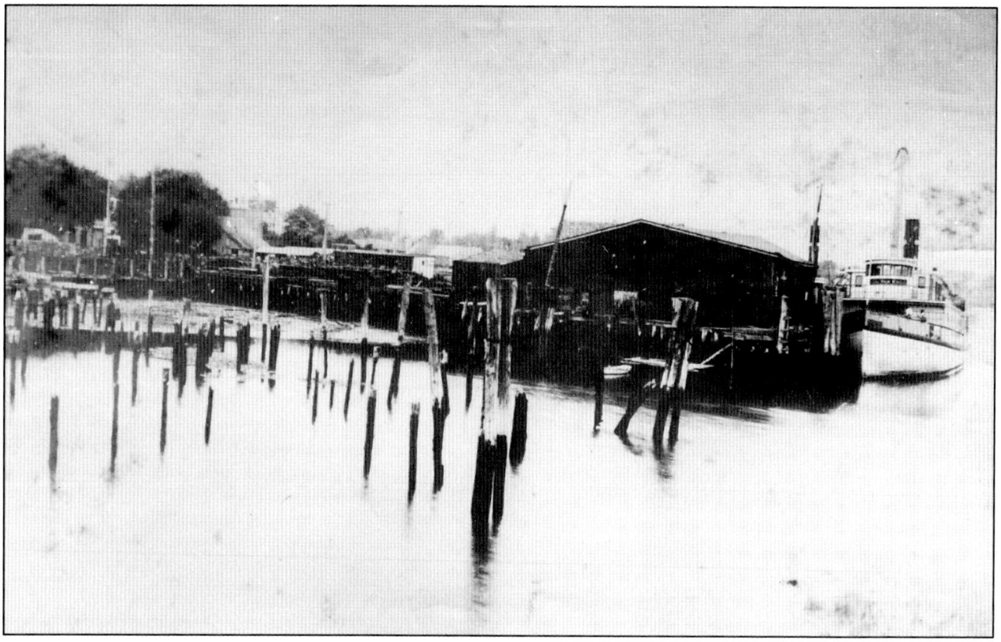

THE STEAMBOAT DOCK, *c.* 1886. Built in 1858 in New York City, the *Kill Van Kull* was 252 feet long and is shown here tied up at the Keyport Dock. The ship was scrapped in 1889, which makes this one the oldest known views of the Keyport waterfront.

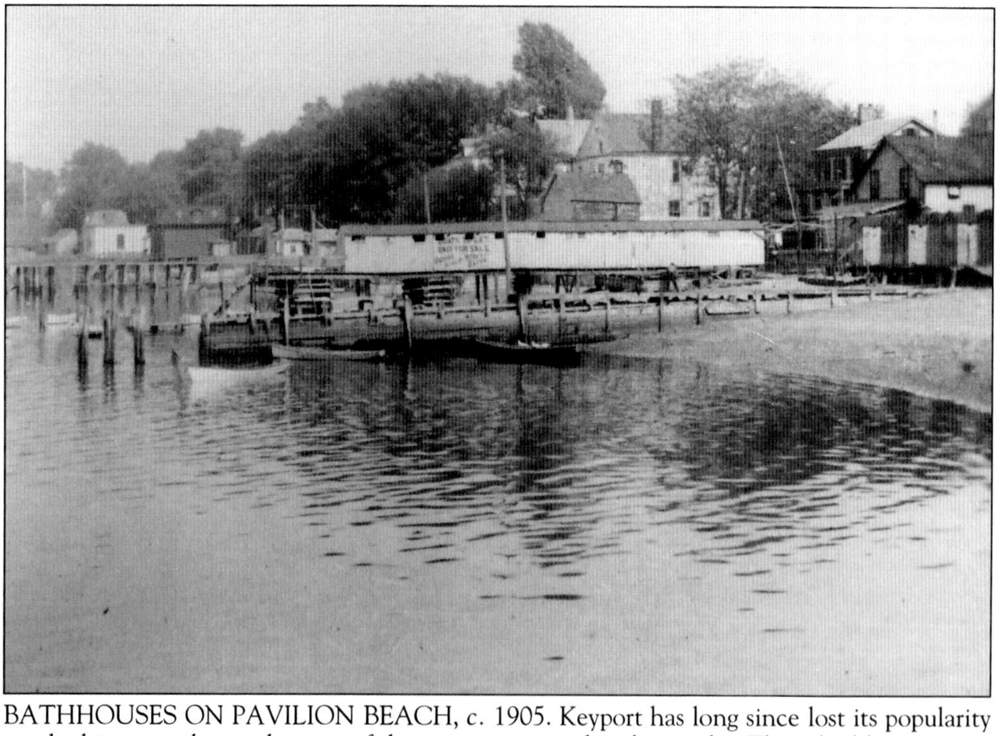

BATHHOUSES ON PAVILION BEACH, *c.* 1905. Keyport has long since lost its popularity as a bathing spot, but at the turn of the century it was the place to be. These bathhouses were erected from scrap lumber, and after years of standing along the beach they were lost to the 1944 hurricane.

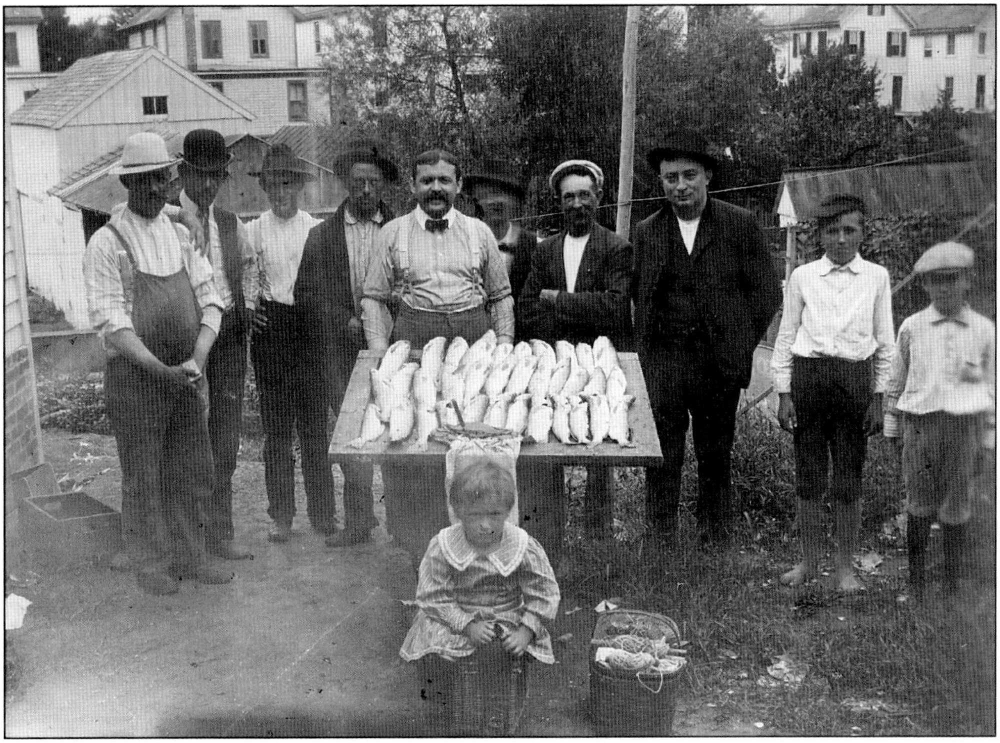

FISHERMEN, c. 1906. Taken in the side yard of the house at the northeast corner of First and Spring Streets, this is how many made their living along these shores beginning in the sixteenth century. These men are extremely proud of their big catch, and after some cleaning and frying, tonight's supper will be most tasty!

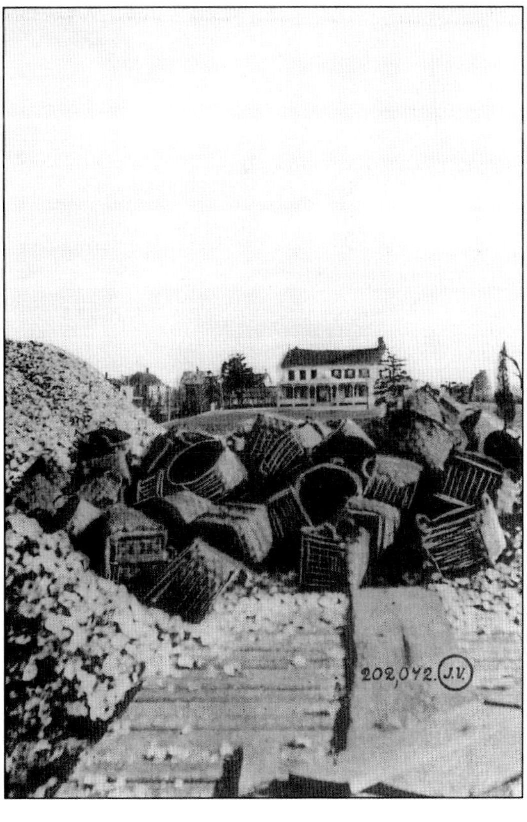

BUSHEL BASKETS, c. 1904. With the Key Grove Plantation house as a backdrop, these baskets have just been emptied on the J & J.W. Ellsworth Oyster Docks along Front and Beers Street. Previous to the 1990s clamming had been banned for over seventy-five years, due in part to heavily polluted waters.

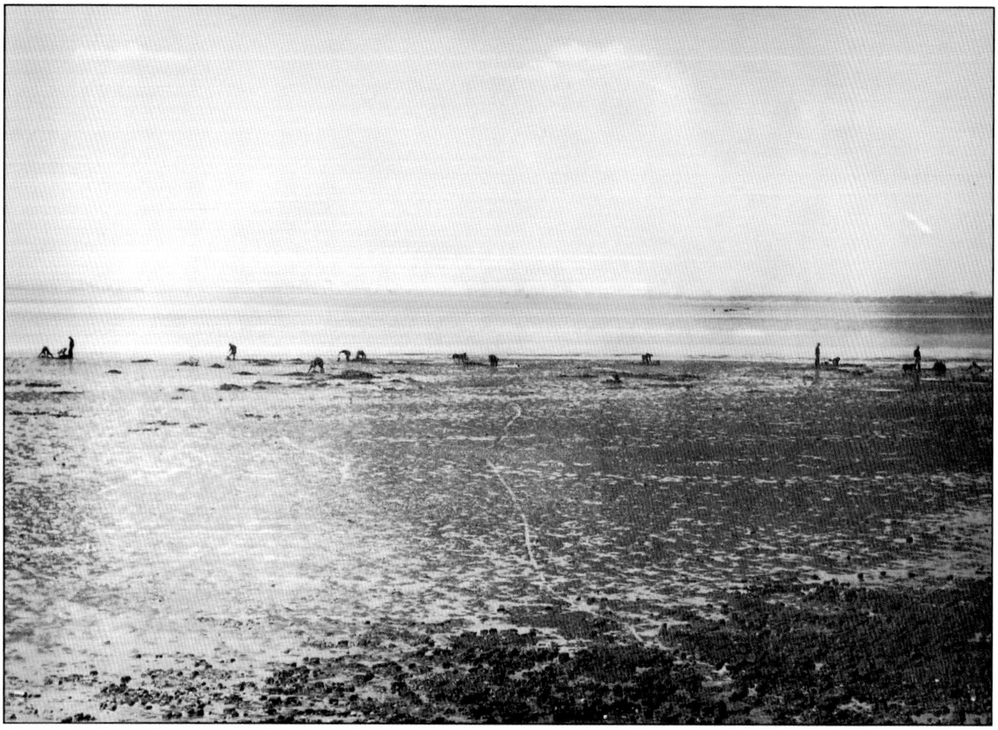

CLAMMING AT LOW TIDE, *c.* 1912. It is unusual to see a photograph of men actually clamming (it was always more glamorous to show the catch), and this one is especially welcome. It is believed to have been taken off the end of Beers Street during a full moon low tide.

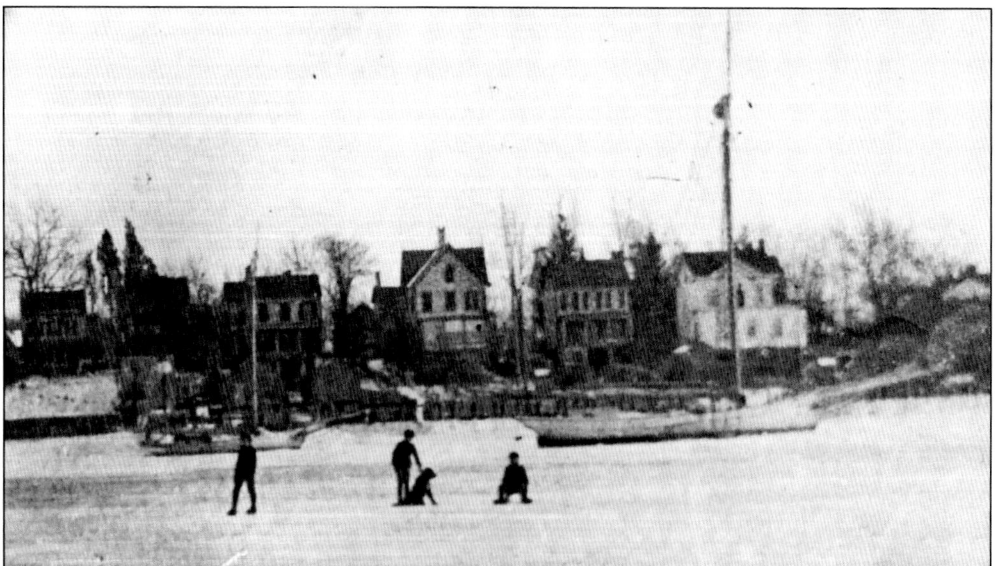

WINTERTIME ON THE BAY, *c.* 1890. I'm sure these young lads were told by mother not to go on the ice, and of course they didn't listen. It could be thrilling to walk up to the oyster skiffs and schooners which always froze in during the deep winter chill. The houses in the background still stand along Front Street.

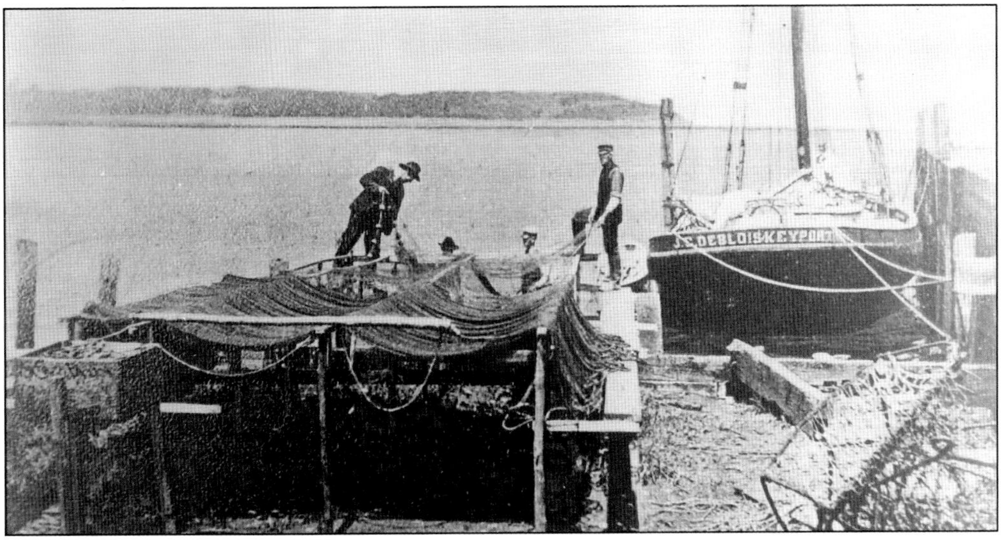

MENDING FISHING NETS, *c.* 1901. The life of a fisherman was not an easy one—it included being up before sunrise, rough seas, and the constant repair of the tools of the trade. A crew from the *J.E. Deblois* is shown here working on some seining nets alongside Thomas Burrowes' lumber yard at the beginning of the new century.

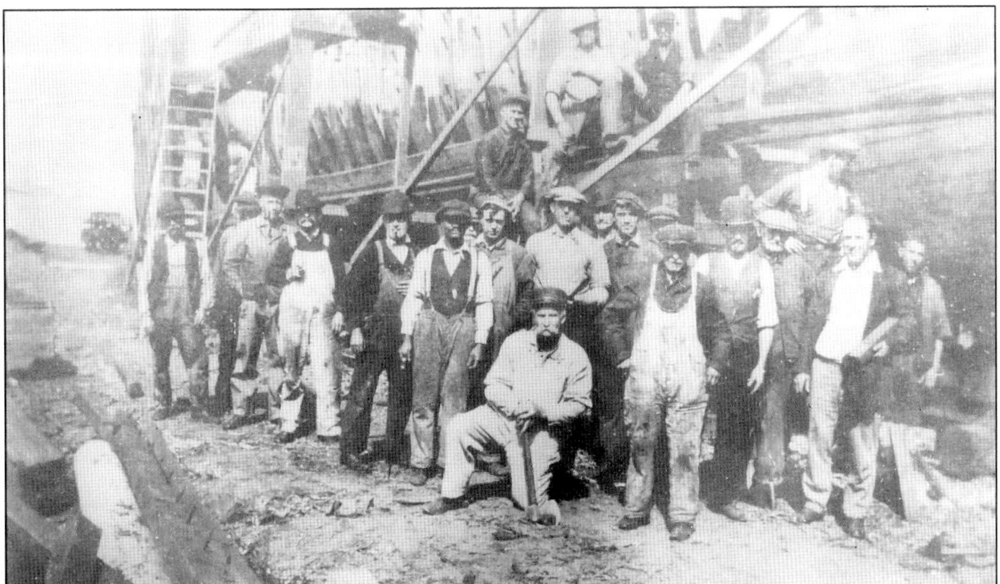

SHIP BUILDERS, *c.* 1901. There appears to be much work that has yet to be done on this schooner before she's ready to sail, but nevertheless all twenty-one craftsmen gathered for this portrait. It sometimes took up to a year for a large vessel such as this to be completed along the beach down at Ben Terry's Lockport yard.

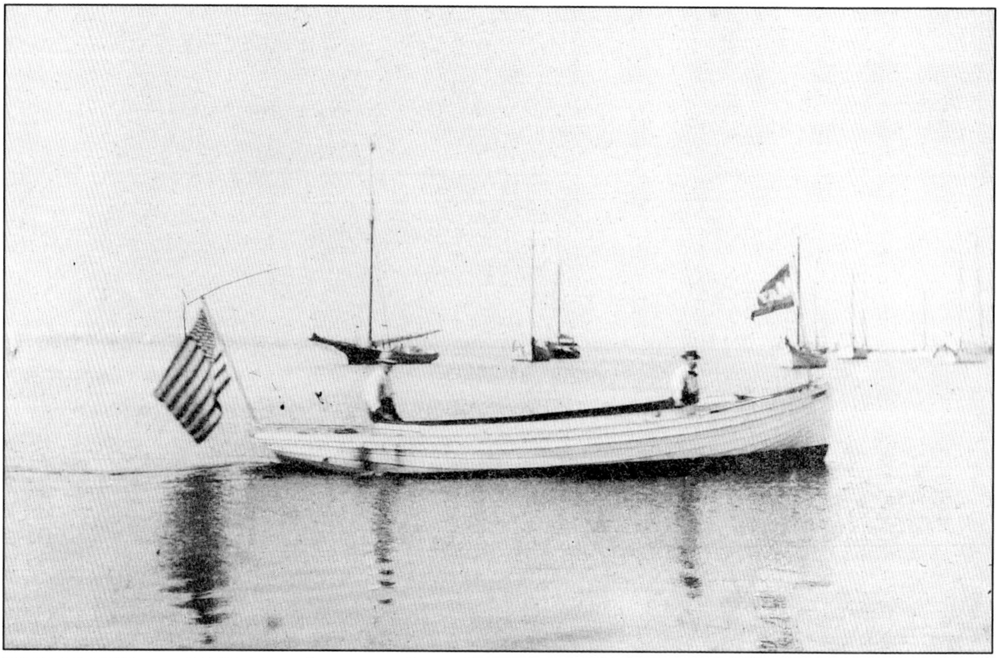

THE MAY *B.*, *c.* 1910. This fine open launch was most likely powered by a small four-cylinder engine, which would be capable of moving the vessel along quite nicely, even against the tide. One of the men in the boat is believed to be John Dougherty.

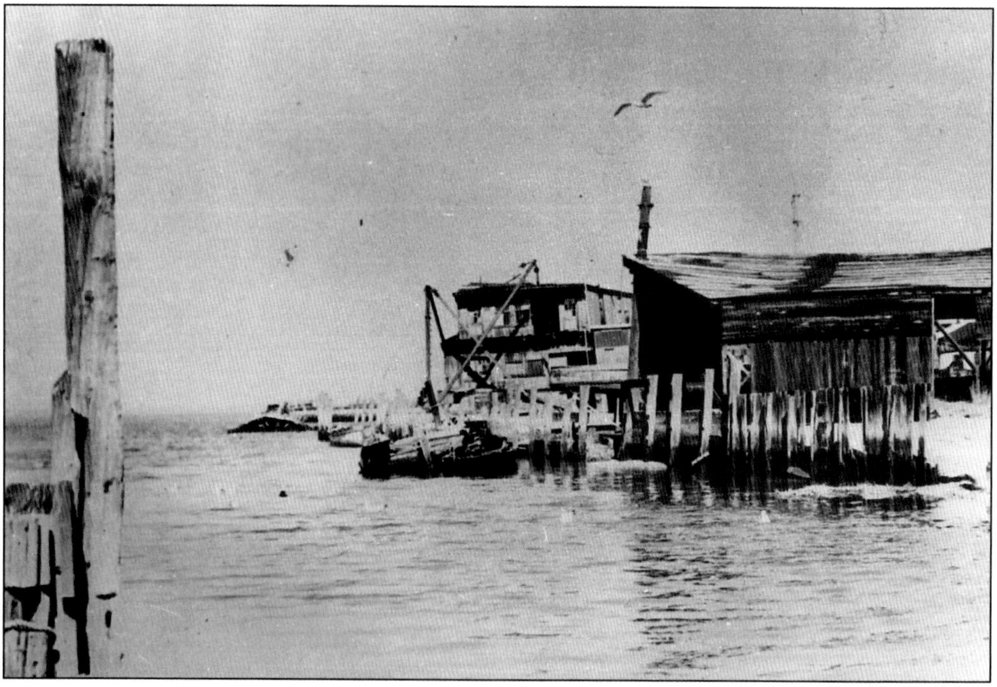

THE OLD COAL DOCKS, *c.* 1917. The old coal docks were crumbling just as fast as the photographer could snap this picture. Today, a walk along the shoreline by Veterans Park affords one a view of the old docks and even the barges themselves which repose silently beneath the high water mark, where they have laid since the 1940s.

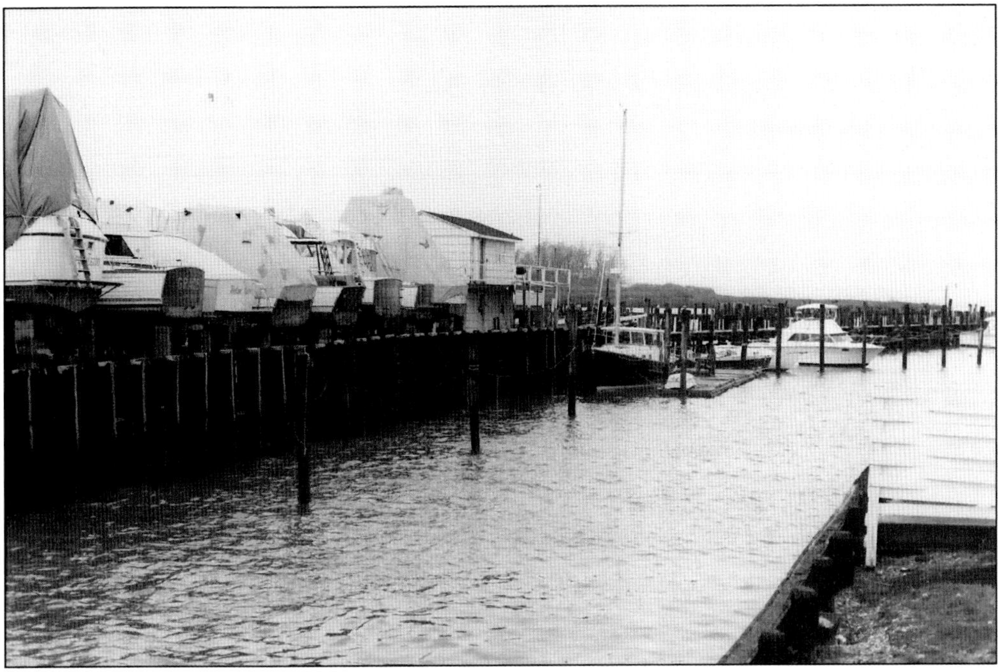

PEDERSEN'S MARINA AND CREEK, *c.* 1970. Every autumn, boats in Keyport's marinas are taken out, winterized, and put upon cinder blocks until mid-April, when work starts for a new season of boating. This photograph was taken at just about the same location as the bottom photograph on p. 62, albeit sixty years later.

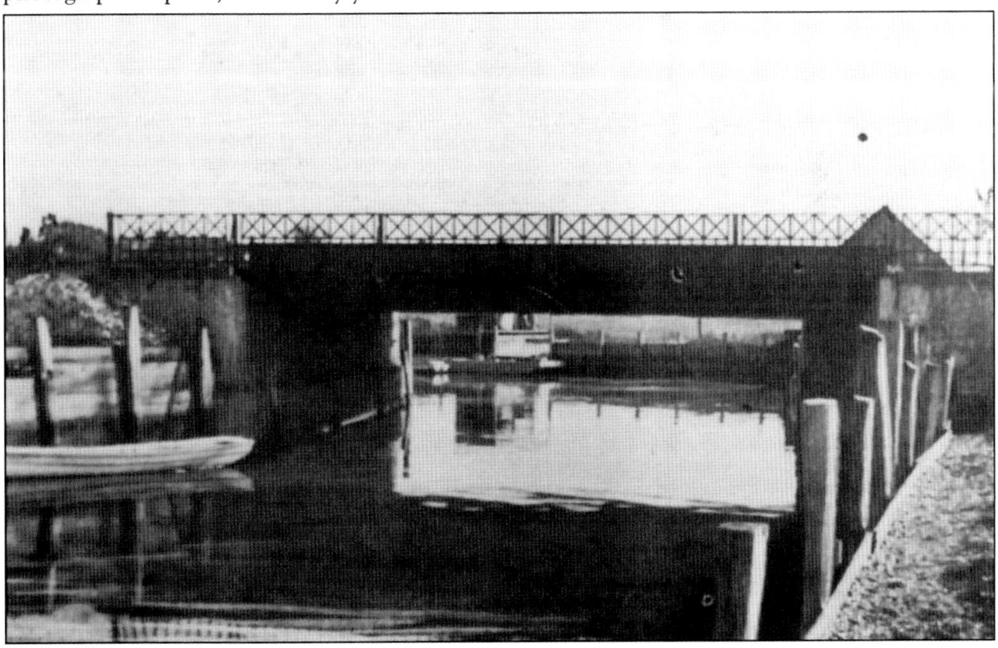

THE FRONT STREET BRIDGE, *c.* 1916. Keyport's historic bridge on Front Street is due to be replaced in 1997 after nearly ninety years of constant use! Through the years it has been known as the Oyster Creek Bridge, the Luppattacong Creek Bridge, and the Front Street Bridge. This view is looking south from the bay.

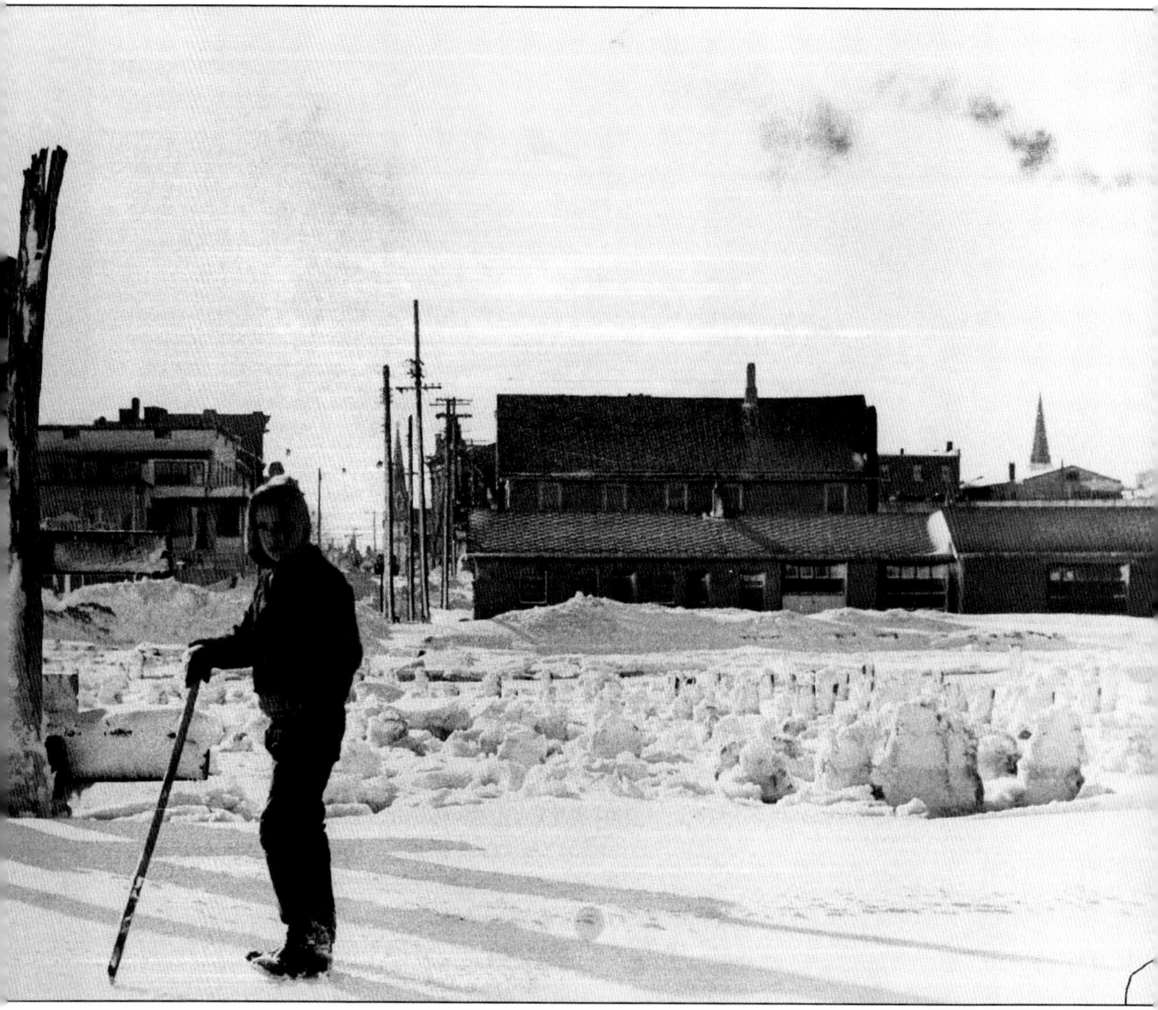

BROAD STREET AND THE FROZEN BAY, *c.* 1959. Some things never change, and if they do they change very little. This shot, which looks up Broad Street from the old steamboat wharf, shows the former Keansburg Steamboat Co. building (to the right), which through much hard work and dedication became the Steamboat Dock Museum of the Keyport Historical Society in the mid-1970s.

Five

Uptown-Downtown

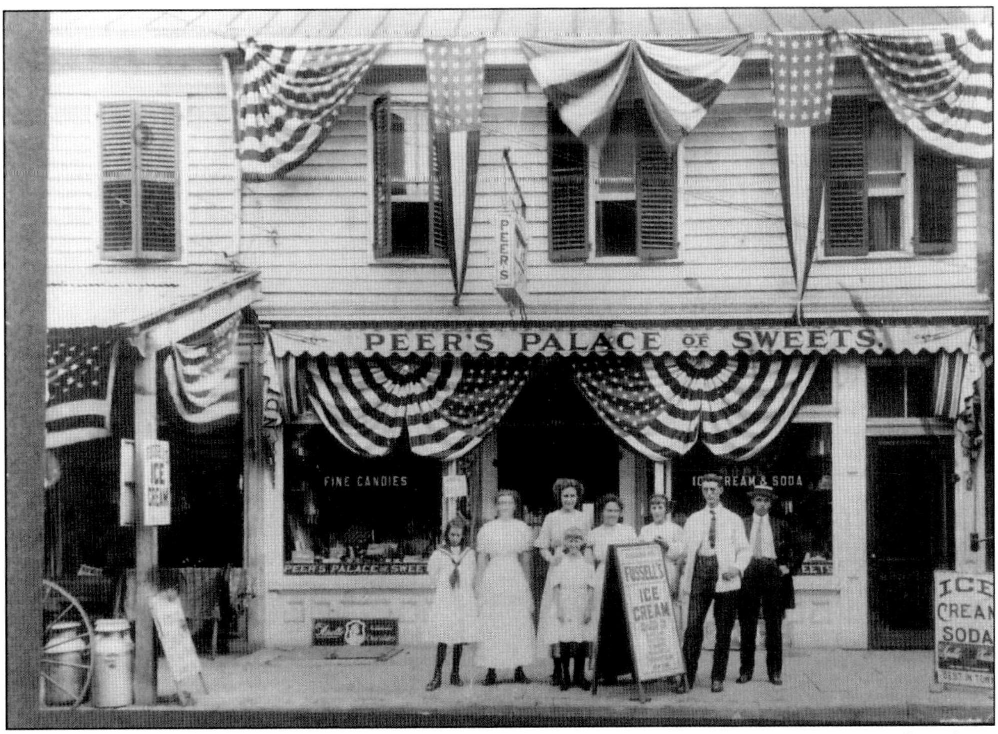

PEERS PLACE, *c.* 1906. During the early twentieth century Front Street was graced with at least three ice cream parlors. Peer's Palace of Sweets opened in this *c.* 1840 store on the south side of Front Street around 1900. The building's second story was removed in the 1960s.

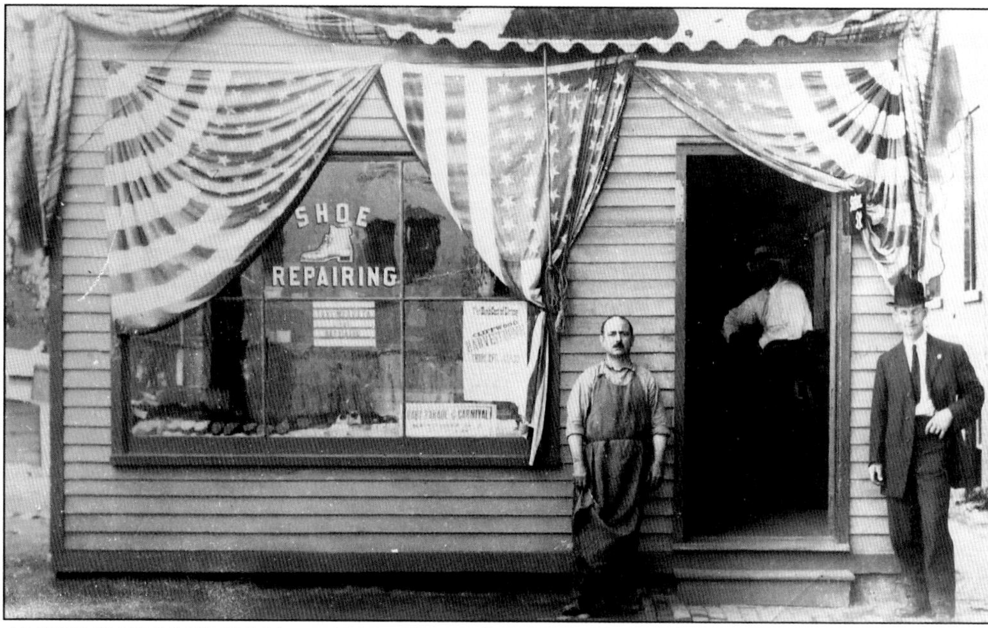

ANTONINO MAROTTA, *c.* 1914. Shoemakers were plentiful around the Front Street area during the twentieth century. Mr. Marotta had his shop on Broad Street next to Bedles Funeral Home, while Anthony Sidoti competed for your shoe business two doors away at the corner of Broad and Front.

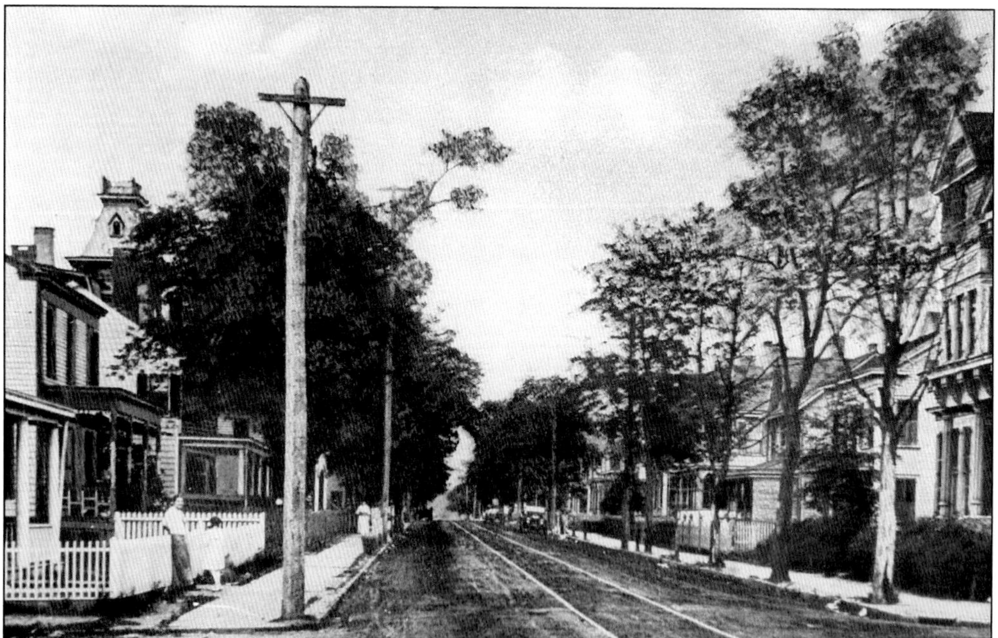

FIRST STREET, LOOKING EAST, *c.* 1905. Taken from the corner of First and Atlantic Streets, this photograph captures some of the oldest houses in town. The second house on the right was built by Asher Tilton in 1838. Mr. Tilton was an accomplished carpenter, who was responsible for building most of the dwellings in town. On September 9, 1905, at the age of ninety-one, Asher Tilton passed away at his beloved First Street home.

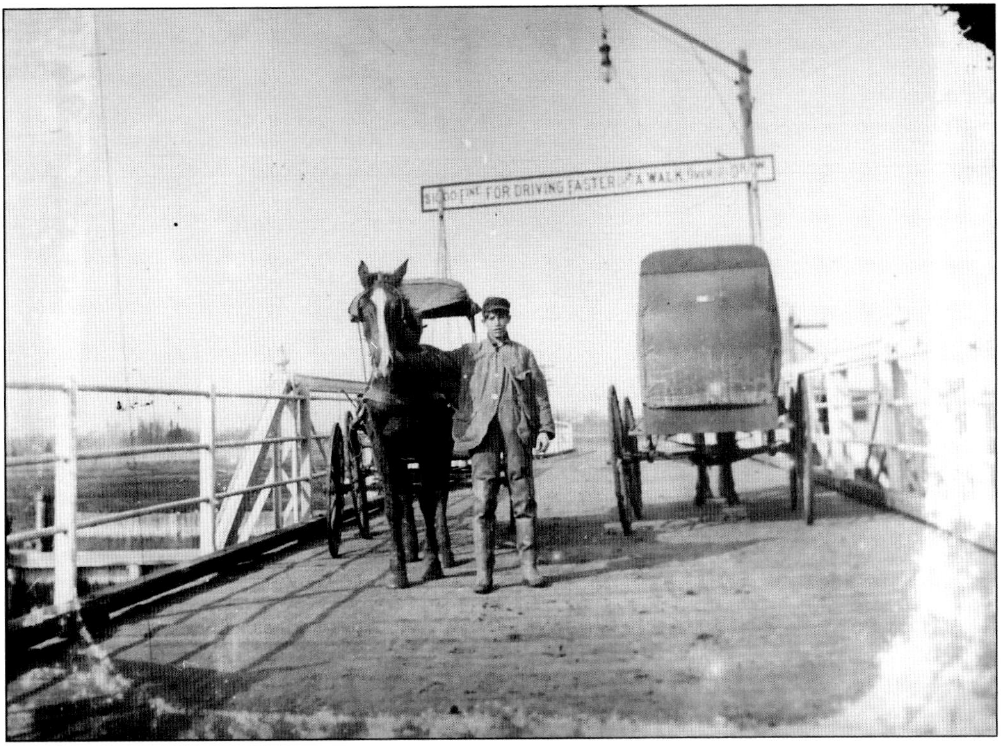

THE MATAWAN CREEK BRIDGE, *c.* 1890. Completed in 1888, this was the second bridge built to span the Matawan Creek, which connects Keyport with Cliffwood. The bridge was constructed of an iron truss with wood decking. By 1915, the structure was replaced with a bascule bridge. This in turn gave way to the fourth bridge (see p. 115). Around 1965, the current bridge (below) was built, making it the first non-drawbridge on the site since 1857.

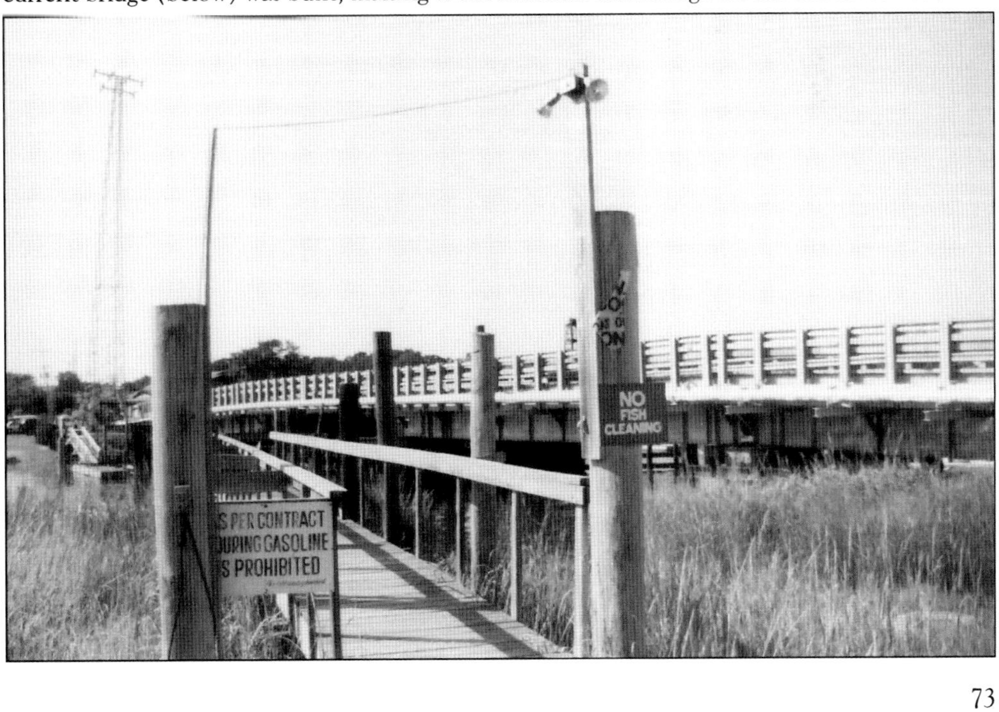

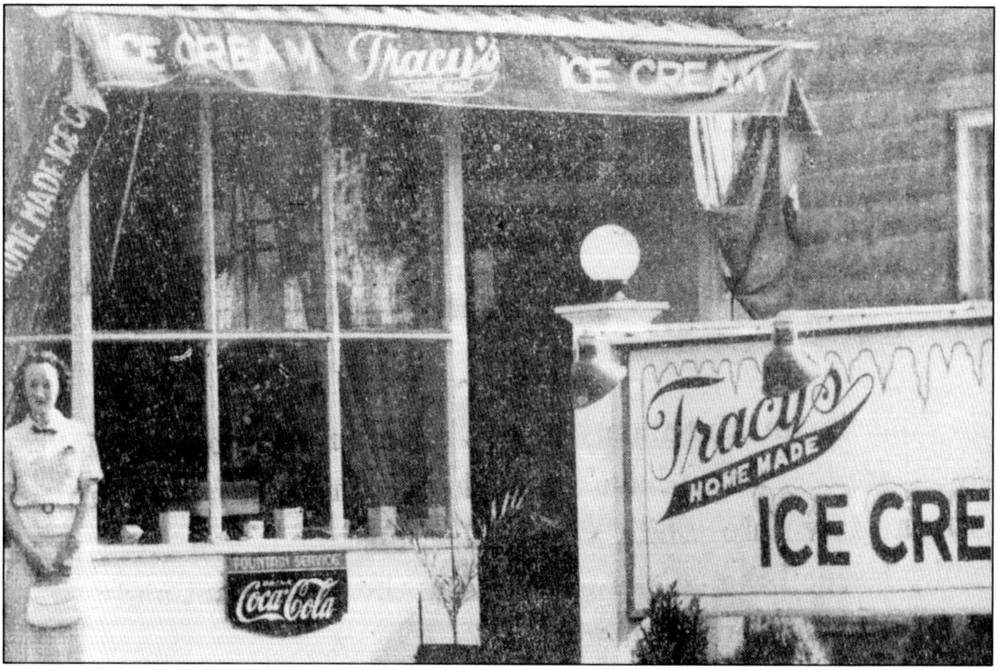

TRACY'S ICE CREAM PARLOR, 1936. This shop, which once stood on Second Street near Atlantic, was in operation during the Depression. Along with ice cream and milk shakes, a soda fountain rounded out the menu.

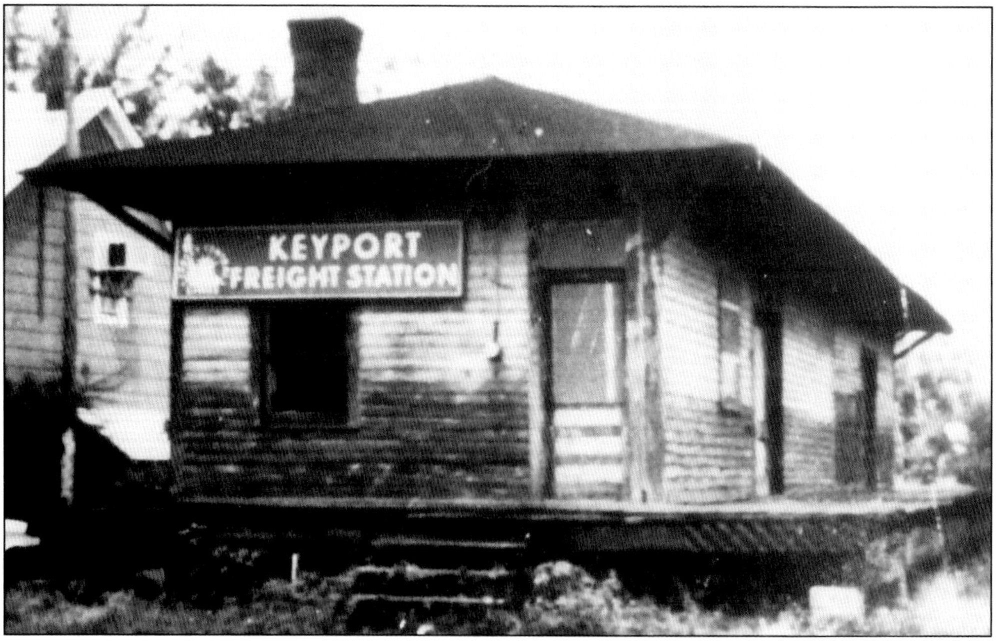

THE FREIGHT STATION, *c.* 1970. Aside from the railroad tracks themselves the old freight depot was the last reminder of the iron horse's existence. It was built in 1902 by the Central Railroad of New Jersey on the right-of-way near First Street. Sadly neglected and vandalized, the old depot was removed shortly after this photograph was taken. The site is now owned by the Board of Fire Wardens.

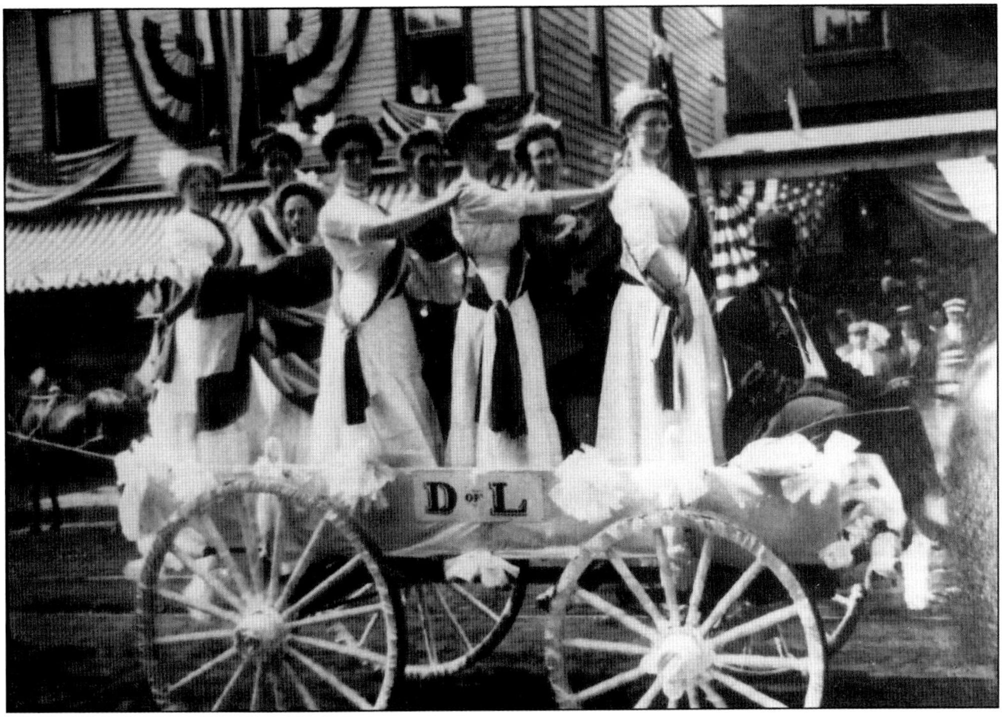

A 1903 PARADE. The Daughters of Liberty parade down East Front Street, in front of John Templeton's store. Mr. Templeton began his dry goods and clothing business in the village in 1875. After moving several times, he settled in the wooden building in 1906, where he remained until closing a few years later.

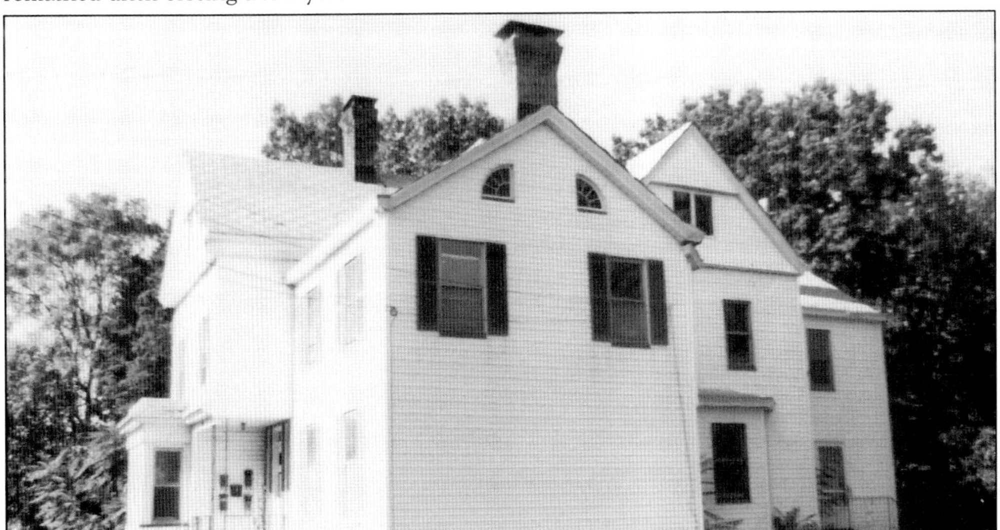

THE SPROUL HOUSE, 1995. John Sproul arrived in Keyport around 1832, and after purchasing a large sum of property on the east side of town, erected this dwelling on First Street, near Atlantic. In 1872 the house was moved to the corner of Second (John) and Church Streets to make room for the new home of Captain Samuel Fairchild. This house, which was rebuilt many times, was best known as the office of Doctor O.C. Bogardus during the first half of the twentieth century.

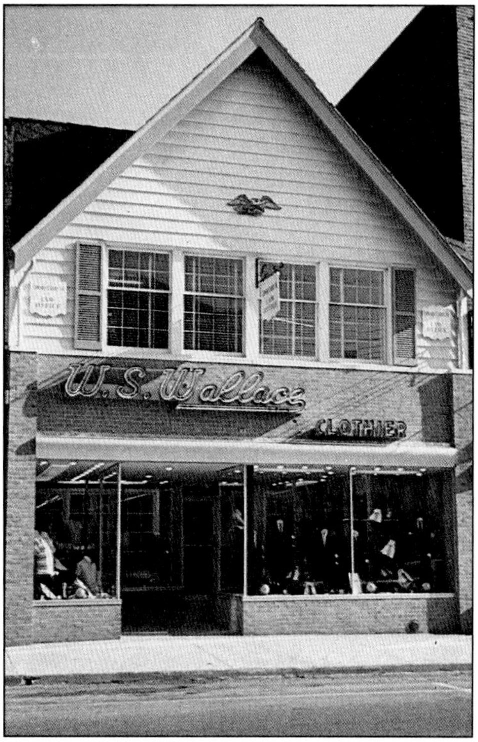

NUMBER 24 W. FRONT STREET, *c.* 1961. What a history this store has! It was opened in 1835 by William and Joseph Hoff and R.B. Walling as Walling and Hoff. In 1836 Leonard Walling became postmaster and the building became the first post office. In 1839 Henry Seabrook purchased the building and it was then operated by the Wallace family for nearly eighty years. It is today the oldest commercial establishment in the town.

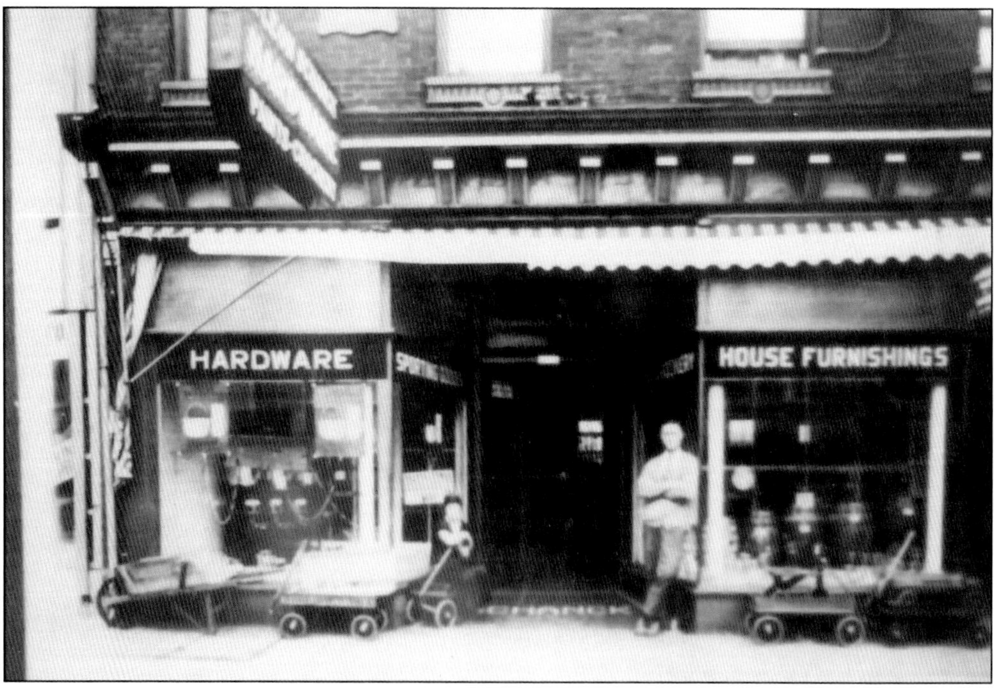

KEYPORT HARDWARE, 1928. This building has been a hardware store since it was first opened by T.H. Roberts, *c.* 1875. The brick, three-story building escaped both great fires and has stood strong season after season. It was owned by J.L. Schanck at the time of the photograph and has since been operated as an industrial hardware store by the Gale family.

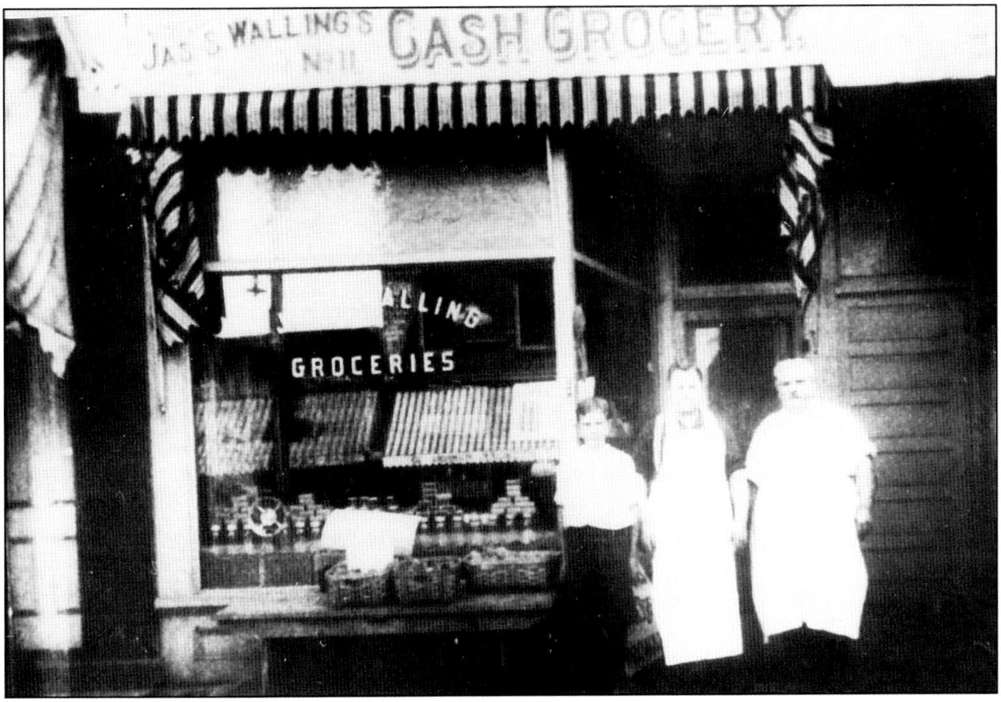

THE WALLING GROCERY STORE. It is difficult to imagine having groceries delivered but during the nineteenth and early twentieth centuries it was big business. Keyport, like all other towns, had many grocers who delivered their goods with an enclosed wagon and horse. James Walling's store was located on Front Street in the structure known as the Sproul building to the east of the old road leading to the municipal lot.

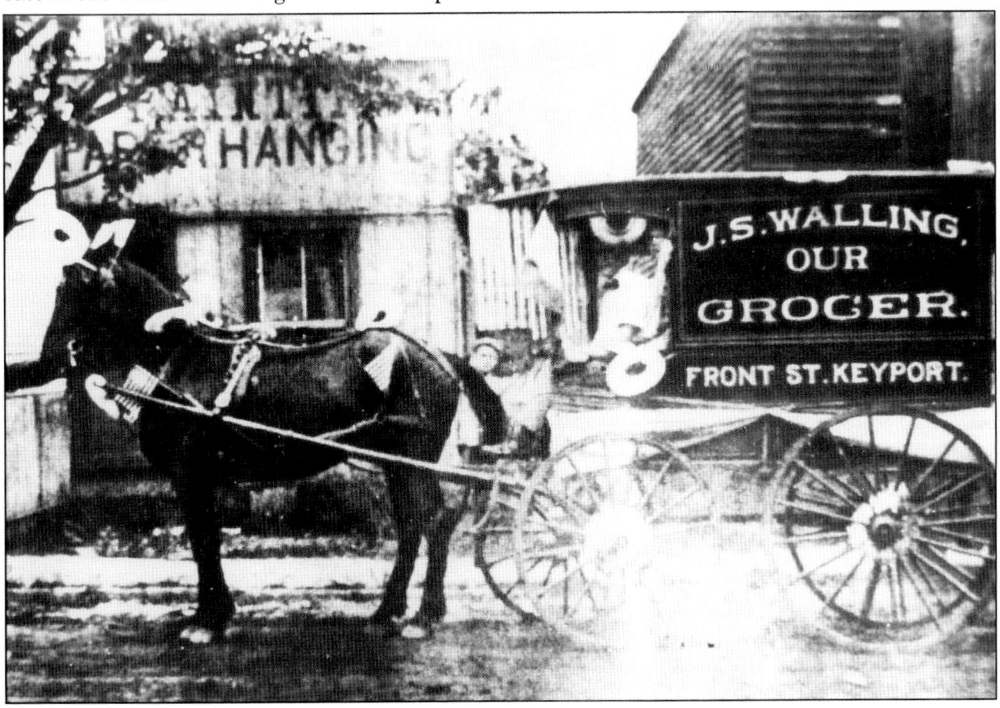

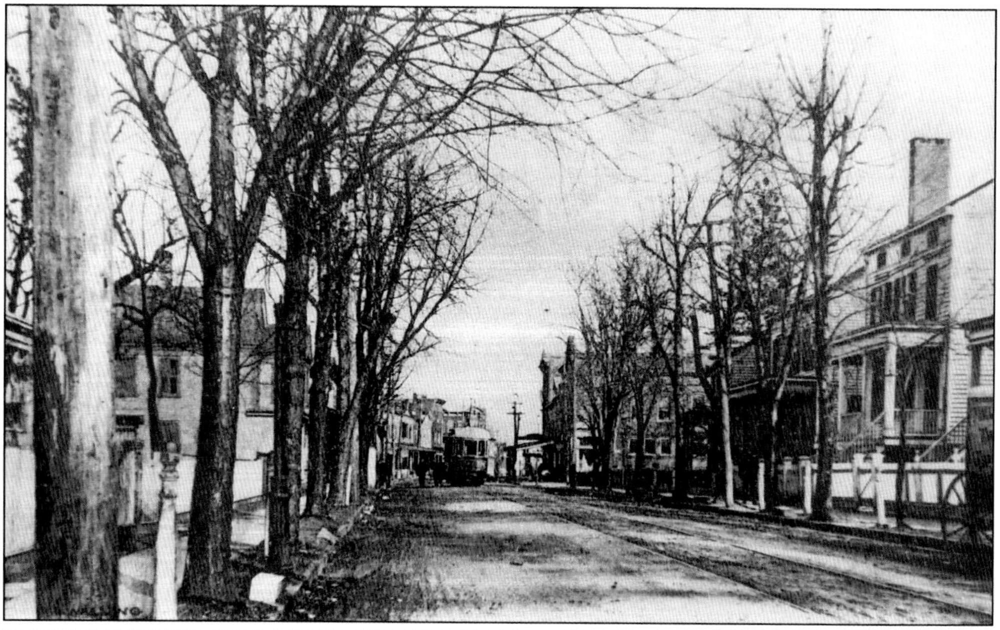

FRONT STREET LOOKING TOWARD MAIN, *c.* 1897. With a trolley headed through town and Phelps Cherry making his deliveries, Front Street bustled with activity around the turn of the twentieth century. Starting in the right foreground are the houses built by J.H. Conover, S. VanMater, Peter Metzsger, and Captain Crawford. By 1970, all but Mr. Conover's house had met the wrecker's hammer, his being converted into retail space.

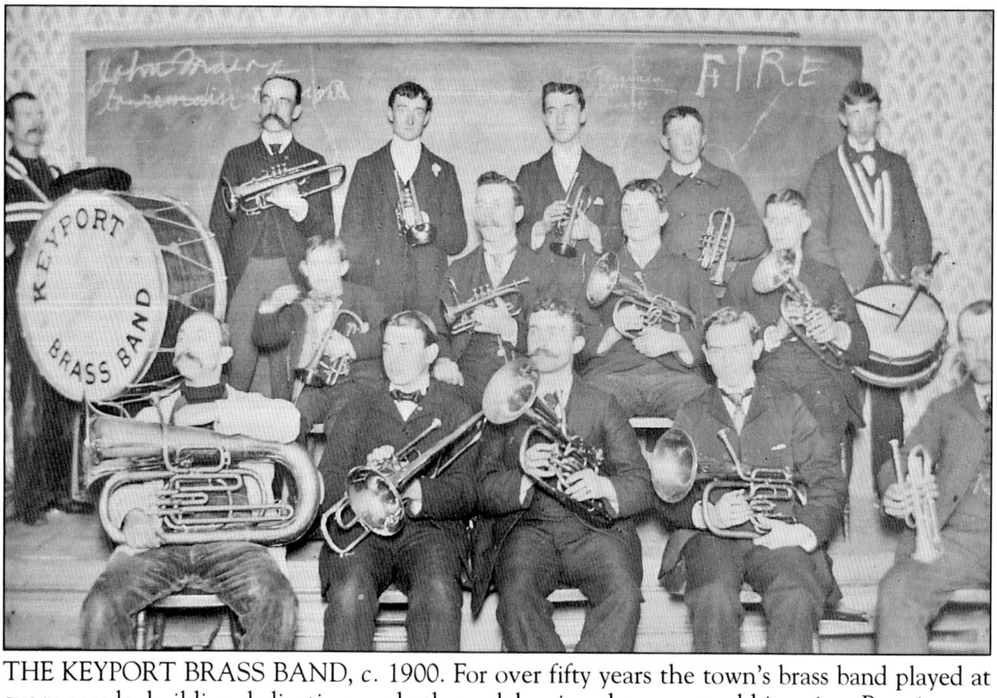

THE KEYPORT BRASS BAND, *c.* 1900. For over fifty years the town's brass band played at every parade, building dedication, and other celebration that one could imagine. Practice was held in various buildings whose owners not only liked music but had neighbors who enjoyed the sounds as well.

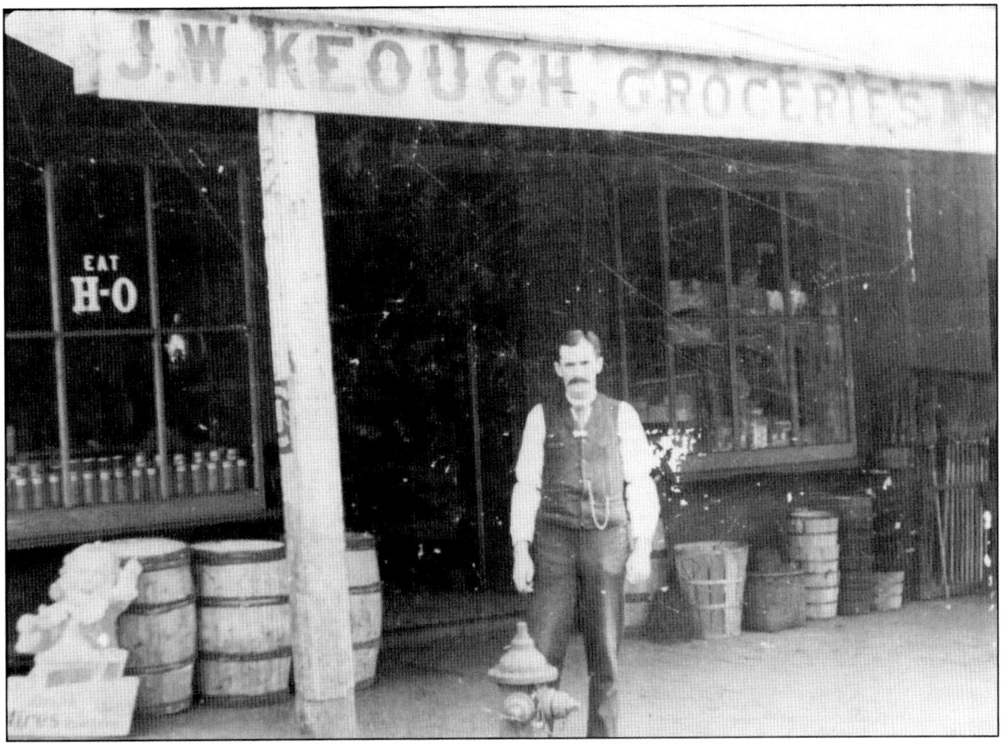

J.W. KEOUGH, *c.* 1895. John Keough opened his grocery store in the agricultural hall (see below) in the spring of 1875. He remained here until 1896, when he completed the Keough building directly north of the old one. In later years both buildings became part of the West Furniture complex.

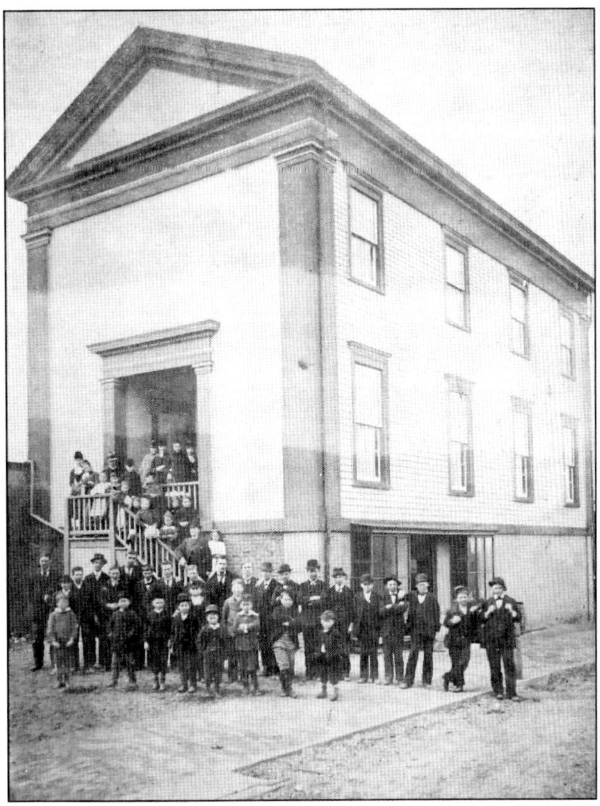

THE AGRICULTURAL DEPOT, 1885. This building served the old village in a variety of important roles and still stands on the southwest corner of Front and Church Streets. It was opened in 1857 by George W. Holmes, who conducted the town's largest private school on the second floor. This is one of Mr. Holmes' class pictures taken at the rear of building around 1885. Mr. Keough sold all types of farm implements, fertilizers, and groceries here, and it quickly became known as the agricultural depot.

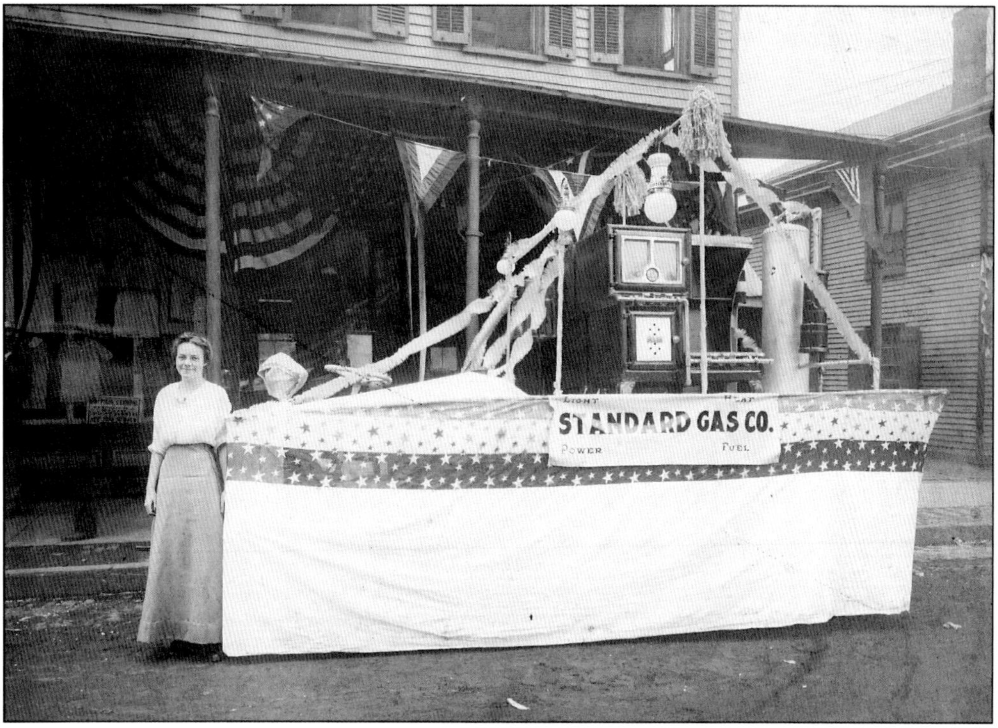

A 1913 FOURTH OF JULY FLOAT. The Standard Gas Company entered this float in the July Fourth parade of 1913. Standing by is Edna S. Bennett, who decorated the float for the day's festivities. It is seen here on Broad Street, in front of the gas company's office and Jaffes Clothing Store, which once stood to the north of Bedle's Funeral Home.

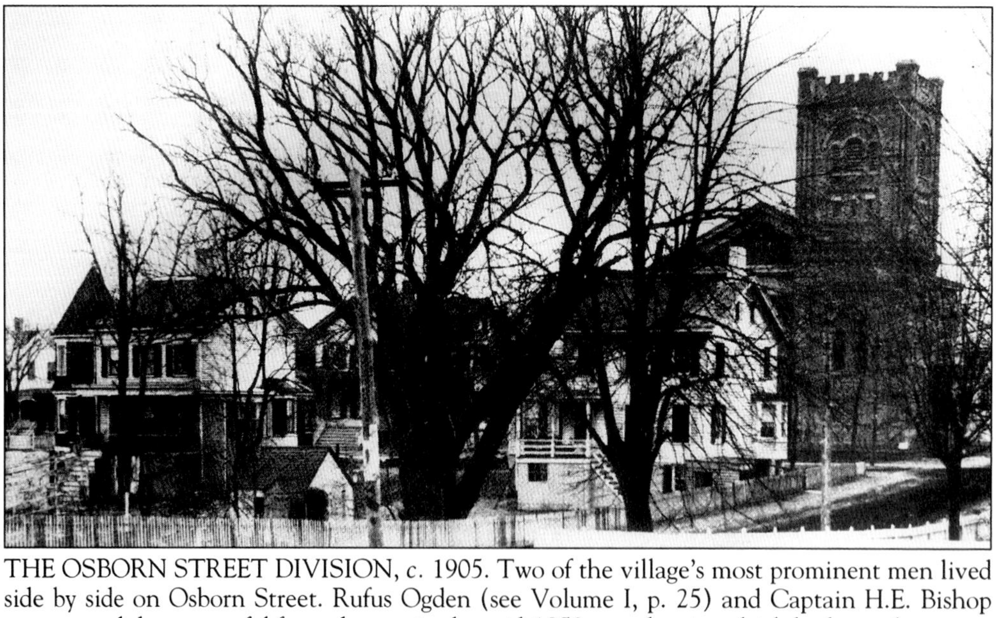

THE OSBORN STREET DIVISION, *c.* 1905. Two of the village's most prominent men lived side by side on Osborn Street. Rufus Ogden (see Volume I, p. 25) and Captain H.E. Bishop constructed these graceful frame houses in the mid-1850s, on the site which had once been part of Necius Pond. The houses still stand, although the miranet-like tower on the Captain's house has been removed.

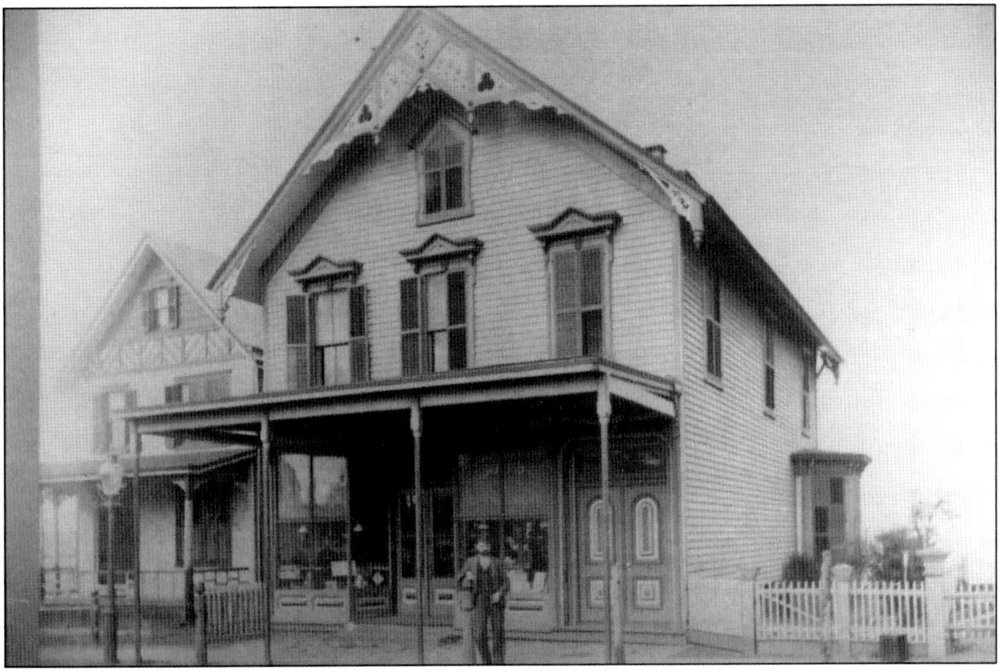

WARN'S DRUG STORE, *c.* 1890. Grab a stool and pull up to the counter, let's see what's new about town and hear the history of this place. The town's first drug store became a reality when this Victorian pharmacy was opened by Asher Holmes in 1872. Shortly after, William Warn bought Mr. Holmes out and operated the store until 1920, when it was purchased by Henry T. Hopkins. The store, which also contained a large fountain (below), remained opened for nearly one hundred years at 55 First Street. Tragically, Mr. Hopkins was killed in front of his store in the early 1970s after being hit by a car on a foggy night.

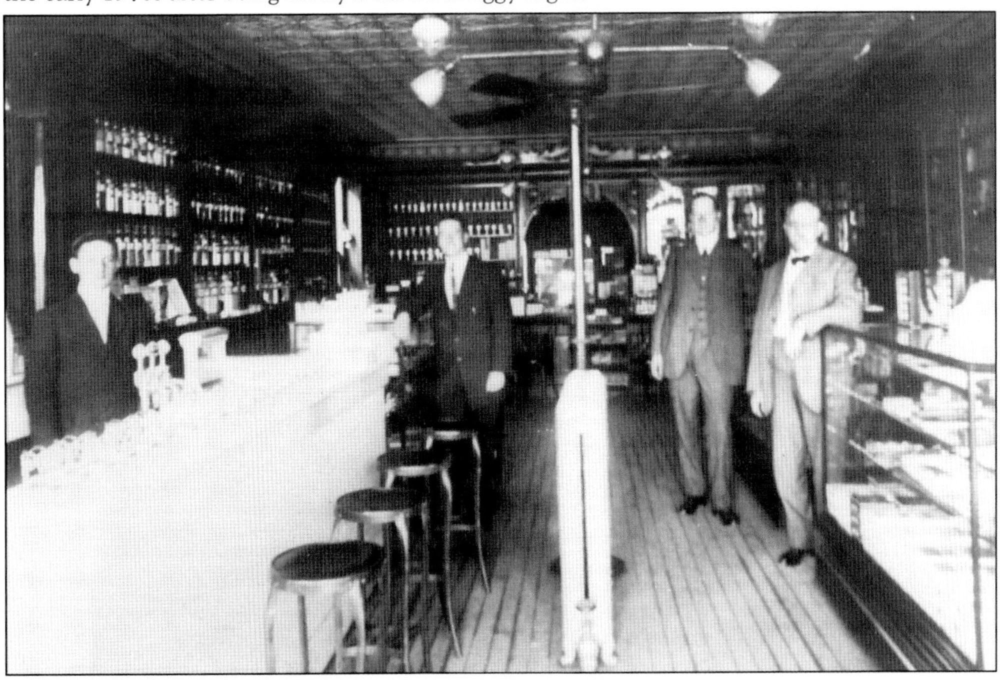

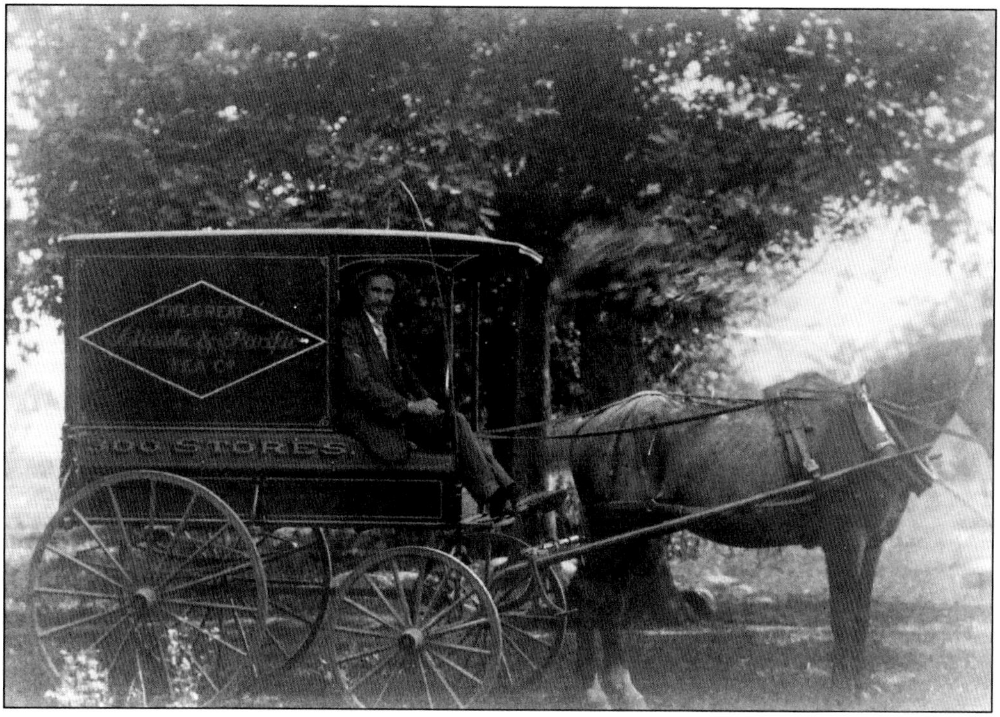

THE A & P WAGON, *c.* 1891. Ready to make his daily rounds, this driver of the Atlantic and Pacific Tea Co. takes a minute out for a photograph. Originally two separate companies; they later merged to better serve their customers across the county as well as in town.

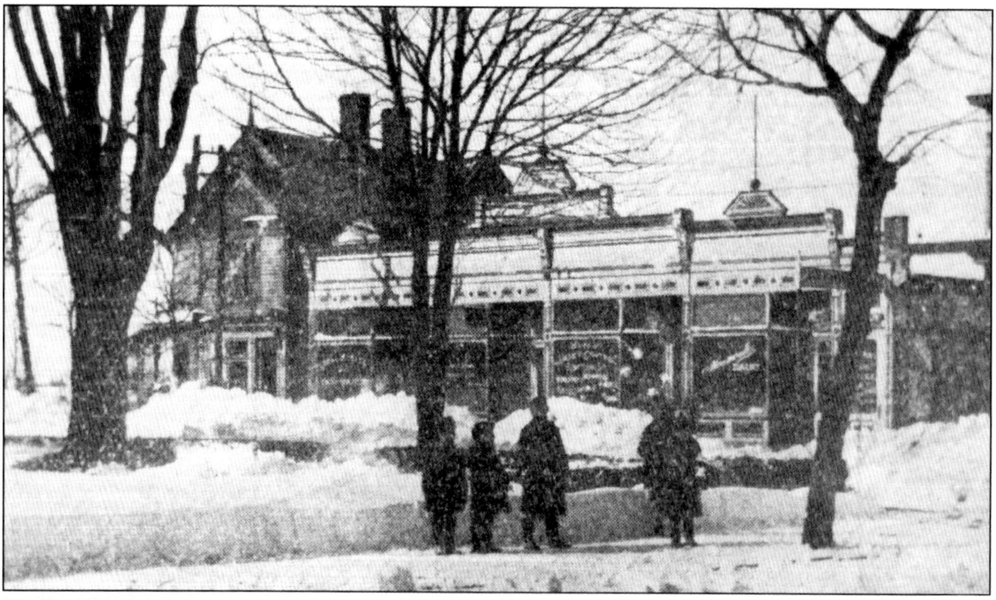

THE *KEYPORT WEEKLY* OFFICE, *c.* 1900. Located on the south side of Front Street from 1880 until 1930, this is the spot the *Weekly* called home. Started in January of 1871, the *Keyport Weekly* was printed non-stop until the last issue appeared, *c.* 1973. For over one hundred years every birth, death, marriage, political event, and tidbit of small town life was captured on its pages, something modern papers simply do not cover!

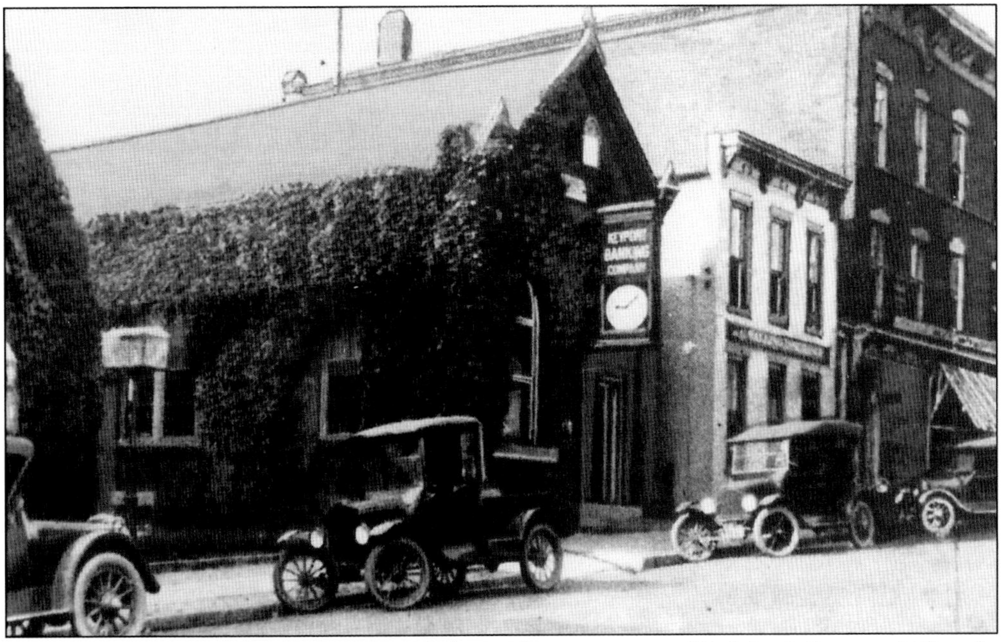

EAST FRONT STREET, *c.* 1924. From left to right we see part of St. Mary's Episcopal Church, the old Keyport Banking Co. building, A. Wallings insurance office, and Dr. McKinney's Drugstore. The bank was one of two nearly identical buildings built in 1884 by the Keyport Banking Co. and in 1889 by the People's National Bank. Prior to 1884 all local banking was carried on in Matawan, which is what forced the town's most prominent citizens to start their own financial institution.

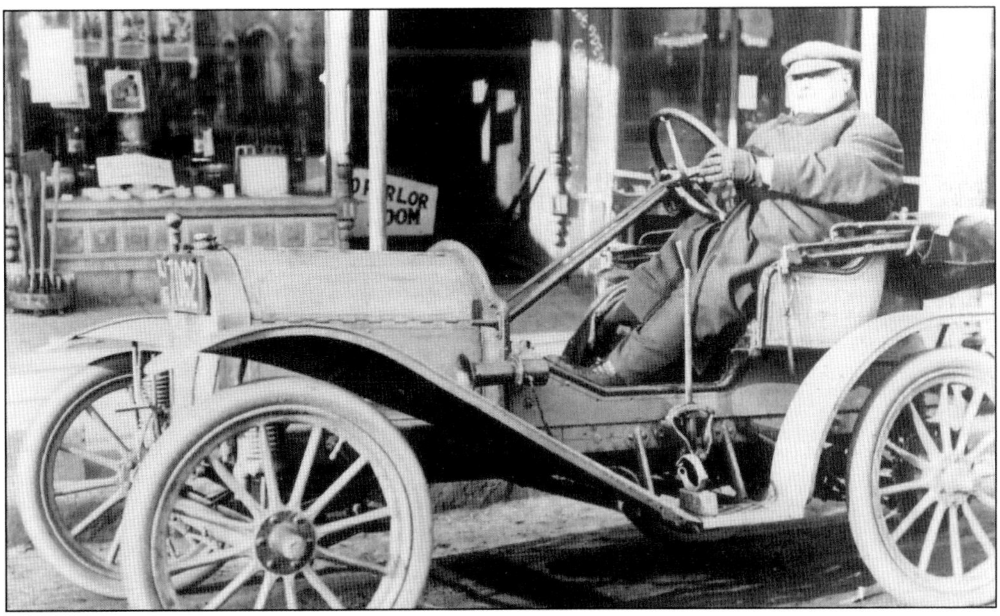

A MAN AND HIS CAR, *c.* 1916. This rather large gent in a rather small car is parked on Front Street near Main. It is not known who the man is or what type of car it is, but one thing is for sure: nighttime driving must have been mighty tough, for the car had no headlights, just a klaxon horn!

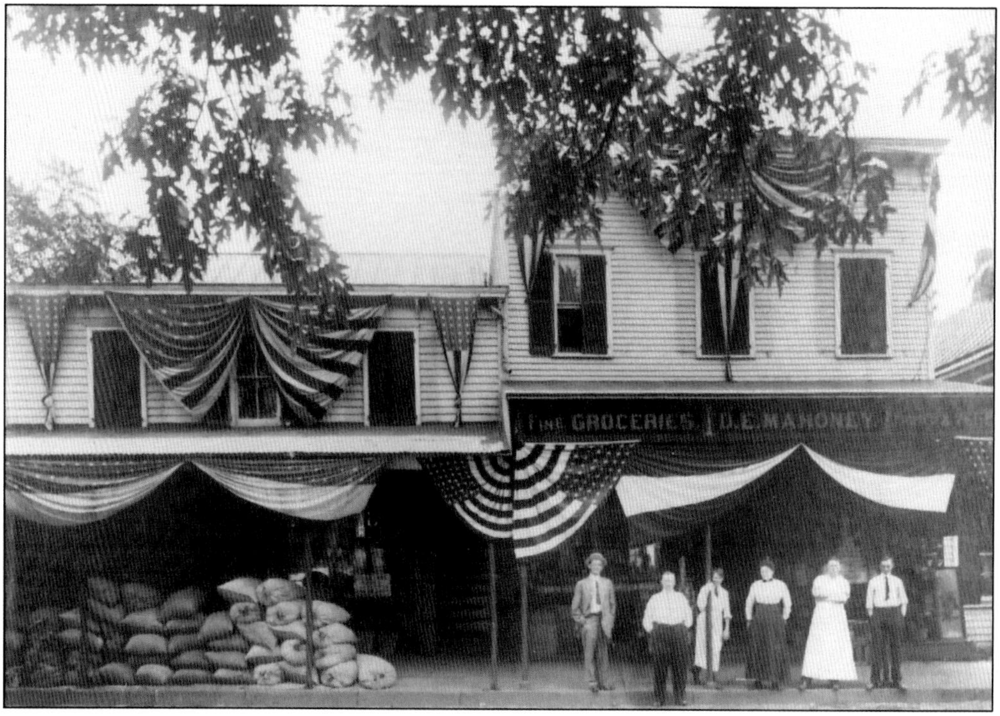

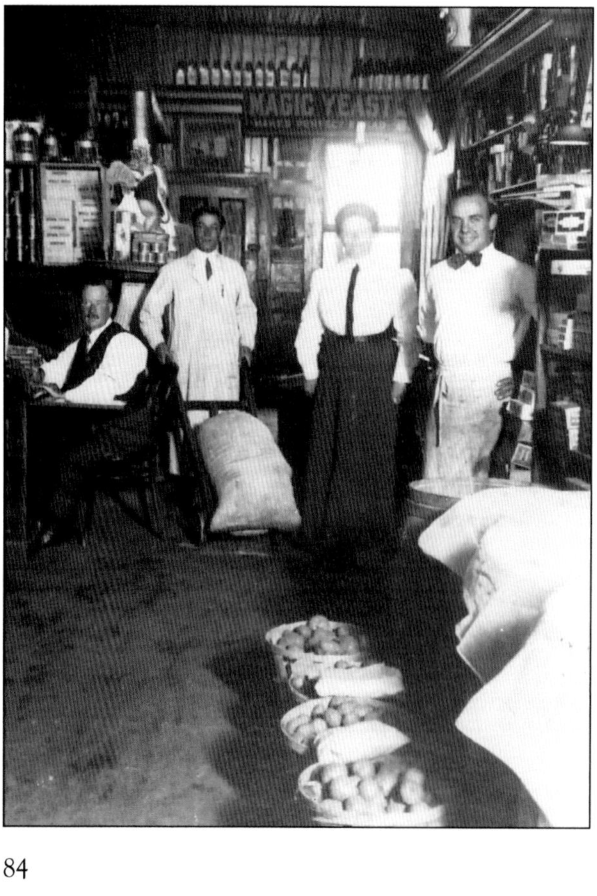

D.E. MAHONEY'S STORE, *c.* 1890. One of the town's best loved merchants was D.E. Mahoney, who operated this large store on the south side of First Street near Church. All types of food, grains, and other staples could be purchased here, including Raritan Brand coffee which "drinks good" according to a 1909 advertisement. Mahoney's was started about 1880 and continued into the 1930s. This building, along with all of the other structures on First Street between Church and Front, were removed by 1976. It is now the site of the Engine Co. and Hook and Ladder firehouse.

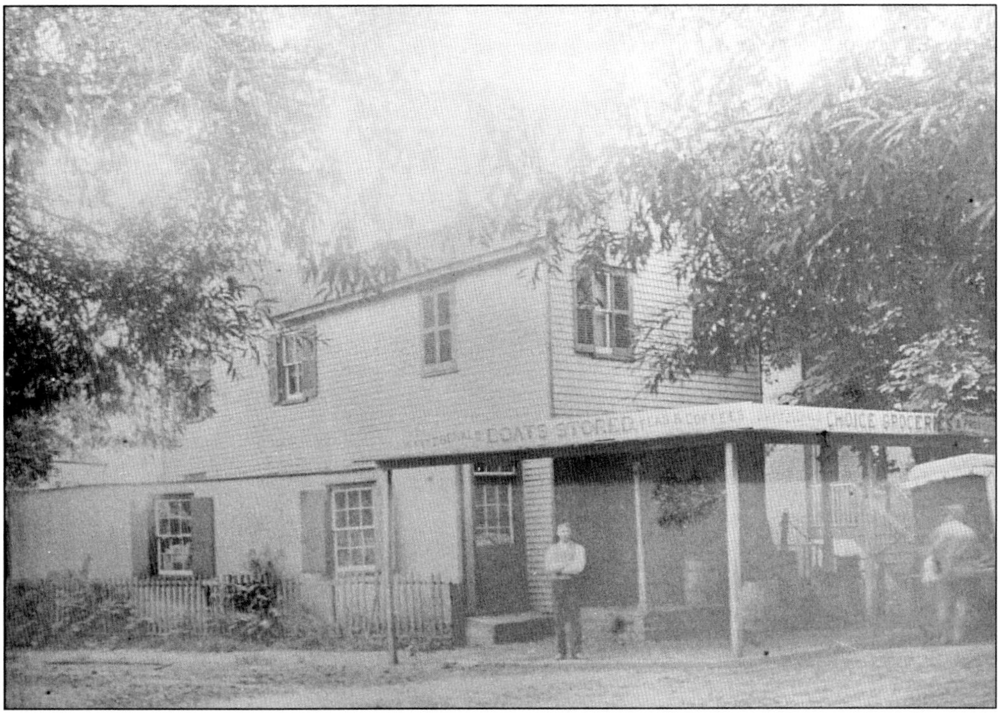

FITZGERALD'S STORE, *c.* 1900. One of the first stores built in Lockport was this one at the northeast corner of First and Cedar Streets. J.H. Fitzgerald opened his grocery store about 1860 and, as his sign read, he also stored boats, which was an uncommon service for a grocery store. The store was closed in the 1930s and still stands as a private residence.

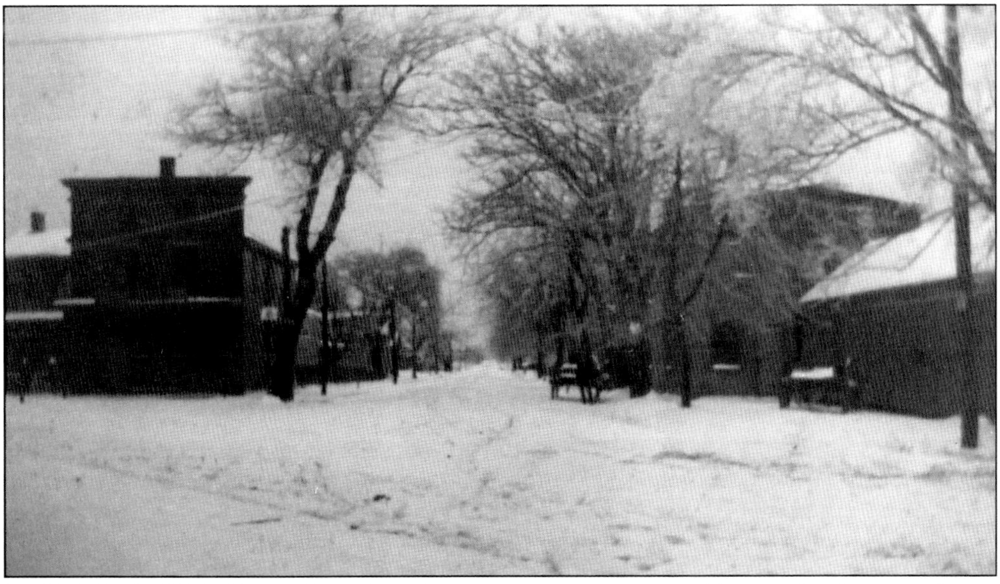

JOHNSON'S STORE, *c.* 1890. Just about a mile from Fitzgeralds was the Johnson Store. Located at the triangle formed by the intersection of Main and Atlantic Streets, this building was an important part of life for people down in Mechanicsville. It stood until the 1950s when it was razed, and the site is now part of the Bethany Manor high-rise property.

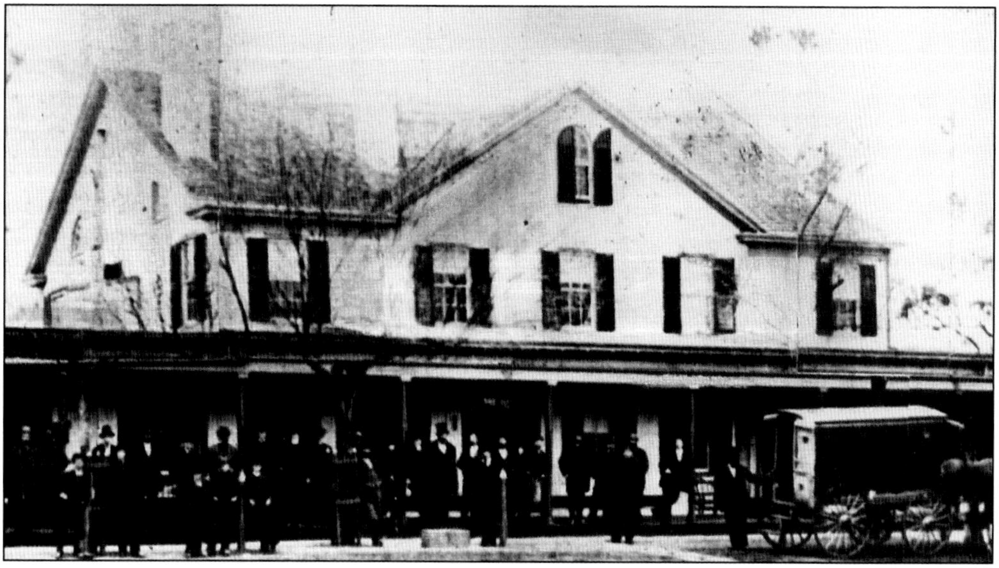

THE ATLANTIC HOTEL. This photographic reconstruction shows how the old Atlantic Hotel most likely appeared during its heyday. Built in 1832 by Primrose Hopping, the Atlantic became the first hotel in the new town. It stood on the south side of Front Street about halfway between Broad and Main Streets, until September 21, 1877, when it was destroyed in the great fire. It was never rebuilt.

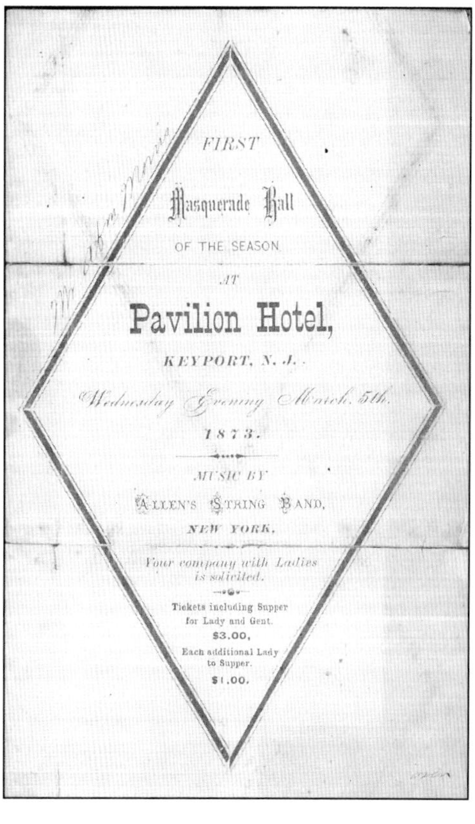

FIRST

Masquerade Ball

OF THE SEASON

AT

Pavilion Hotel,

KEYPORT, N. J.

Wednesday Evening March 5th.

1873.

MUSIC BY

ALLEN'S STRING BAND,

NEW YORK.

Your company with Ladies is solicited.

Tickets including Supper for Lady and Gent.

$3.00,

Each additional Lady to Supper.

$1.00.

A TICKET TO A BALL, 1873. Mr. Abraham Morris was cordially invited to attend this event, which was surely a grand affair at the old Pavilion. You and your lady could get in for a mere $3 for dinner, but for each extra lady you brought you had better fork over another buck. It is ironic that this old ticket belonged to Mr. Morris, for the great fire of 1877, which almost destroyed the Pavilion Hotel, began in Mr. Morris' apartment building.

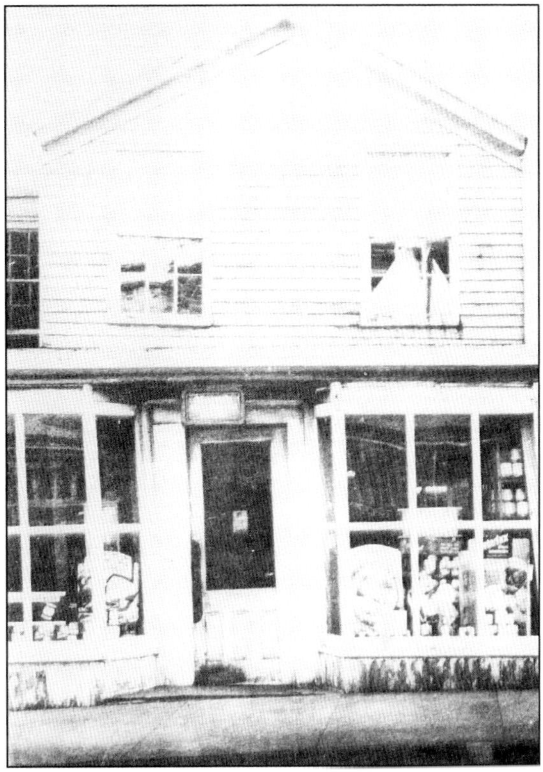

THE KEYPORT PAINT STORE, *c*. 1900. For nearly one hundred years, anyone who needed painting supplies or glass came here, to Bedles. Located on the corner of Front and Division Streets, Albert M. Bedle opened the shop in 1864. It is said that by 1910 over 600 tons of white leaded paint was sold to local customers.

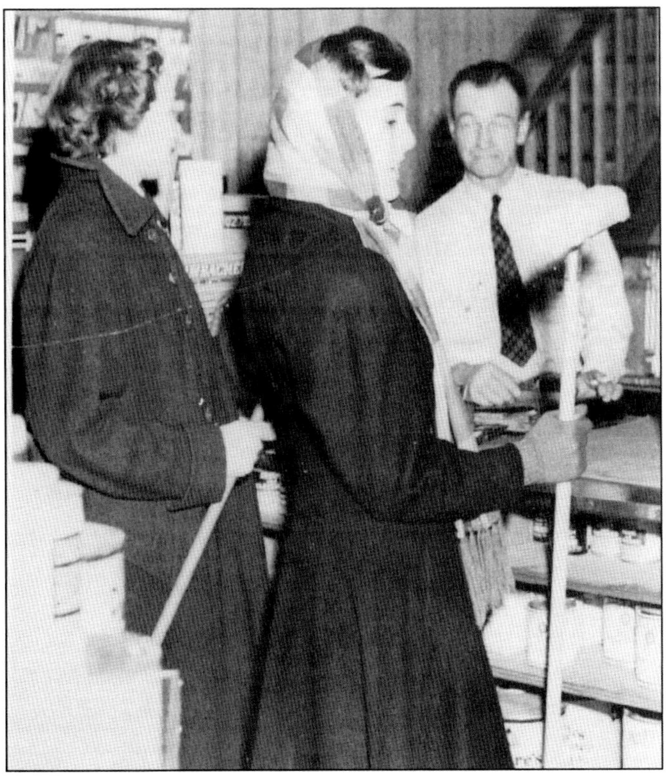

THE KEYPORT PAINT STORE, 1954. Albert M. Bedle died in 1919, at which time his son, J.D. Bedle, became the proprietor. Here Yvonne Seabury (foreground) and Diane Wilson pose for a 1954 Keyport High yearbook photo. The building has been rebuilt several times and was rebuilt into a deli in 1989 after serving as a church in the 1970s.

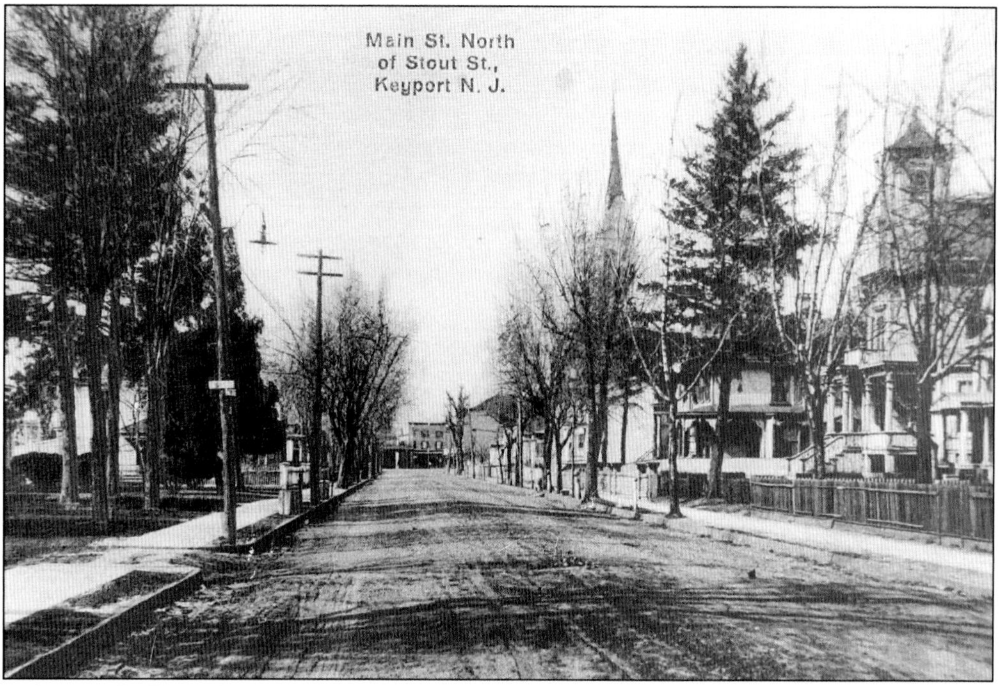

MAIN STREET NORTH FROM STOUT, *c.* 1905. Main Street became the first official thoroughfare in the village when it was laid out in 1830. Upon it quickly rose several of the towns first houses, such as the Nimrod Bedle House (completed in 1831). By 1834 Jacob VanPelt took up his residence and shoemaking business south of Mr. Bedles house, near Warren Street.

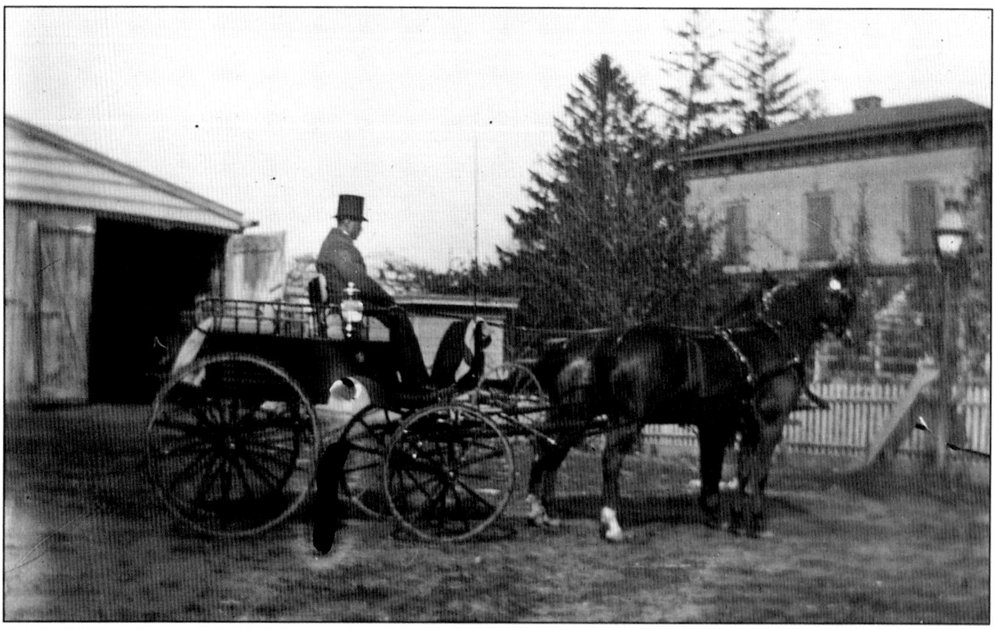

A CARRIAGE, *c.* 1890. With a black top hat, black carriage, and a black team, this carriage takes on a sinister appearance. The man, who was likely a driver, would be in charge of not only maintaining the carriage but of grooming and general stable duties for the steeds.

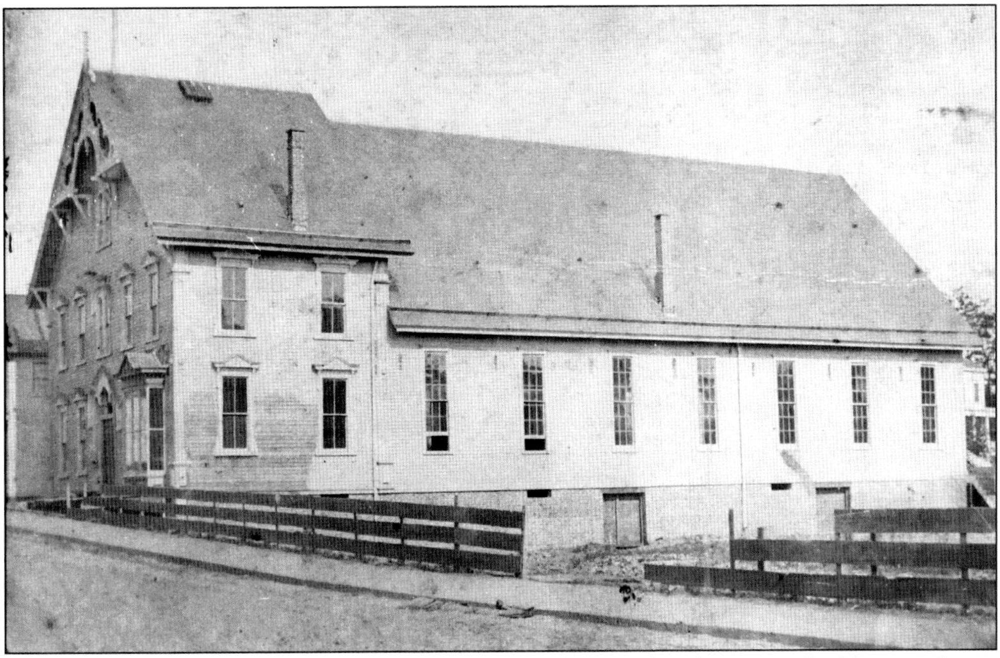

THE RARITAN GUARD ARMORY. The recently completed Armory building is shown above. When finished in 1879 it became the largest wooden structure in the village. The timber given for its construction was donated by local farmers and the rest of the building was finished at a cost of about $7,000. After the 1909 fire (see Volume I, p. 118) the building became the Armory Theater. By the 1970s the old timbers could take the weight no more and the old drill room area came crashing to ground in the dead of night. The entire structure was removed soon after for safety reasons.

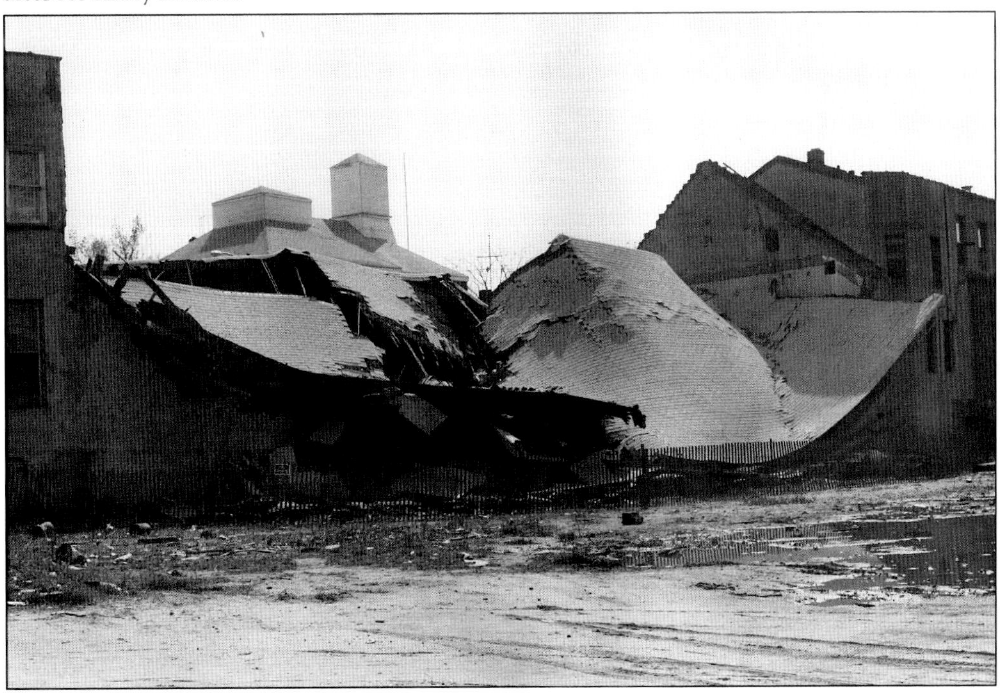

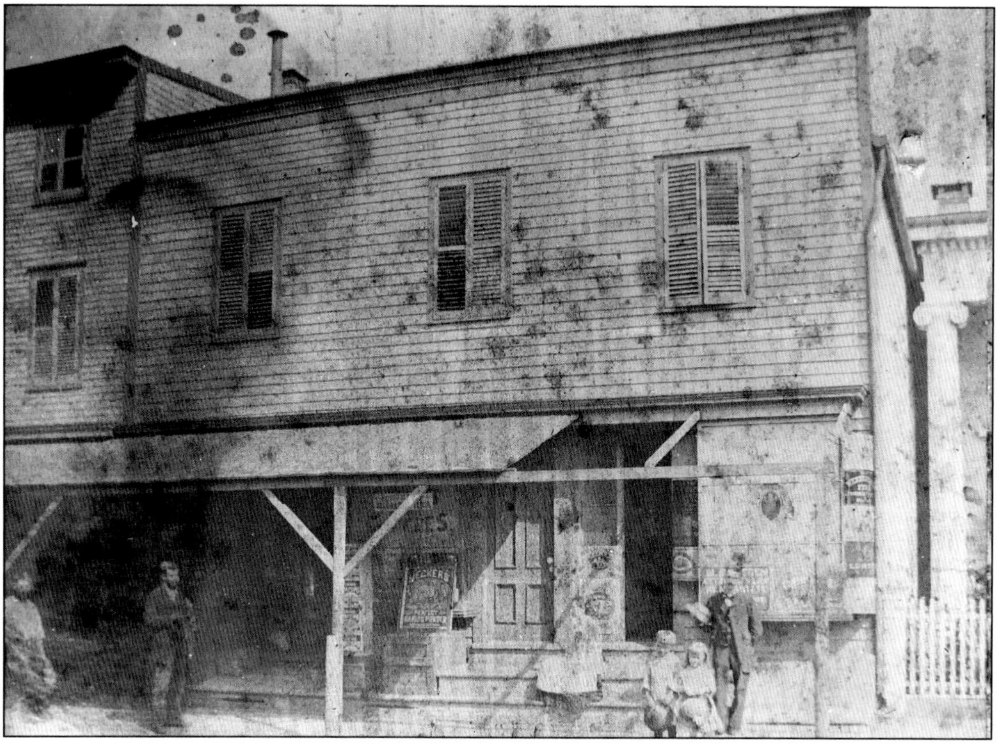

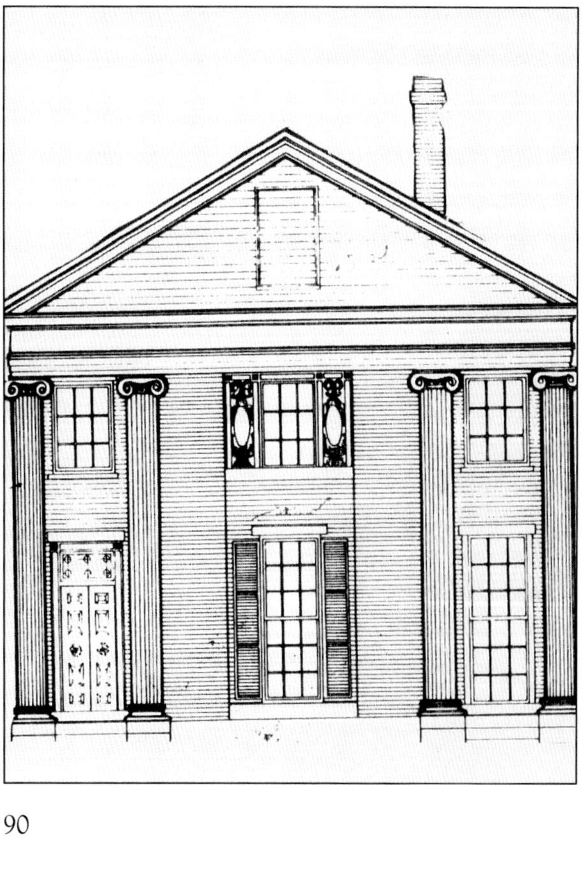

THE T.B. STOUT BUILDINGS, 1874. Both of the frame stores shown were built in the 1840s on south side of Front Street, opposite the Atlantic Hotel. They stood until 1906, when they were removed for the Bogardus building, best known for its longtime tenant J.J. Newberrys' five and dime. The column to the right belonged to the house of Captain Fred Decker.

THE CAPTAIN DECKER HOUSE, *c.* 1840. If the historian or lover of old houses has one enemy, it must be fire. Fires in Keyport have taken a great toll on our historic buildings, destroying valuable links to our rich past. Ironically, Captain Decker's house did not burn at all—it was torn down during the fire of 1877. Local citizens, in a heroic attempt to save the rest of Front Street, stopped the flames; nevertheless, the grand Greek Revival house was lost and Captain Decker rebuilt.

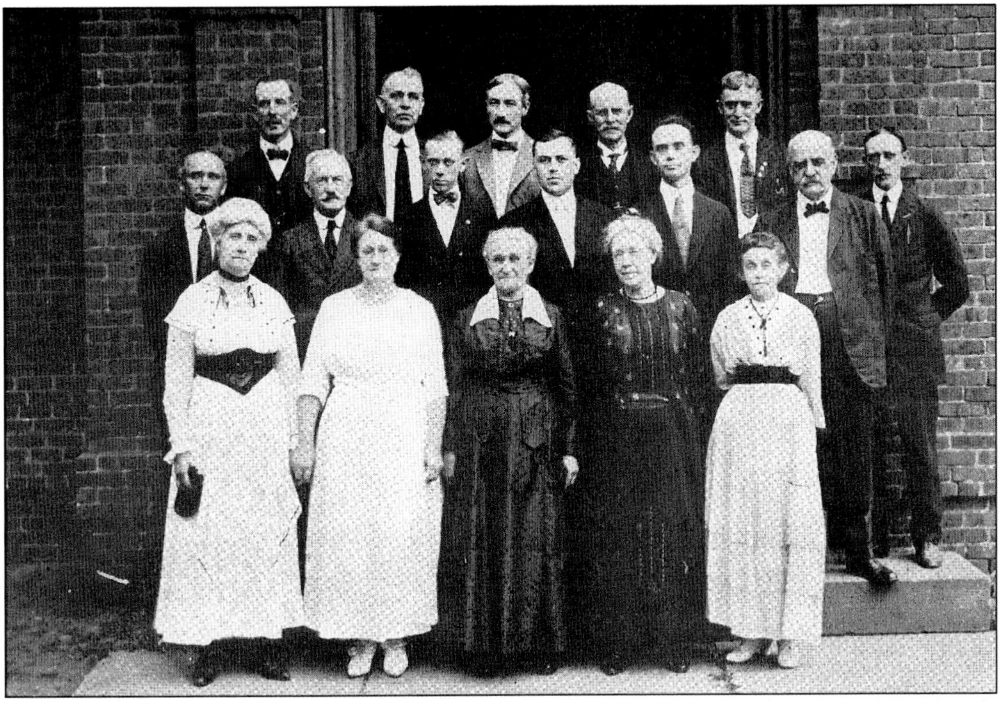

THE CALVARY METHODIST CHURCH BOARD, 1909. Posing on the steps of the church house on Osborn Street are, from left to right, as follows: (front row) E. Dey, Mrs. Dawson, Emma Black, M. Bedle, and Mrs. Madden; (middle row) C. Kruser, S.P. Dey, W. Lambertson, Reverend Brady, E. Hyrne, and W. Tilton; (back row) T. Walter Snyder, Phelps Cherry, E. Wharton, D. Decker, W. Brower, and L. VanGieson.

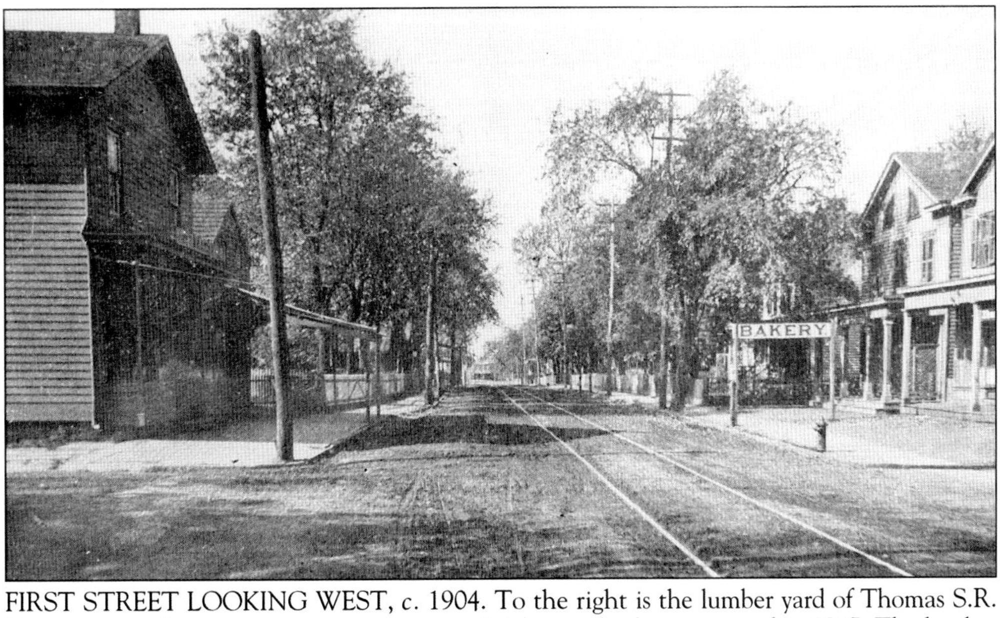

FIRST STREET LOOKING WEST, *c.* 1904. To the right is the lumber yard of Thomas S.R. Brown; across the street are two more stores which were both constructed in 1847. The lumber company has been replaced by condos, while the store in the right foreground was razed. Only the old bakery remains, long since renovated into a residence.

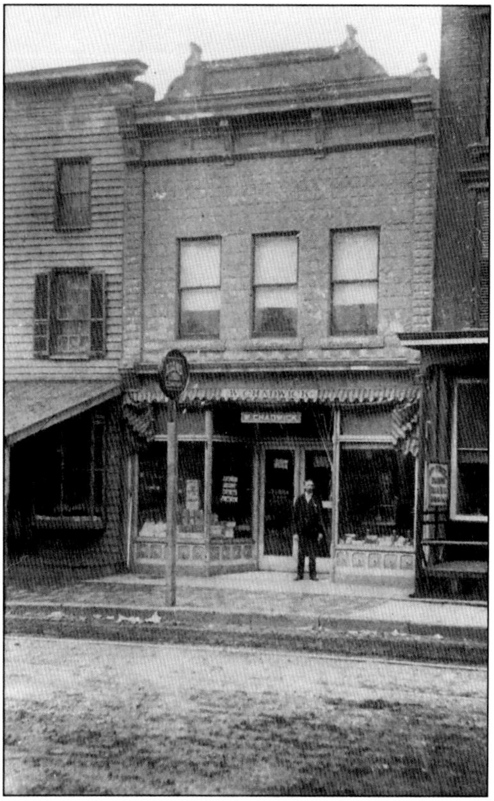

CHADWICK'S, *c.* 1905. William Chadwick built this unique masonry stationary store on the south side of Front Street in 1897. He sold all types of postal cards, fountain pens, and stationary. Over one hundred years later it is still a stationary store, but the fountain pens have been replaced with a lottery machine. The building to the left was built in 1838 and removed, *c.* 1940.

BROAD STREET LOOKING SOUTH, *c.* 1900. Taken near Elizabeth Street, we can see the old fence of the grade school on the left, while in the distance is the old covered coal trestle. Built by J.G. Schanck in the late 1880s, this covered building was the scene of an accident around 1920 when a railroad coal car failed to stop and crashed out of the building, precariously hanging over the Broad Street sidewalk until workmen could rerail it.

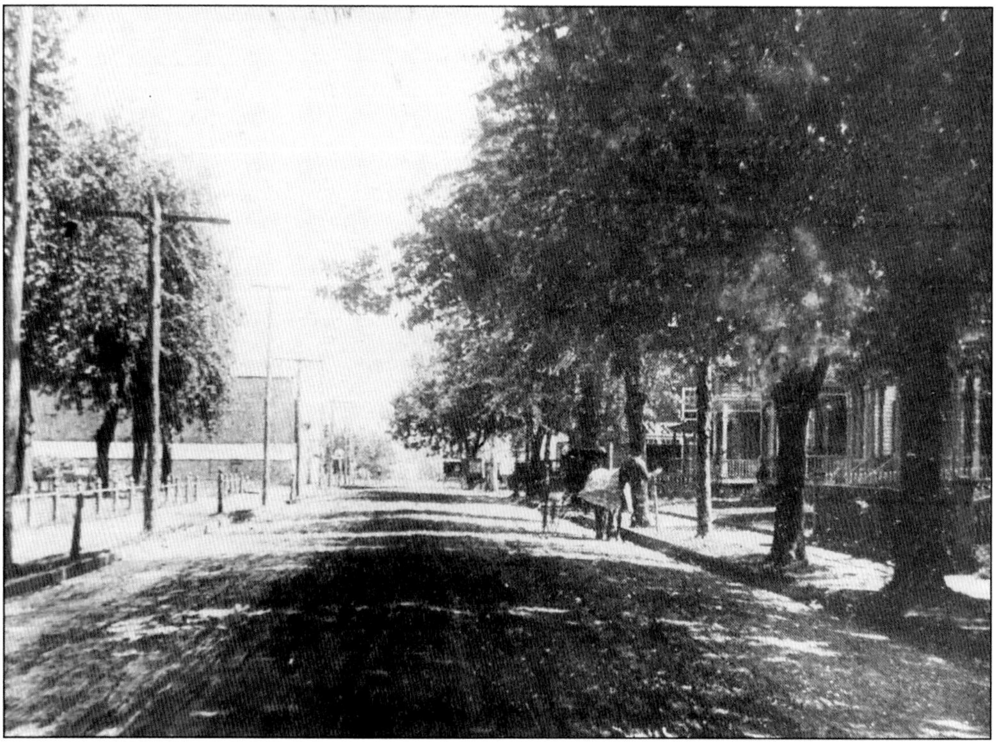

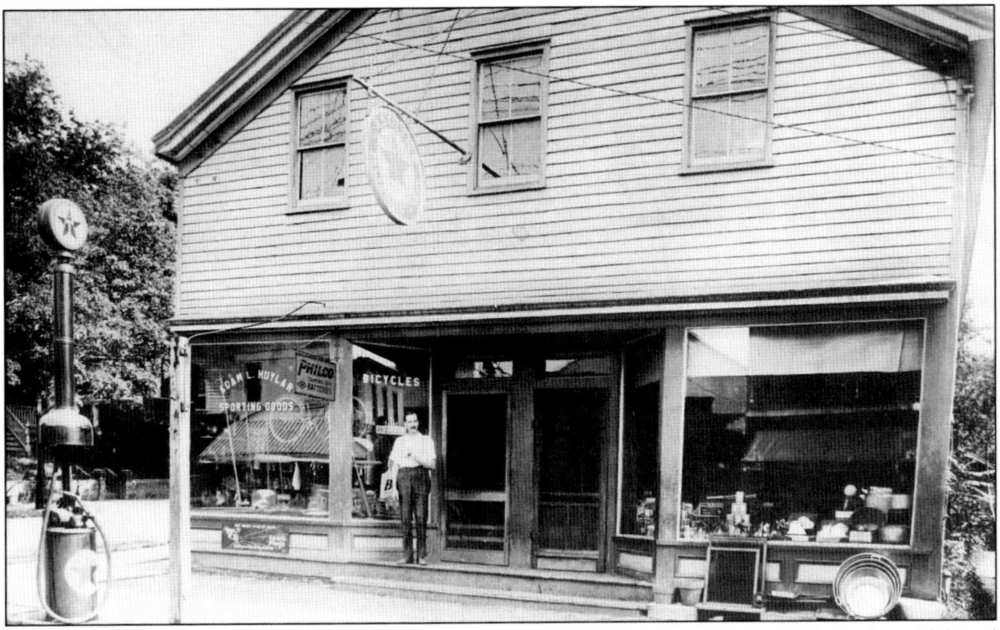

HUYLAR'S STORE, *c.* 1920. The sign reads "Gasoline Filling Station," while the old hand pump waits for the next customer and his tin lizzie. Gasoline companies had yet to begin building the fancy stations which graced America after the 1920s. No service, just gas at Huylar's, and it sure beat the old way of pouring it into your tank from a can and funnel. Huylar's was located at the corner of Front and Osborn Streets.

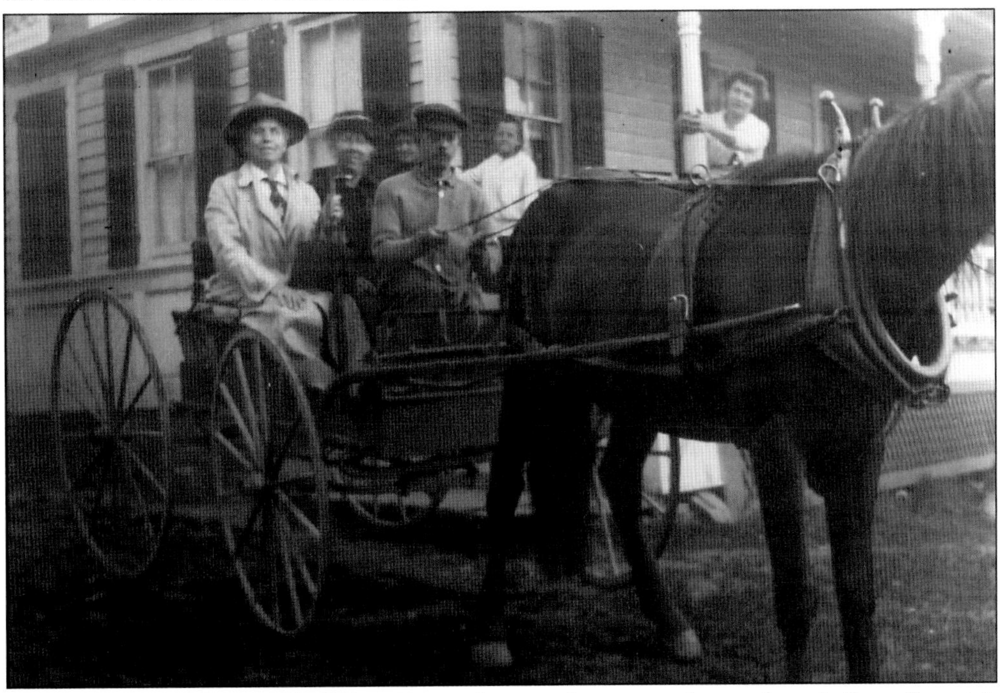

OUT FOR A RIDE, *c.* 1907. Off we go, maybe to pick up some dry goods up in "town" or visit some friends who lived at Browns Point. Either way everyone could not go as the old carriage just didn't have room. Looks like Dad has to take both of his mothers (in-law too) on this trip.

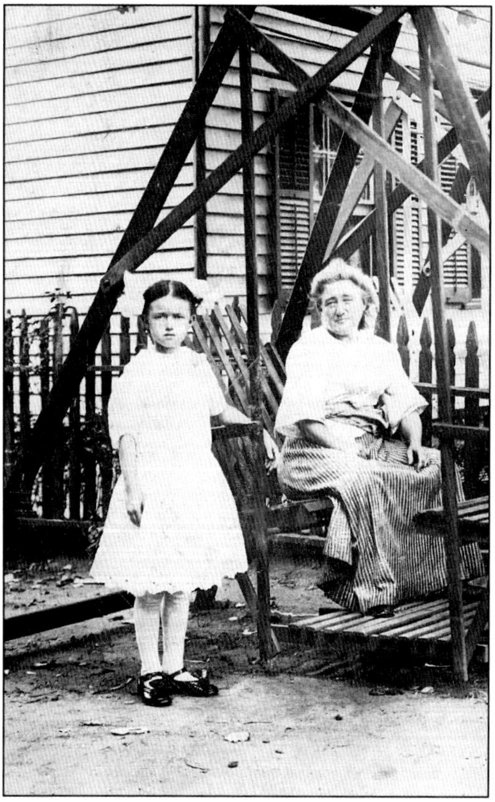

MOTHER AND DAUGHTER, *c.* 1912. In this photograph, taken at the old home in the yard on Second and Fulton Streets, Mrs. Catherine Evans and her daughter Gladys pose near the old swing.

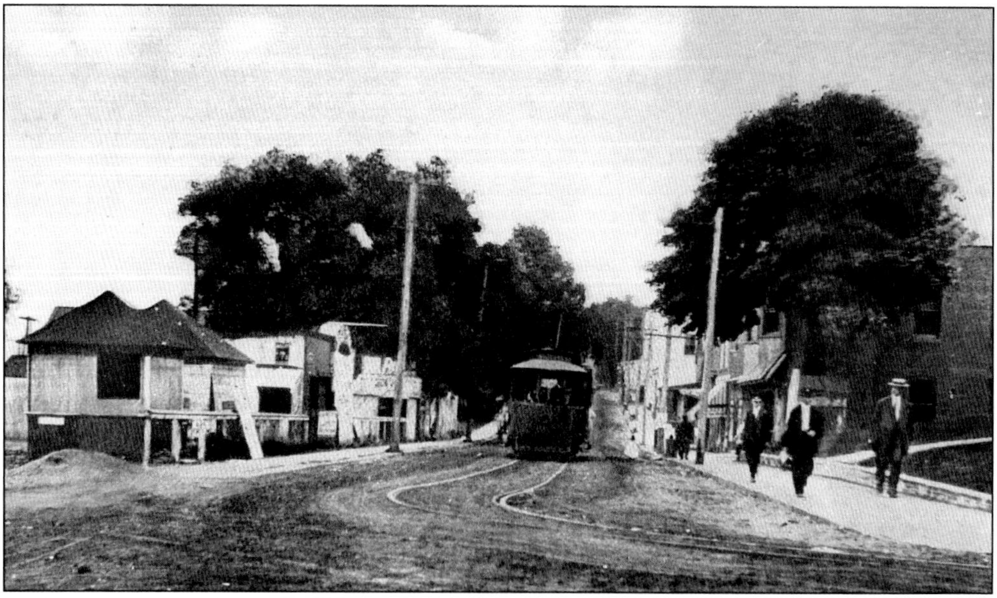

FIRST STREET, LOOKING EAST, *c.* 1904. Summertime was here! It was time to play and maybe even take some time off from work. All of the buildings to the left were amusement games and concession stands. Behind them, in Beach Park, was a wading pool and sometimes a traveling merry-go-round, which caused great sadness among the young ones when it left for good in 1921.

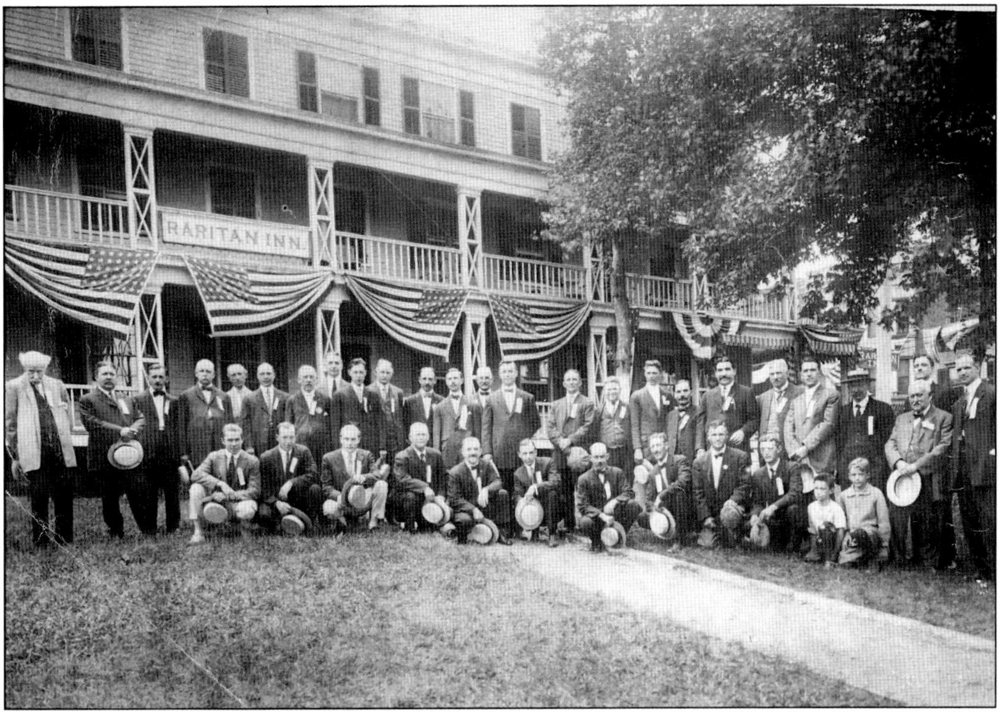

A GATHERING, 1920. It was done, the Women's Suffrage movement was over. Legislation had just been passed to allow women to vote and these group of men turned out to protest the new law. Compare this view to the one on p. 116, which was taken about forty years later in the same general area.

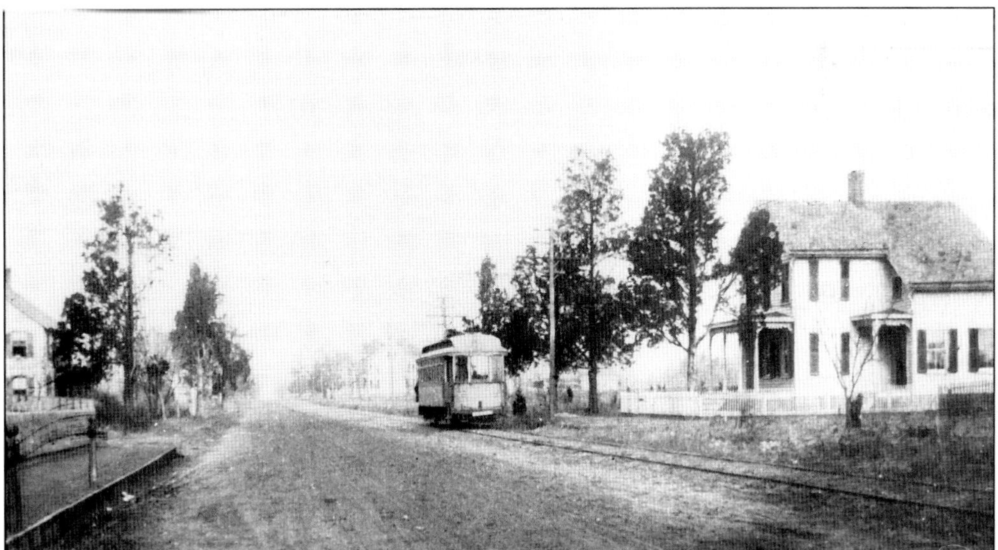

BROADWAY, *c.* 1905. This view looking north gives a good idea as to how sparsely populated West Keyport was during the early twentieth century. The house to the left was built *c.* 1889, while the house diagonal was of 1840s vintage. It has since been destroyed.

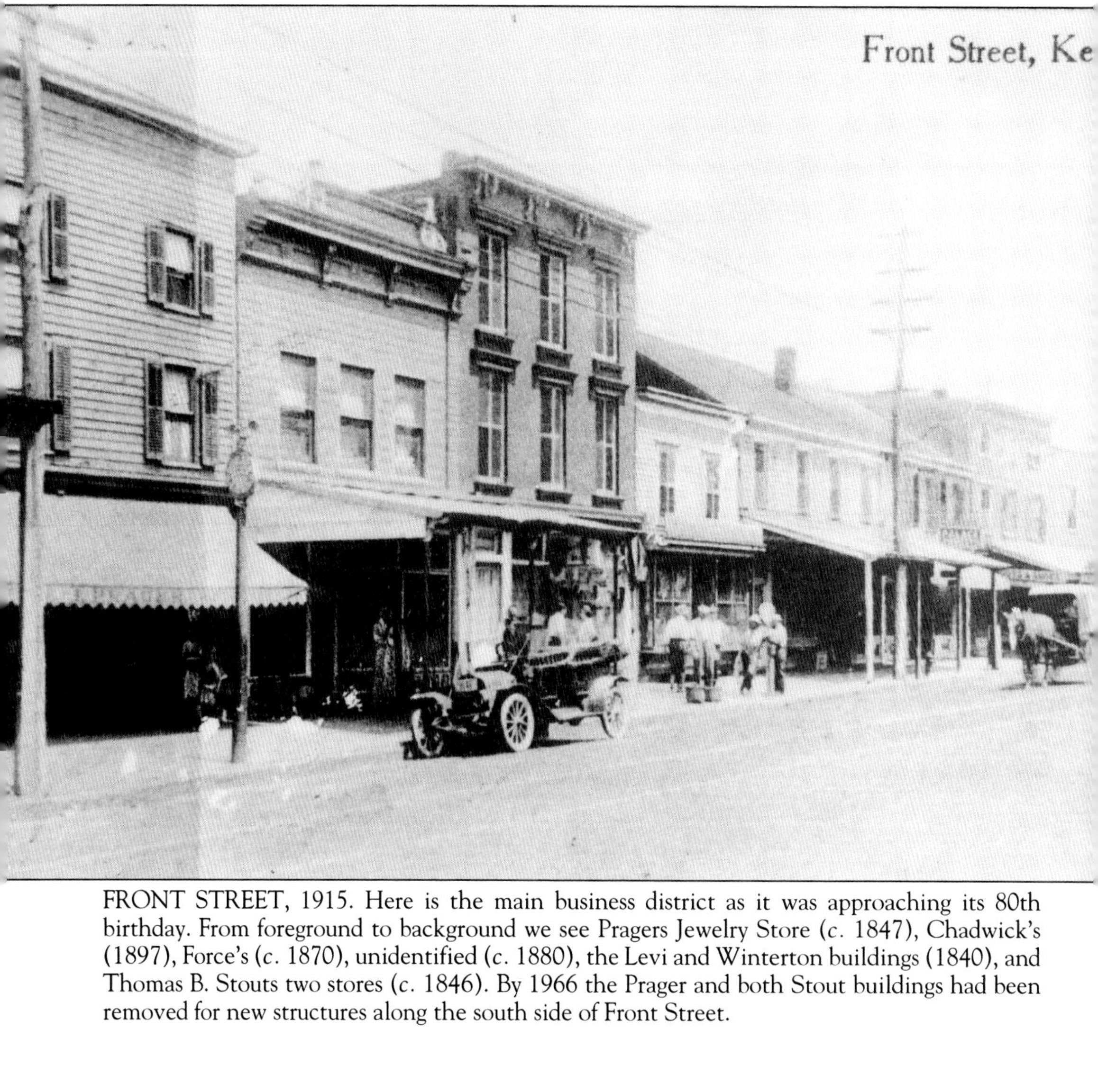

FRONT STREET, 1915. Here is the main business district as it was approaching its 80th birthday. From foreground to background we see Pragers Jewelry Store (*c.* 1847), Chadwick's (1897), Force's (*c.* 1870), unidentified (*c.* 1880), the Levi and Winterton buildings (1840), and Thomas B. Stouts two stores (*c.* 1846). By 1966 the Prager and both Stout buildings had been removed for new structures along the south side of Front Street.

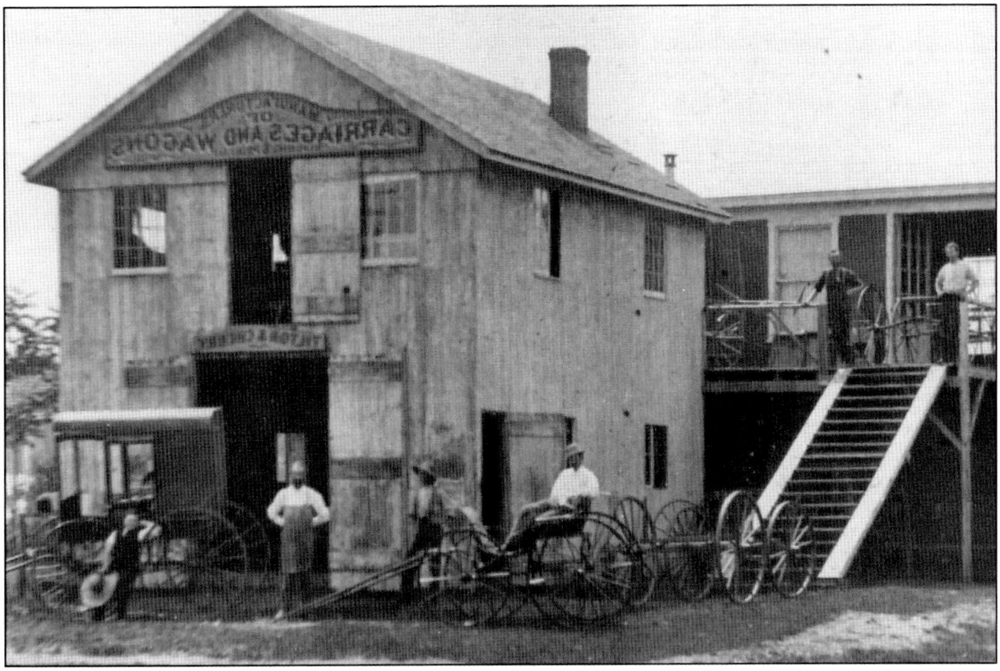

TILTON AND CHERRY, 1868. Francis W. Tilton and Henry Cherry built their blacksmith and carriage factory on the southeast corner of Elizabeth and Main Streets in 1860. Around 1877 it was decided to move the old building to a new site at Broad and Mott Streets (see Volume I, p. 41). Three days later the job was done and the building was being added on to.

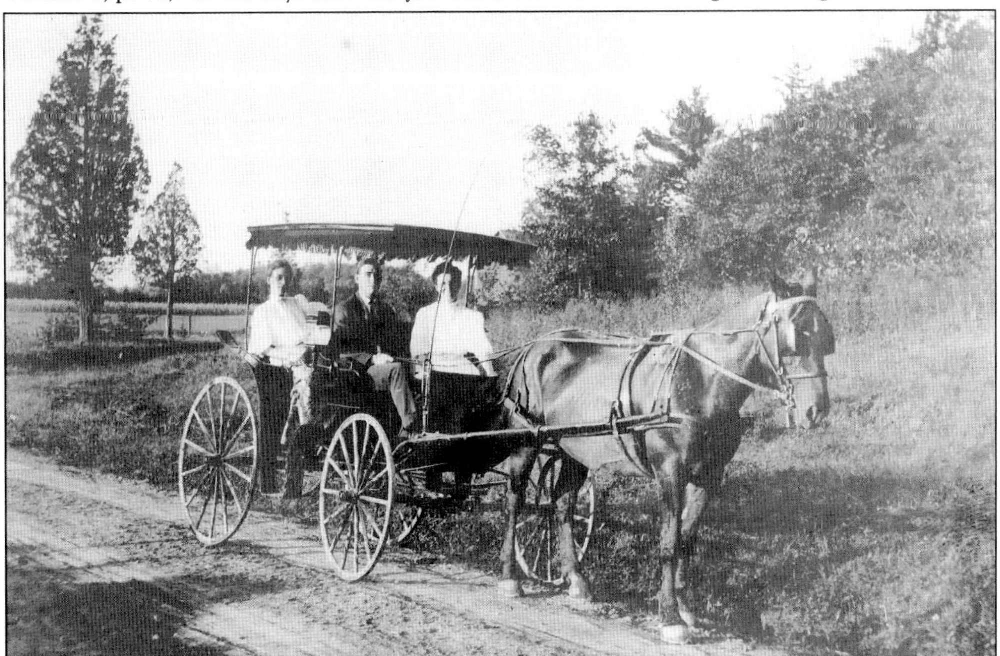

A TILTON AND CHERRY CARRIAGE. Henry and Francis did quite a business at the old shop, finally selling out to the Galbraith Company around 1915. Tilton and Cherry were among the finest of Monmouth County's wagon builders as well as one of the oldest.

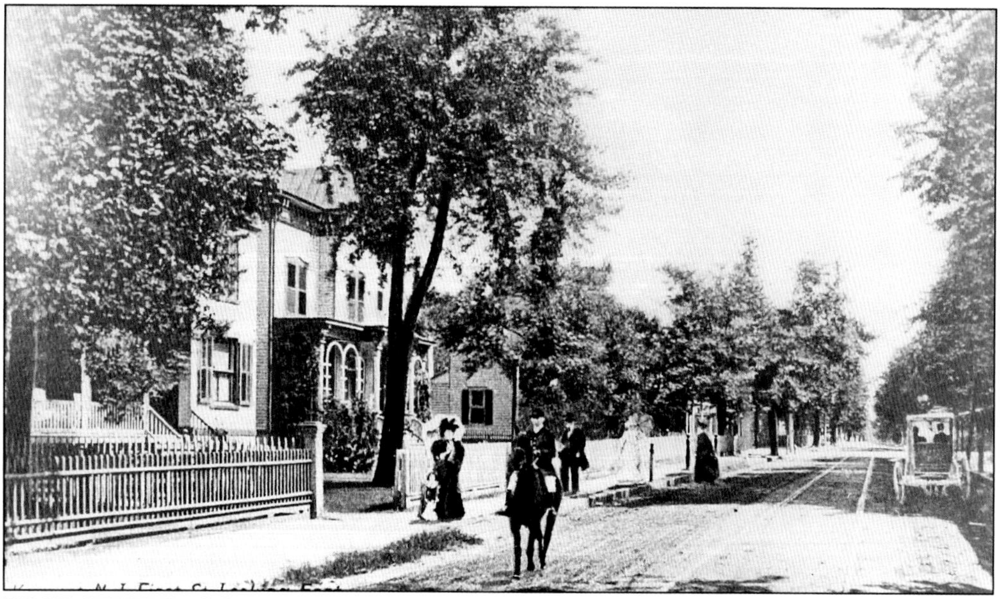

FIRST STREET LOOKING EAST, *c.* 1900. On the right is the fine house completed by J.S. Walling around 1880. With its white picket fence, large open-air porch, and fine view of the harbor, Mr. Walling held his old home dear until his death.

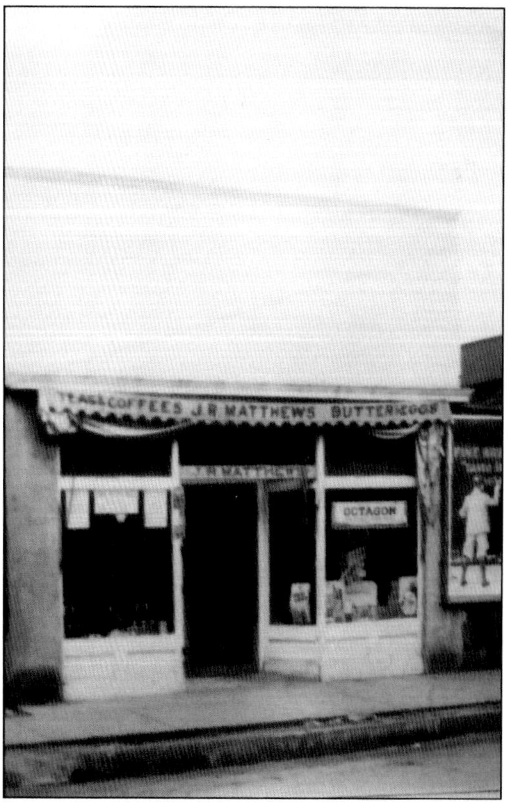

J.R. MATTHEWS, *c.* 1925. This little shop stood at 27 East Front Street, near the old town hall. Mr. Matthews carried a complete line of groceries, teas, and coffees, and orders could be taken by simply calling 178-R on your telephone.

THE SUGAR BOWL STORE, c. 1918. Located in a recently built store, the Sugar Bowl Candy Company was located at 22 W. Front Street during the 1910s. It later became a small supermarket, Vogel's Women's Clothes, and is now operated as a fitness center.

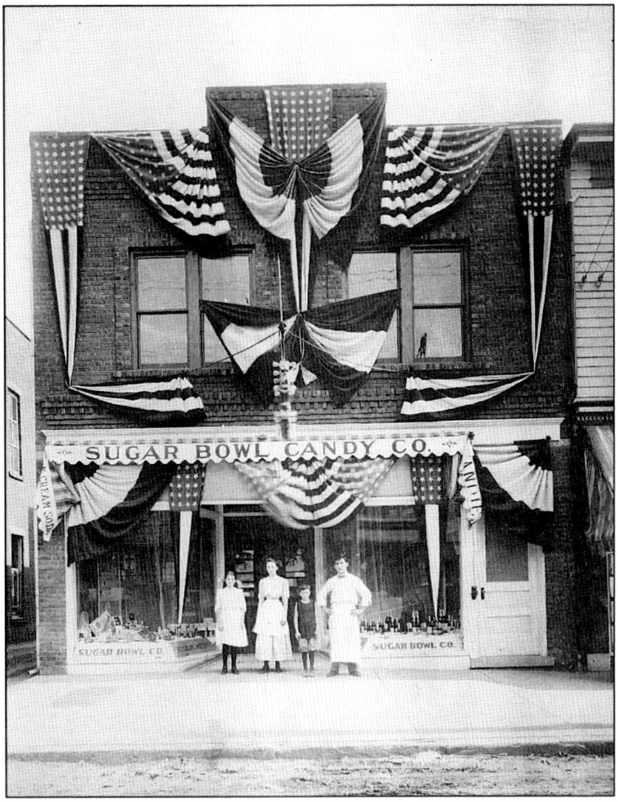

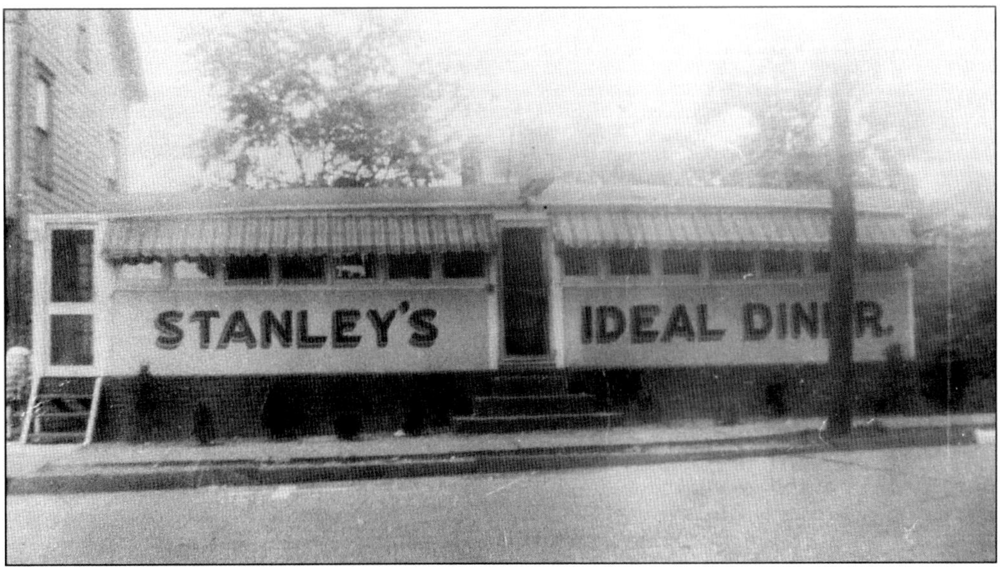

STANLEY'S IDEAL DINER. There have been at least three diners on this property, located in the old "hollow" on Broad Street. The Palace was first followed by Stanley's Ideal, which later dropped the Ideal and simply became Stanley's until the late 1980s. At that time it was rebuilt into the Seaport diner, where the legacy of good cooking and great atmosphere continues.

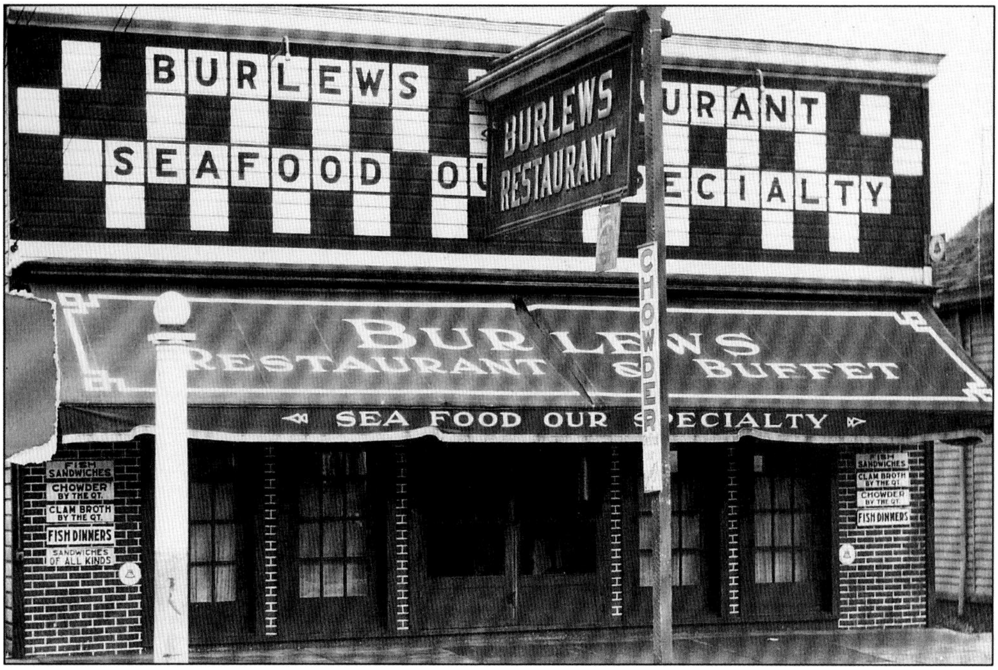

BURLEW'S FISHERY. This classic restaurant was located along "Fishery Row" on W. Front Street. Burlew's was later bought out by the Ye Cottage Inn, and the building was retained as part of the new restaurant. Note the old Bell Telephone signs affixed to the building.

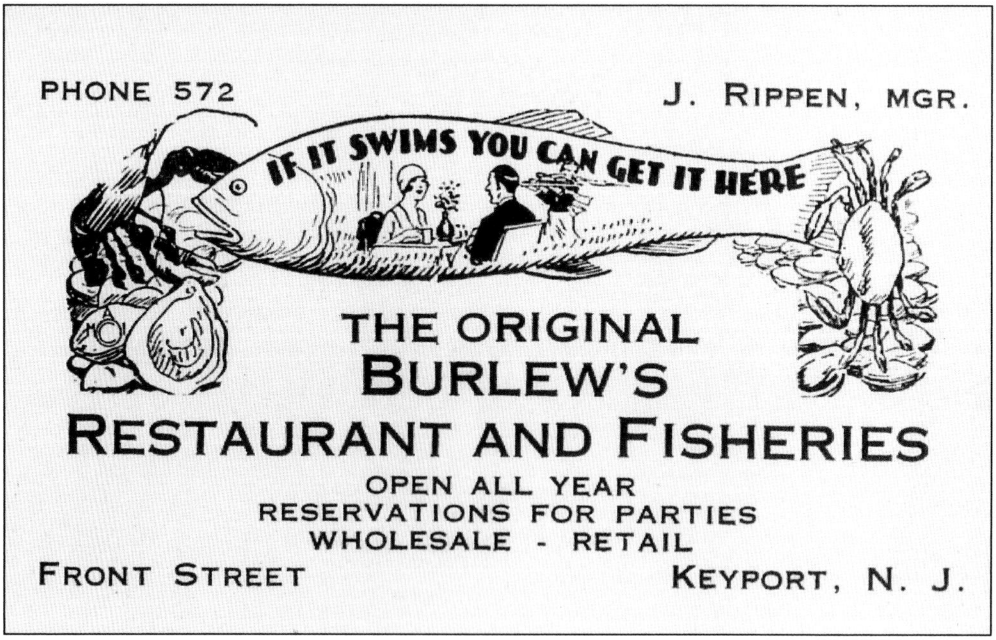

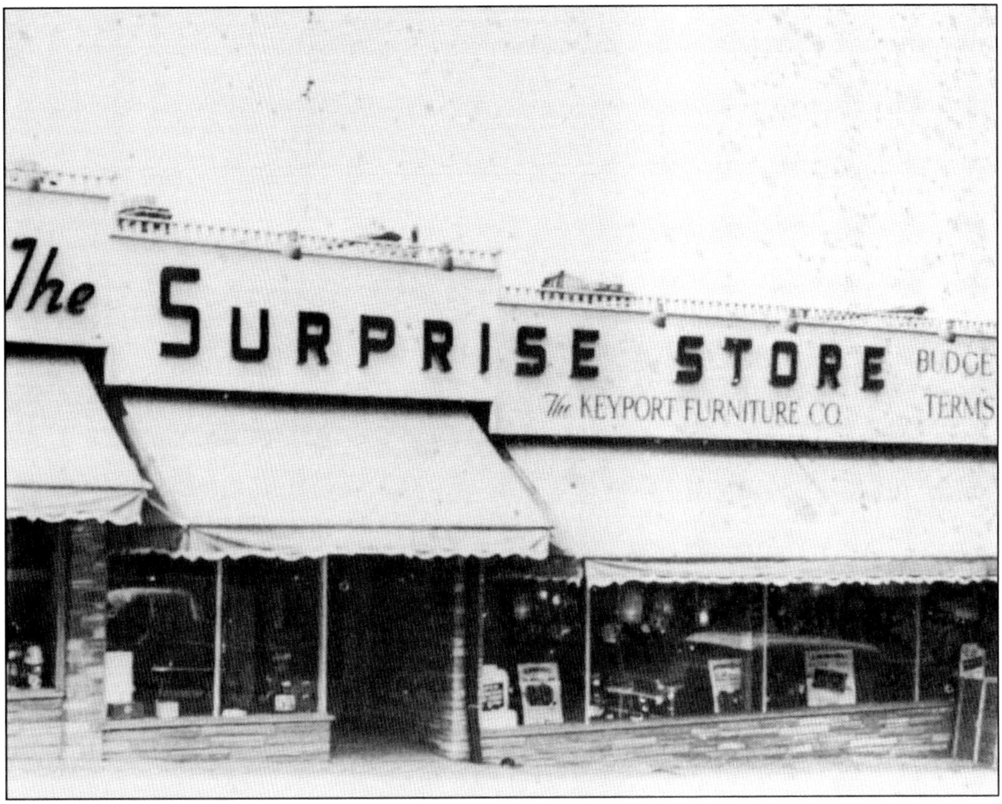

THE SURPRISE STORE, 1958. This Keyport five and dime was bought out by the Keyport Furniture Company in 1956. It stood on the south side of Front Street across the street from St. Mary's Episcopal Church, c.1967.

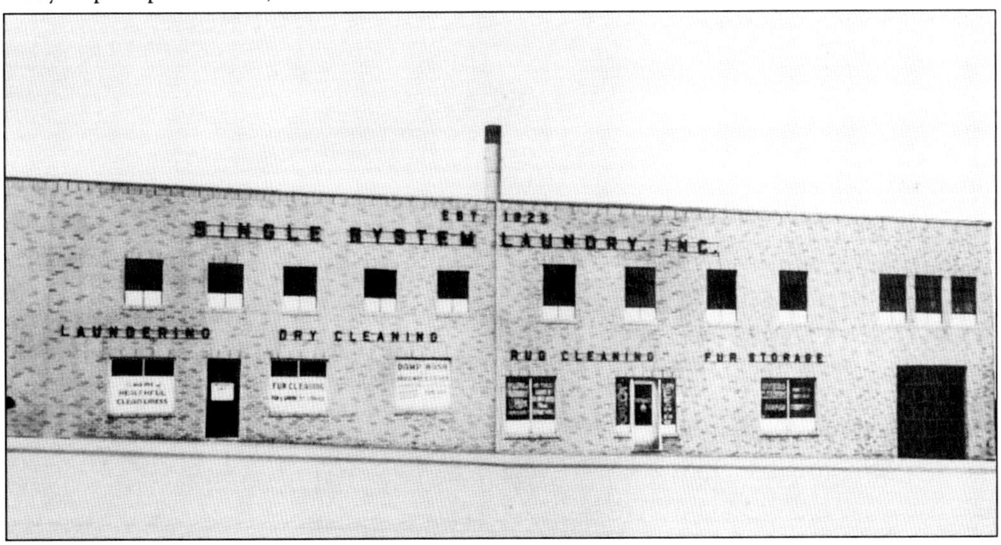

SINGLE SYSTEM LAUNDRY, 1958. The town's largest dry cleaner and laundry was located here, at the foot of Broad Street. Each day the shrill sound of the large steam whistle could be heard throughout the town at 8am, 12 noon, 12:30pm, and 4:30pm. The building still stands, minus the stack, and is now used for commercial purposes.

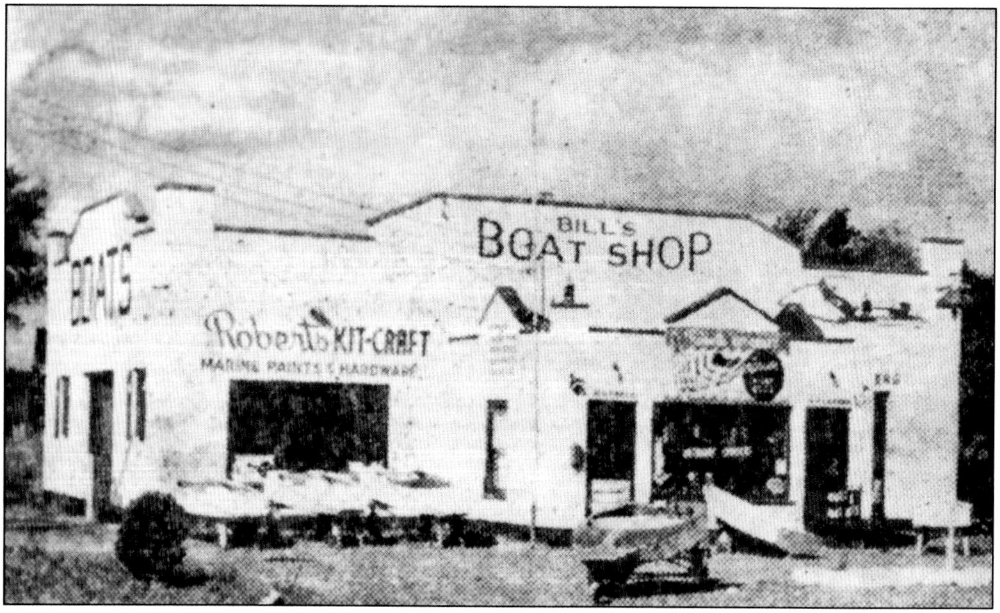

BILL'S BOAT SHOP, *c.* 1950. This structure, now an Army and Navy store, was built as a boat shop around 1949. It was later home to a lighting shop and then served as the headquarters for Dolan's Moving Company. It is located on the northeast corner of Route 36 and Atlantic Street.

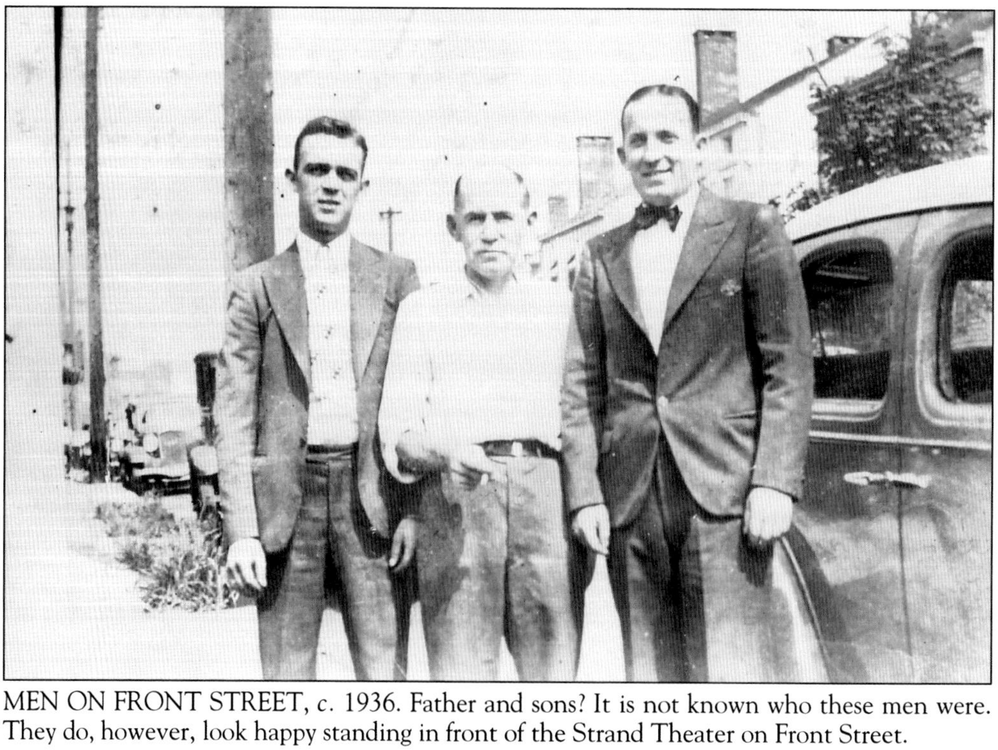

MEN ON FRONT STREET, *c.* 1936. Father and sons? It is not known who these men were. They do, however, look happy standing in front of the Strand Theater on Front Street.

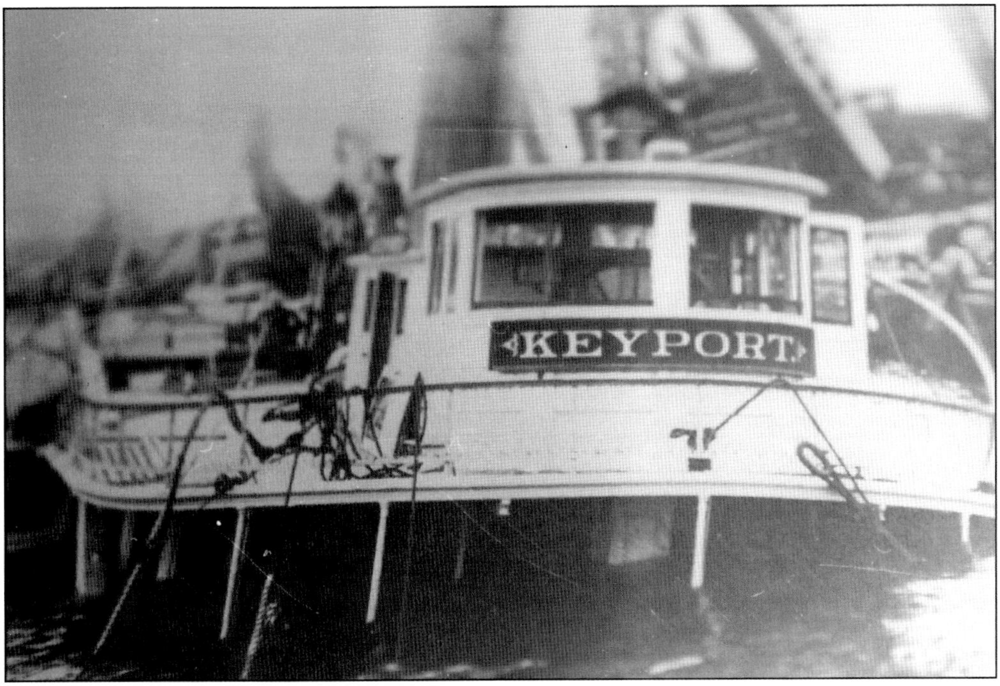

THE *KEYPORT II*, 1917. Tragedy was averted on July 22, 1916, for the seventy-five passengers of the *Keyport*, which was rammed by the ocean liner *Santos* in New York harbor. Seven minutes later the *Keyport* sank in 14 feet of water, abruptly ending her thirty-six-year career as a passenger ship. She was built as the *Martha's Vineyard* in 1871, and had been running out of Keansburg since 1913.

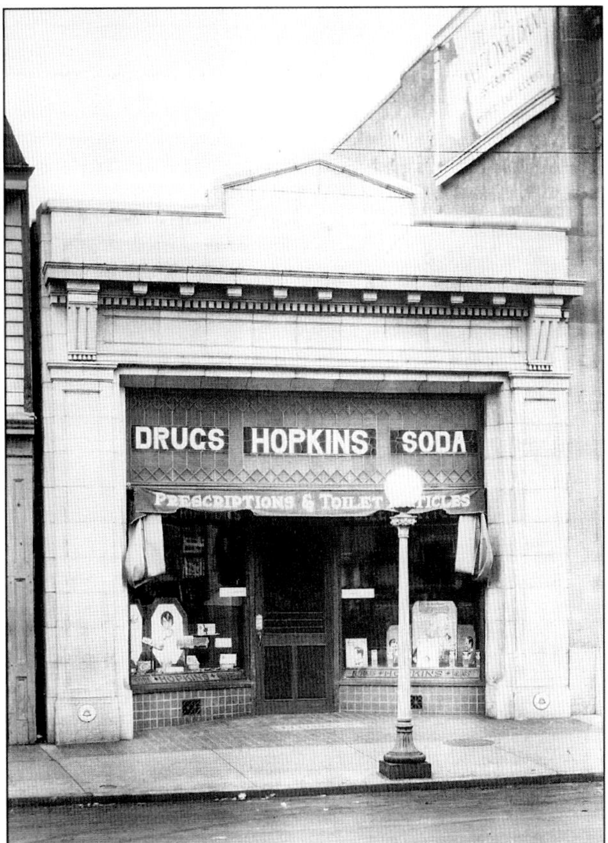

HOPKINS DRUG, *c*. 1925. Business was so good for Henry Hopkins that he opened a second drug store just three blocks away from his First Street store. Several years later he built a third store in Keansburg. As of 1996 the store was still operated as drug store, as it has been since it was built in 1917.

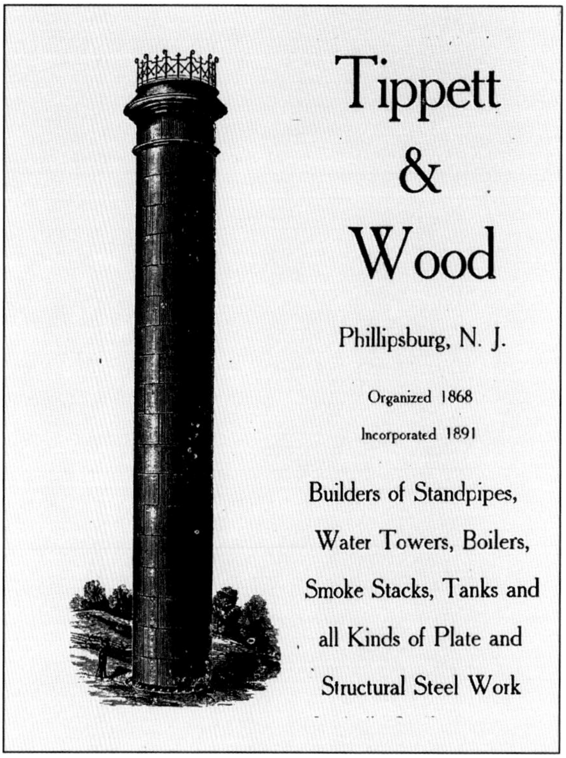

THE 1893 WATER TOWER. The water commissioners quickly went about purchasing property on the southwest corner of Church and Elizabeth Streets to erect a standpipe for the new water system. Six months later, the big steel cylinder was completed, allowing ample water pressure to be supplied throughout the town.

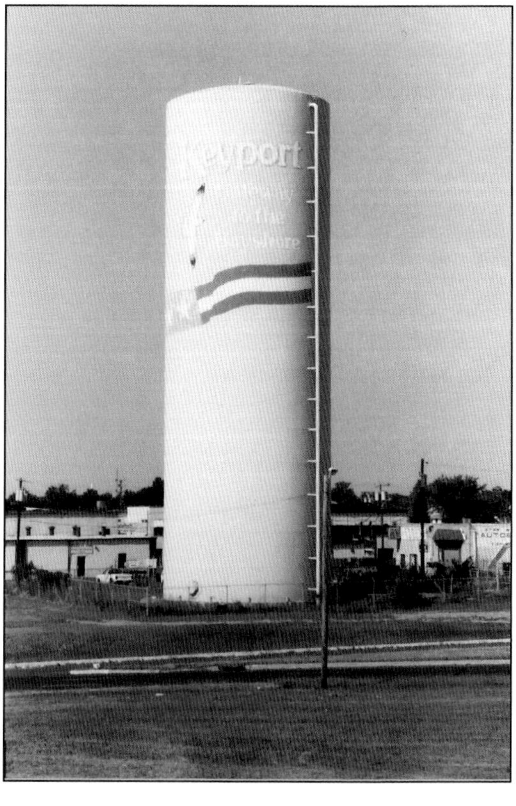

THE 1976 WATER TOWER. After nearly eighty years the old tower just wasn't able to keep up with the increased demand for water. So in 1976 the new tower was completed by the Fisher Tank Co. of Chester, PA, on the southwest corner of Cass Street and Route 35. Upon the tank the logo "Keyport Gateway to the Bayshore" was painted by Vanguard Art Services of Hazlet.

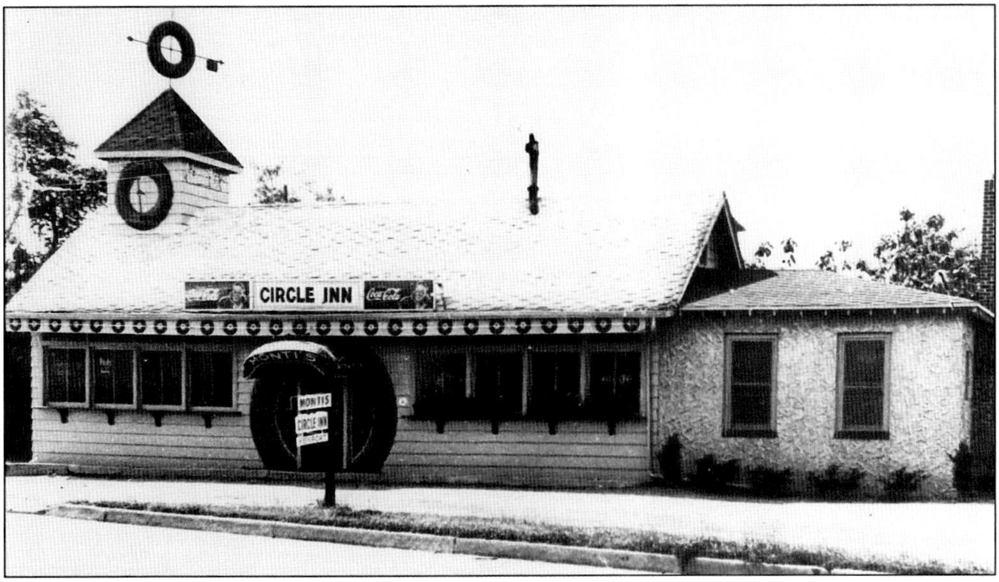

MONTI'S CIRCLE INN. Located on state highway 35, Monti's was a pleasing stop for shore travelers along the old concrete highway in the 1920s and '30s. It stood near the present-day on ramp to the Garden State Parkway near Routes 35 and 36. The Circle Inn could not be mistaken; the circle entrance, circle on the tower, circles below the gutter, and even a circle weather vane left little doubt as to the building's identity.

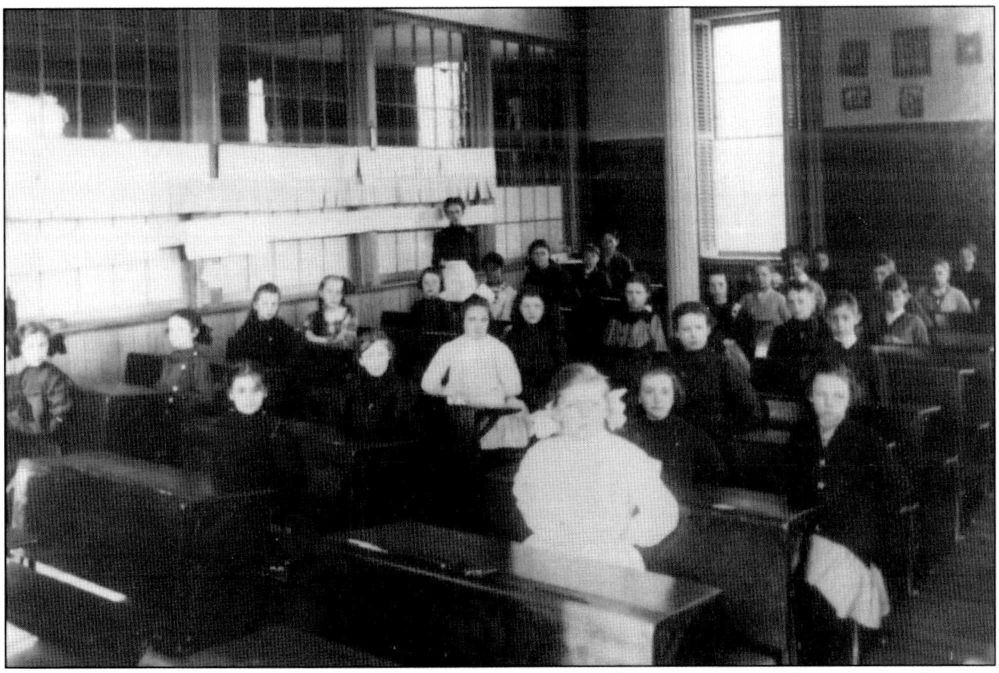

THE INTERIOR OF THE GRADE SCHOOL, 1899. When the new addition was added to the school in 1892–93, this became the common arrangement for all of the classrooms. Each room was divided by a glass partition and had at least two windows facing outside. Builder and architect Henry A. Young claimed that sunlight enhanced learning, making this section superior to the old section, where some classrooms had no windows at all.

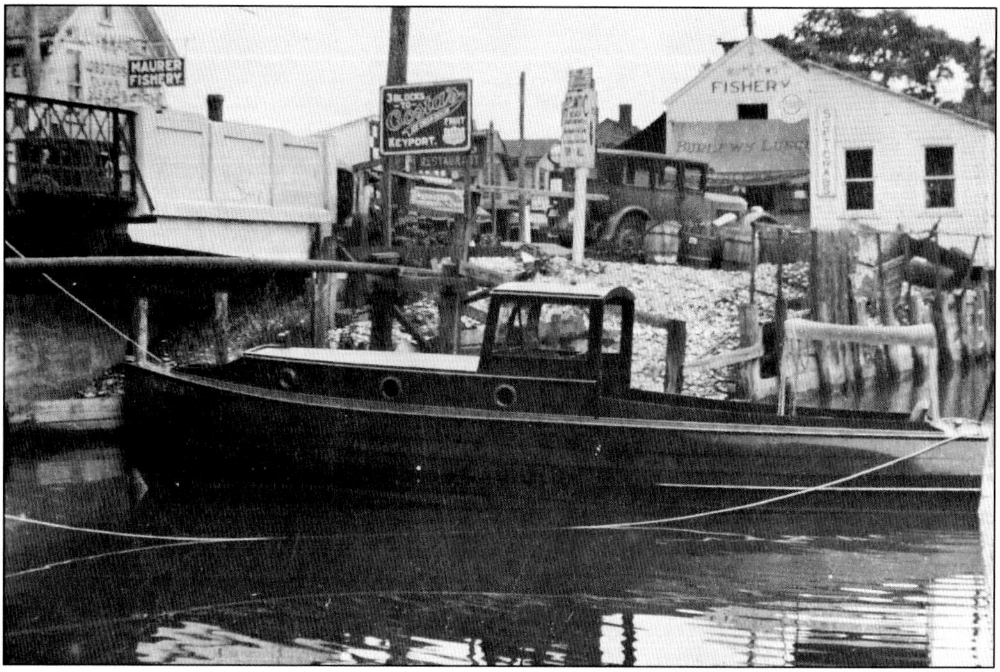

LUPPATTACONG CREEK, *c.* 1925. What could be better than heading to Keyport from the city for a good Sunday afternoon fish dinner? Not much. This scene is from the southwest side of the creek looking toward the business district. The area has changed very little today except that there are a few less shells on the ground, and there aren't too many Kofoed-built boats moored in the creek.

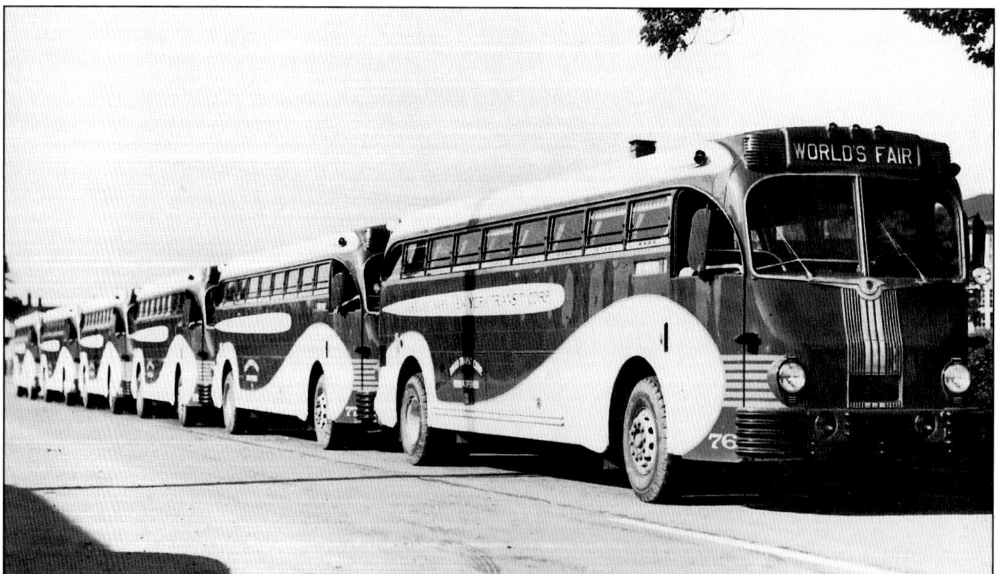

ROLLO BUS LINES, 1939. Rollo Bus Lines was begun by James Rollo in 1923 when he first began service between Freneau in Matawan and Walnut Street in Keyport. By 1924 the line was running through Union Beach and into Keansburg. These buses are shown heading from Keyport to the New York Worlds Fair.

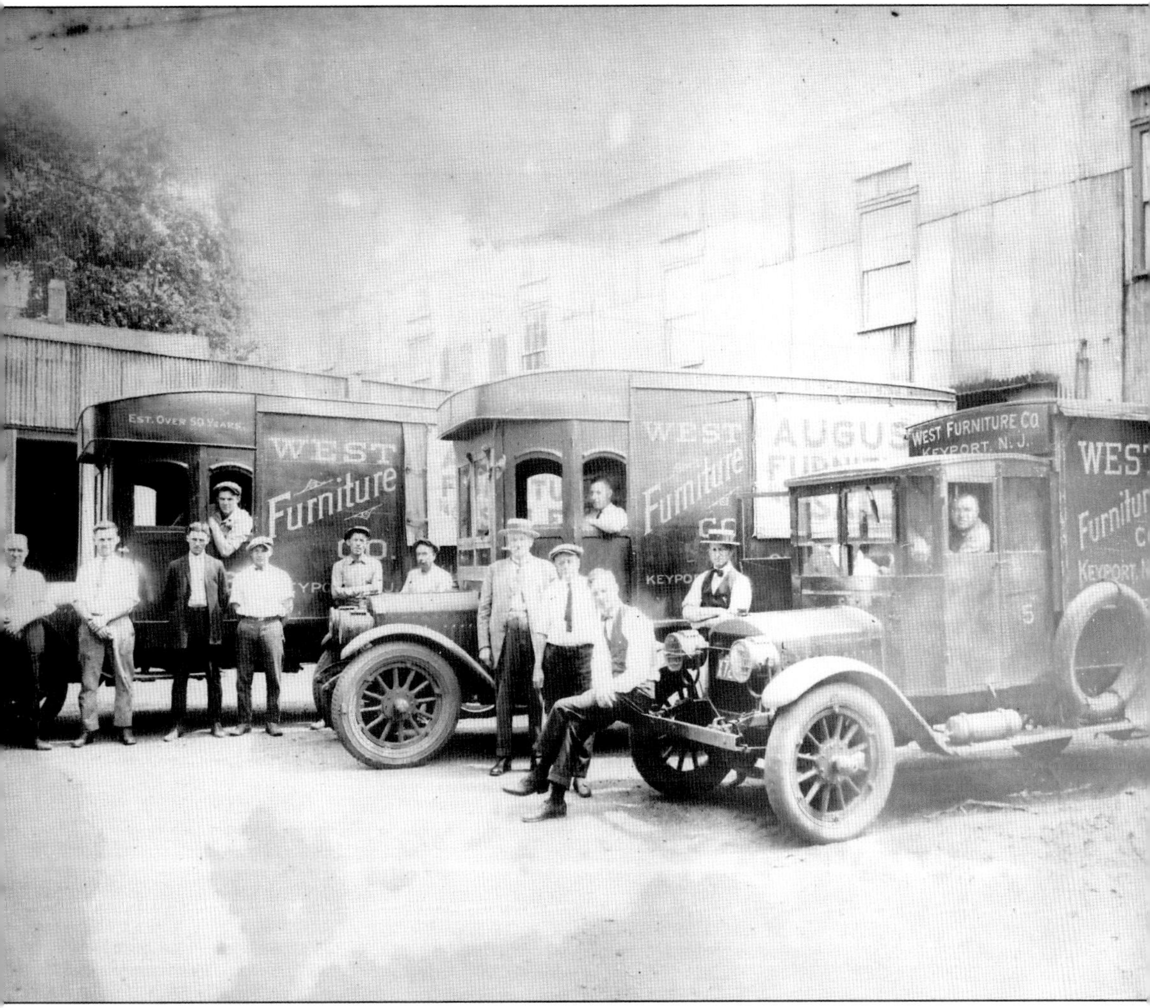

THE WEST FURNITURE CO., 1923. Already over fifty years old, the West Furniture Co. continued to be "the" place to buy your furnishings. With over eight delivery trucks, forty employees, and five buildings, the company prospered for 127 years until they closed their doors for good in 1996. These early moving trucks were mostly hand-built and contained canvas sides so that large furniture could be squeezed in just by rolling up the sides.

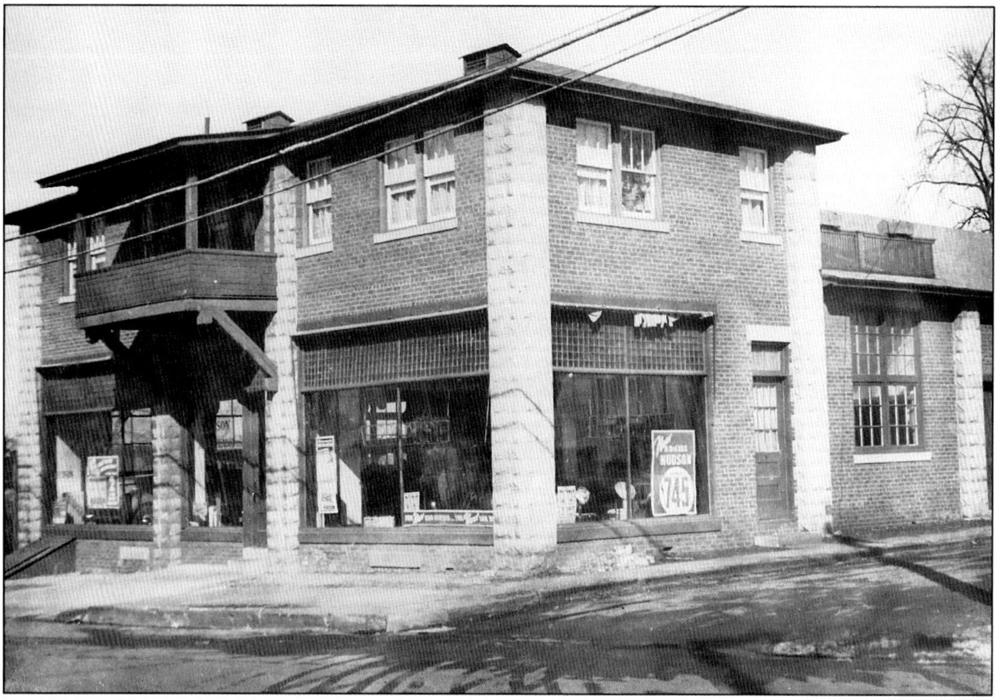

SCHANCK'S GARAGE, *c.* 1927. This unique building was built *c.* 1923 by J.L. Schanck as a automobile dealership. It was later purchased by Buhler and Bitner, and as the car business expanded, it ceased being used as a showroom. The building was also the first home of the Keyport Fire Patrol, who used it for about ten years. It is now an auto body shop.

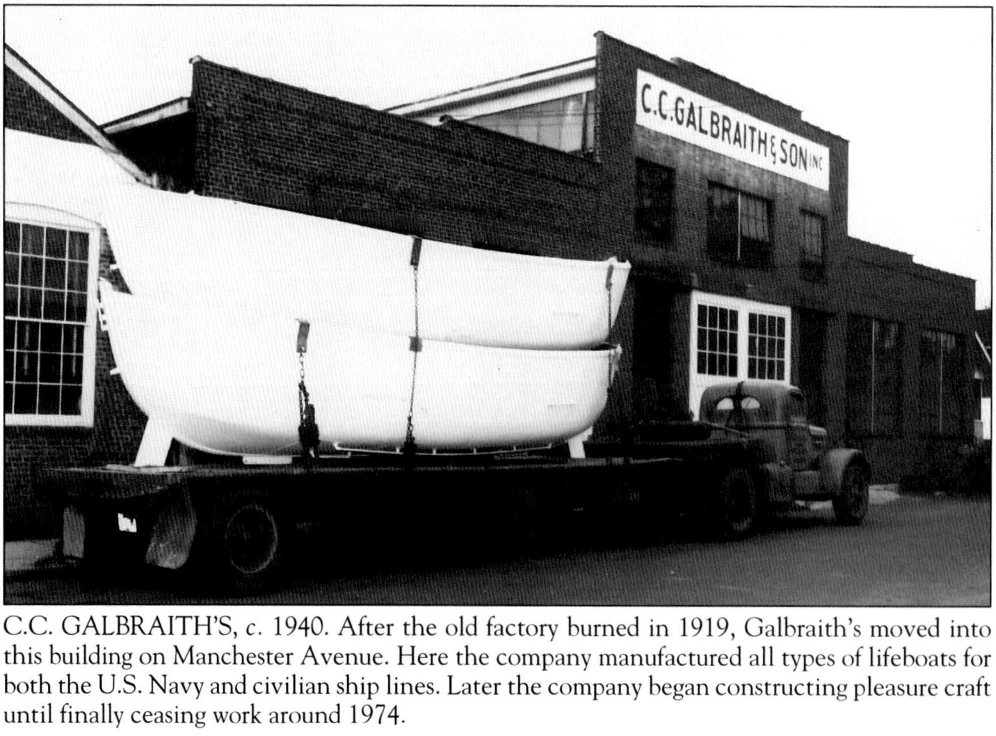

C.C. GALBRAITH'S, *c.* 1940. After the old factory burned in 1919, Galbraith's moved into this building on Manchester Avenue. Here the company manufactured all types of lifeboats for both the U.S. Navy and civilian ship lines. Later the company began constructing pleasure craft until finally ceasing work around 1974.

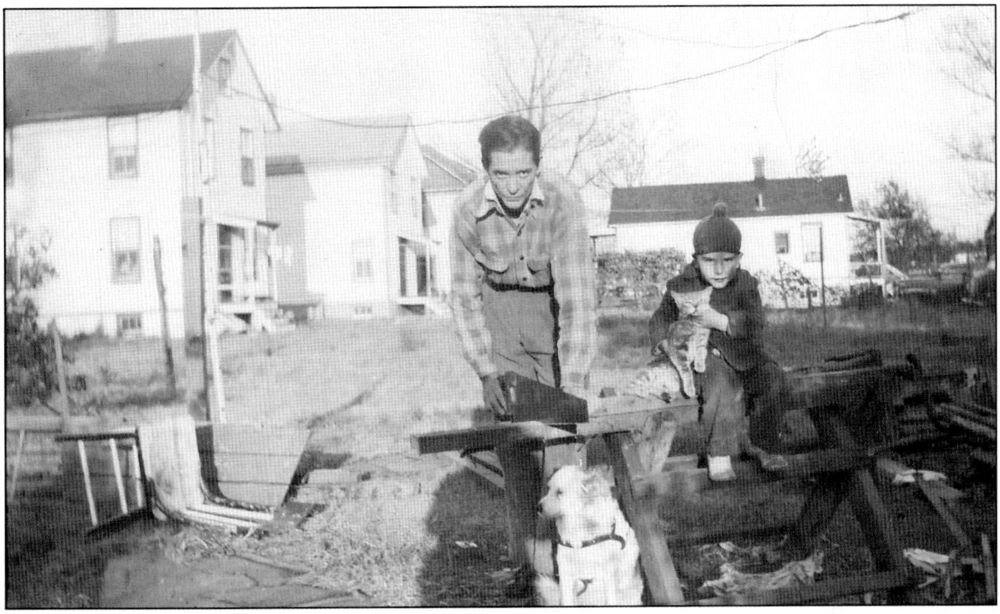

BERT MORRIS AND HIS FATHER, *c.* 1945. Five-year-old Bertram Harry Morris, shown here with his dad, Bertram Frederick, grew up in Mechanicsville with his parents and younger brother. Little did they know that this entire block would be demolished in the late 1960s for the construction of the Bethany Manor high rise. Bert later joined the Liberty Hose Co. on the same block as his house and in 1991 served as the Keyport fire chief.

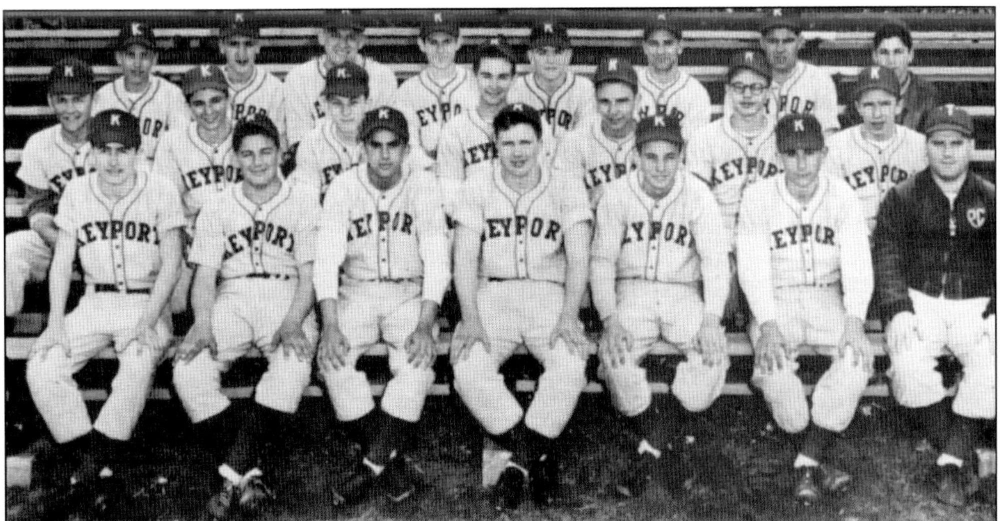

THE KEYPORT HIGH BASEBALL TEAM, 1953. From left to right are as follows: (front row) J. Mullaney, P. Genovese, A. Falduti, H. Shumock, C. Walling , C. Davino, and Coach Zampelle; (middle row) R. Jouneau, B. Arnella, R. Skislak, D. Raynor, J. Clayton, R. LoPresto, and W. Clayton; (back row) B. Donaruma, D. Eastmond, R. Westerdahl, C. Cundey, R. Wharton, J. Trabucco, W. Neihart, and E. Jacques.

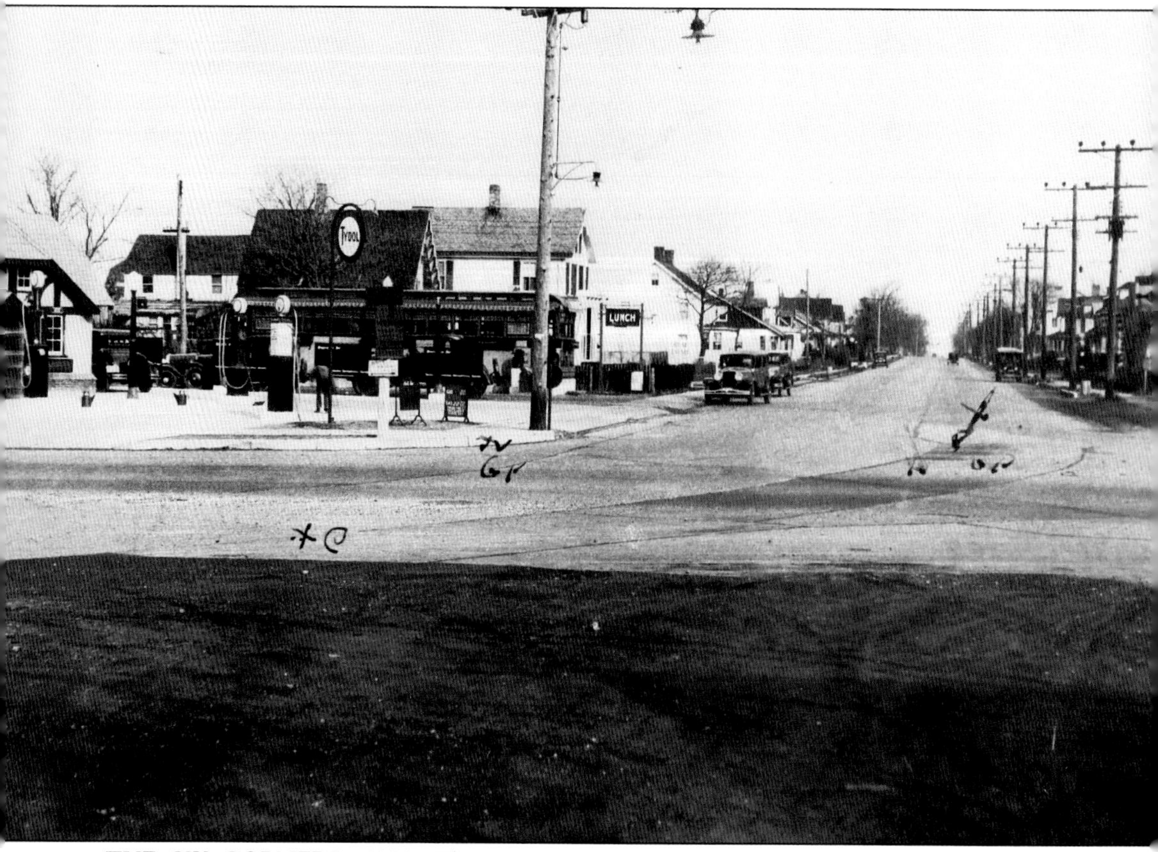

THE SIX CORNERS, 1929. The six corners were undoubtedly the busiest of Keyport's intersections after 1900. Formed by the intersections of Maple Place, Broadway, and Route 35, this area was quickly built up to take advantage of the new shore highway. The railcar diner, Tydol Station, and most of the houses in the view were removed for the construction of the new route 35 overpass in 1966. The site to the left has been the home of a diner since 1921.

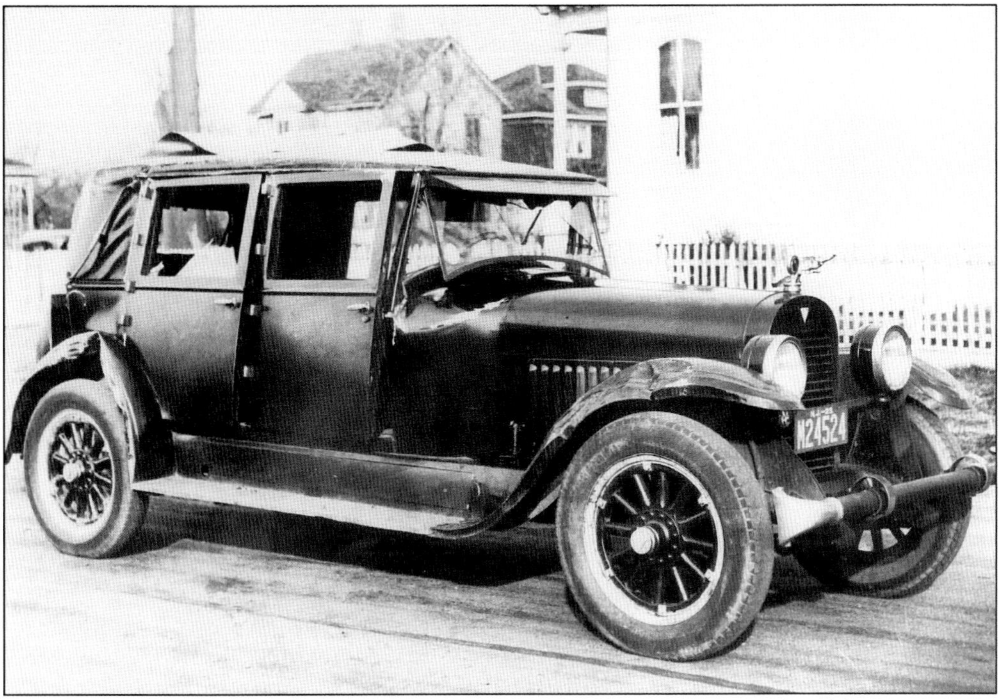

A CAR ACCIDENT, 1929. This auto was involved in a bit of crash at the old six corners in 1929. The x's on the preceding page show the location of the several cars which were involved. The photograph was taken on West Third Street near Broadway, possibly were the owner of the car resided.

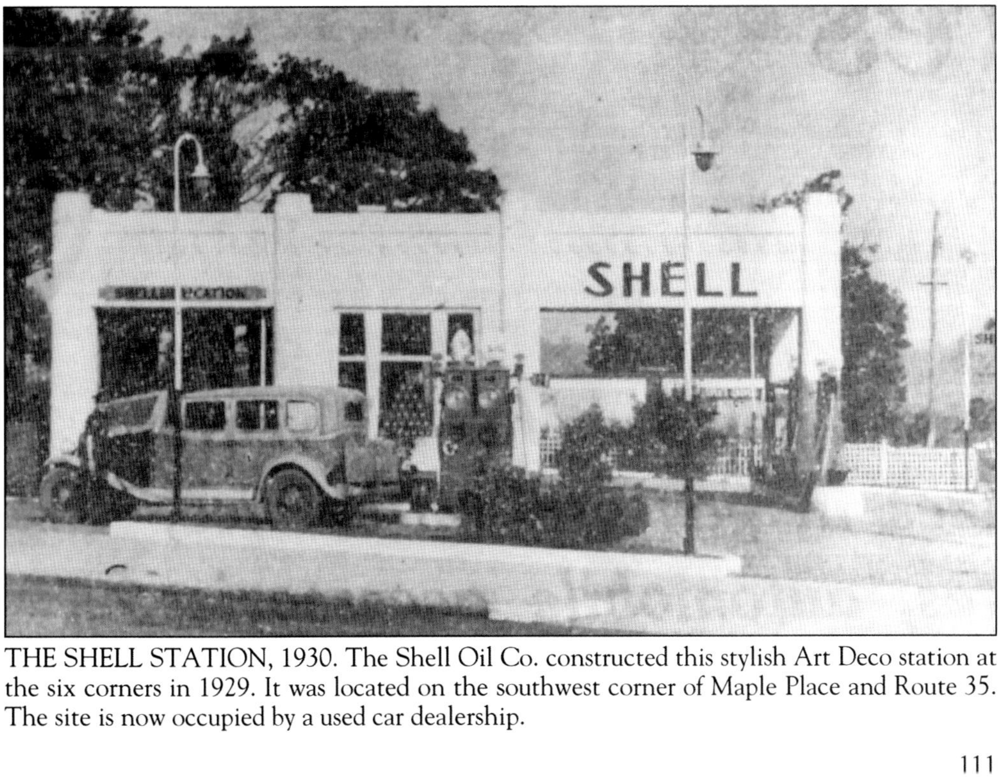

THE SHELL STATION, 1930. The Shell Oil Co. constructed this stylish Art Deco station at the six corners in 1929. It was located on the southwest corner of Maple Place and Route 35. The site is now occupied by a used car dealership.

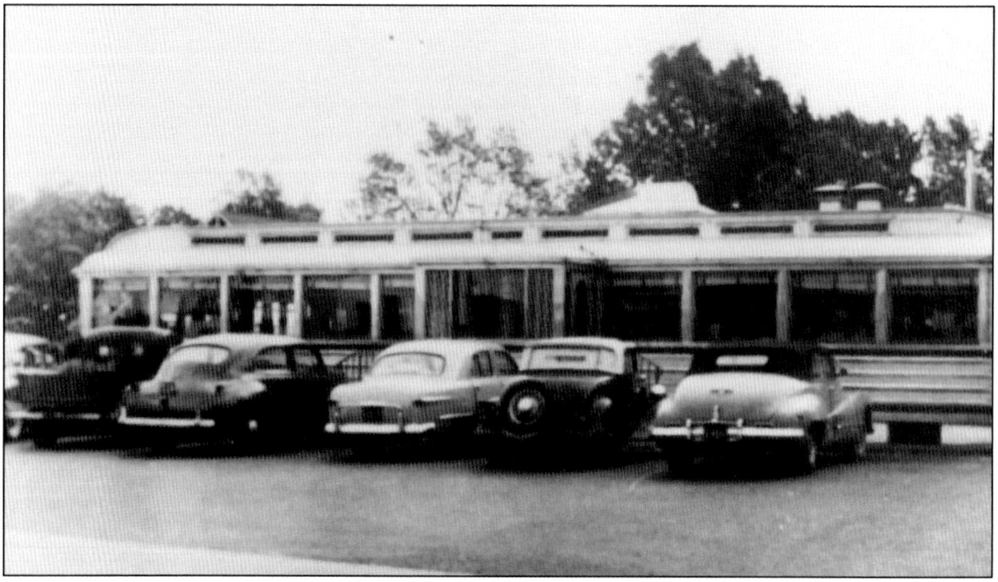

THE KEYPORT DINER, 1950. The second Keyport diner was this stainless steel classic which stood on Route 35 South, near Chingarora Avenue. In the photograph can be seen a 1941 Chrysler, 1941 Buick, 1951 Ford, and a 1934 Ford convertible. The diner was destroyed by a c.1967 fire, a fate which at least three other diners in West Keyport met during the 1960s.

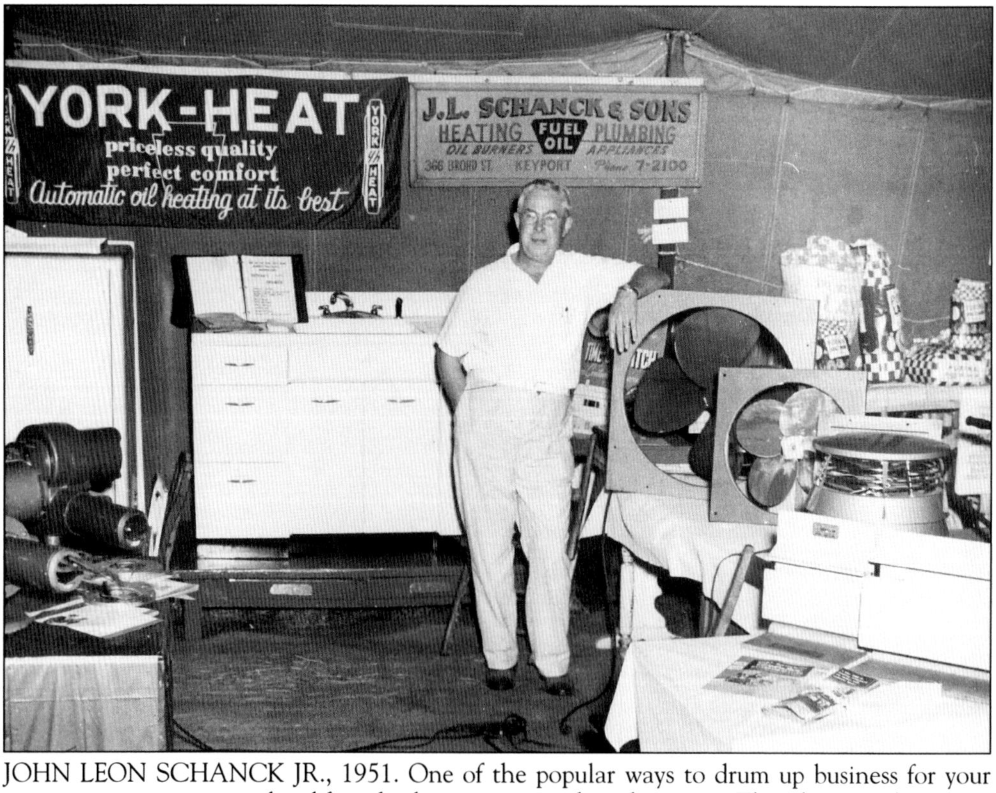

JOHN LEON SCHANCK JR., 1951. One of the popular ways to drum up business for your company was to appear at local fairs displaying your goods and services. This photograph appears to have been taken at a Hazlet Fair on Route 35.

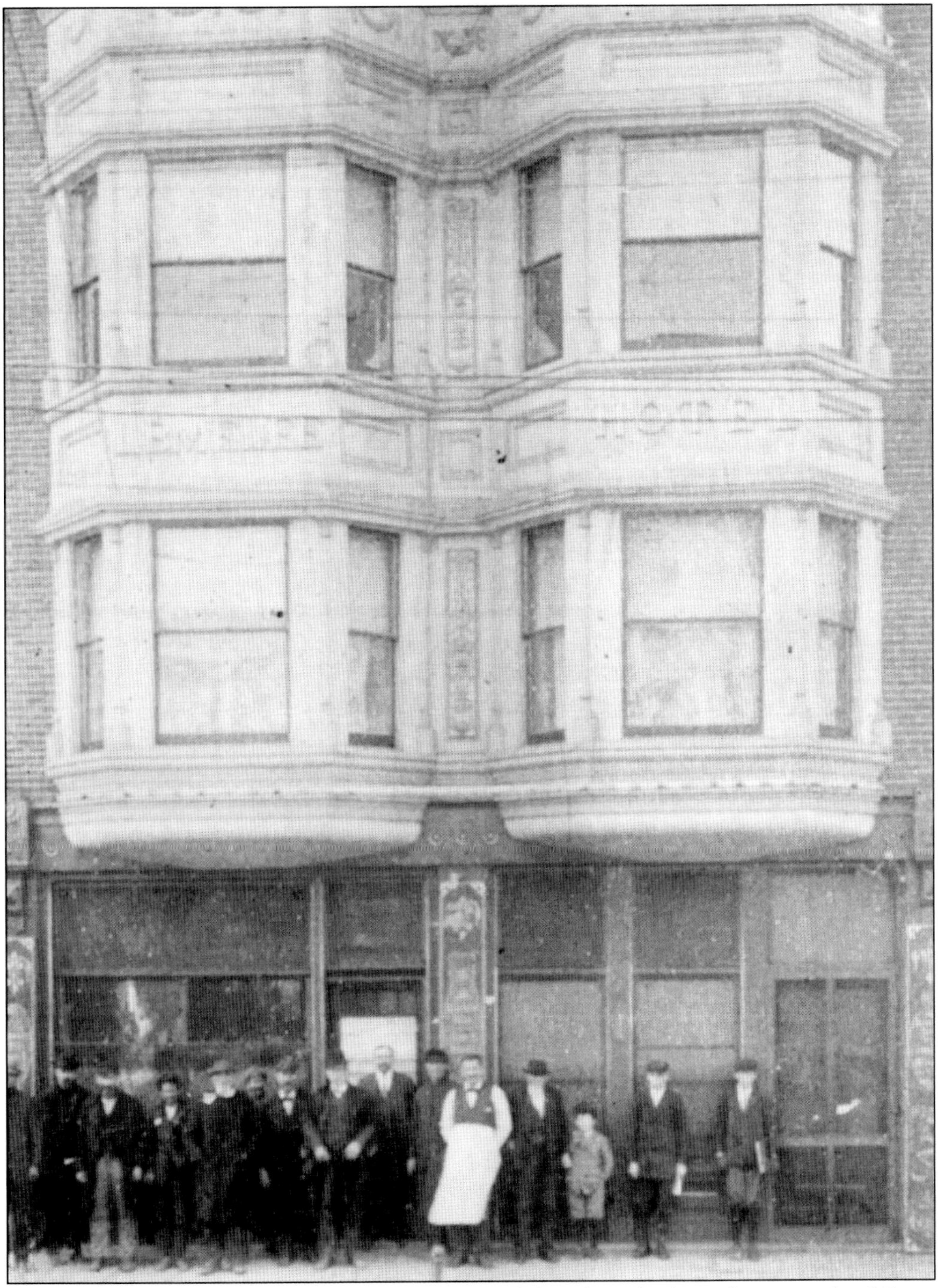

THE LBMELEE HOTEL, c. 1901. Keyport's seventh hotel was built on the west side of Front Street, directly across from the Pavilion Hotel in 1892. The three-story edifice contained a saloon and restaurant on the ground floor while the upper floors were reserved for steamboat and railroad travelers. The building has characteristics of Beaux-Arts classicism, which was popular from about 1890 until the 1920s. The hotel, which has long since been known as the Monmouth, lost its third floor to a tragic 1981 fire where one person lost their life.

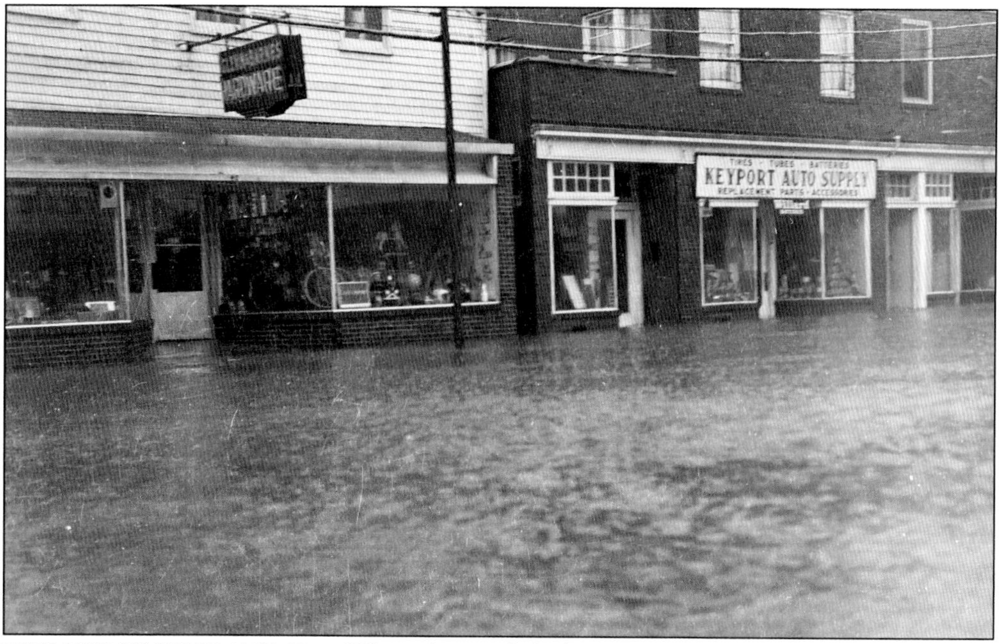

THE 1950 HURRICANE. Top: When the winds kick up and the tides begin to rise even the driest parts of town cannot keep the seawater out. Here along First Street the water is rushing through Beach Park and is creeping up on the old houses which lined the south side of First Street. Bottom: As with First Street, Front Street near the hollow is an old creek bed, and water—like people—likes to return home no matter how long it's been gone. One of the biggest threats during a storm is not the water itself but the large pieces of debris which float through water violently until they are stopped by a building or car.

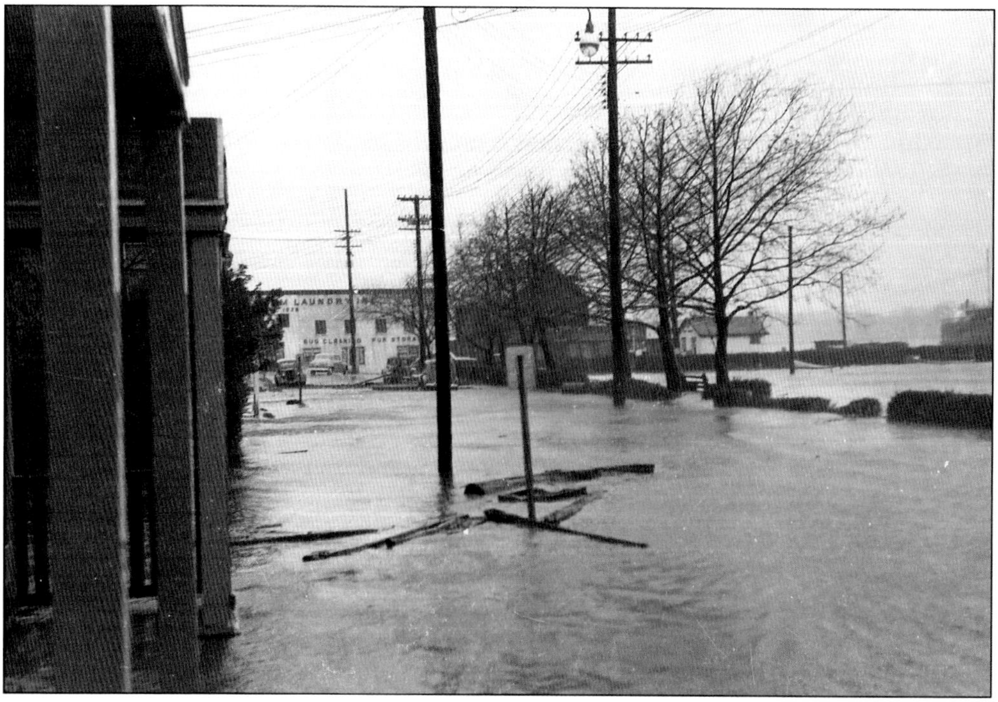

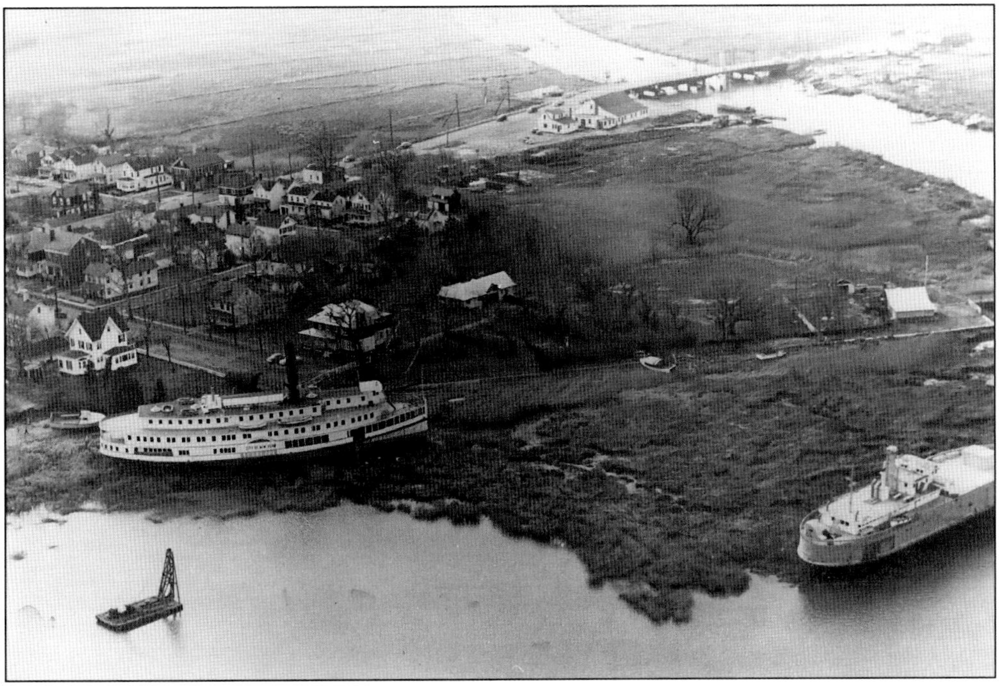

AFTERMATH OF THE 1950 HURRICANE. As soon as the waters begin to recede, it become time to survey the damage and start the repairs. Top: All of the steamships which were moored at the wharf broke loose in 1950, and ended up scattered over the meadows in both Keyport and Cliffwood. All along Browns Point Cove boats broke away, sank, and in this case, came to rest. Bottom: These craft came to rest just over the bridge into Cliffwood. Hurricanes and nor'easters can be a devastating time for boat owners.

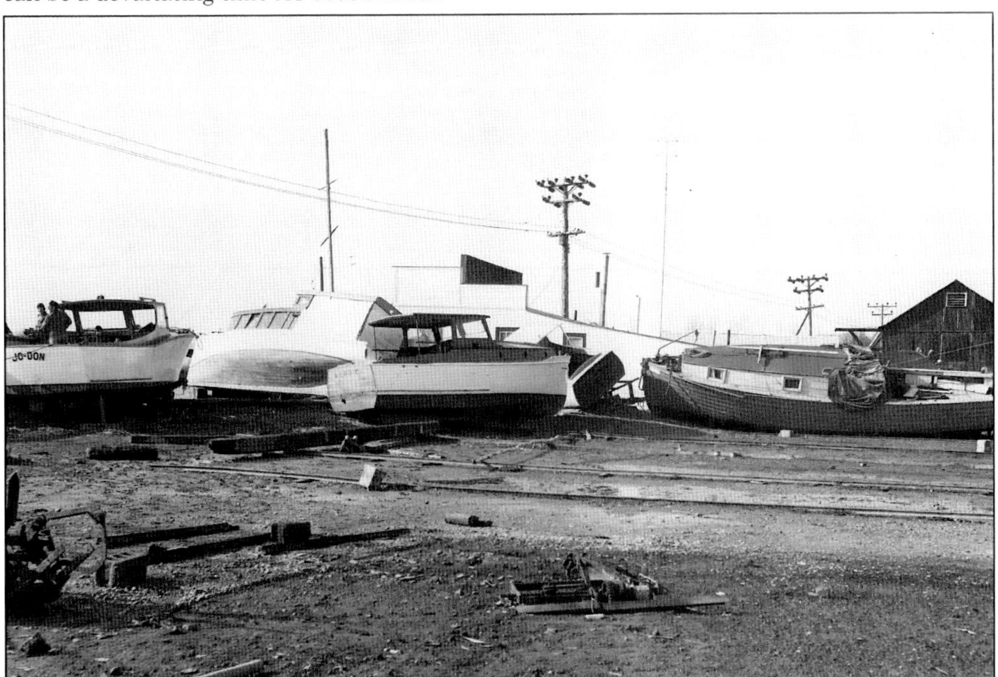

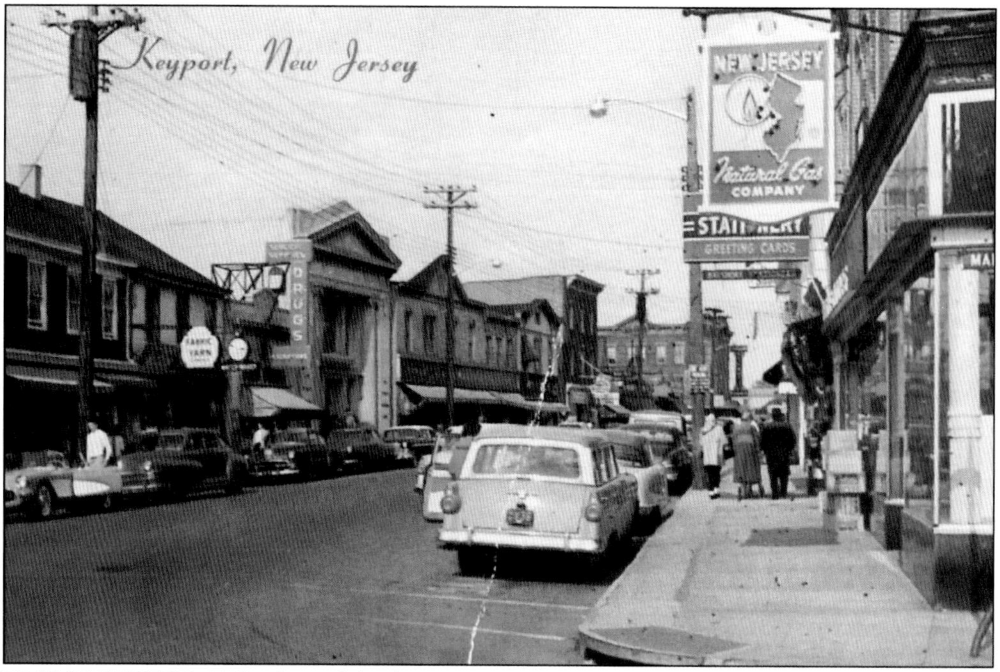

FRONT STREET, 1962. One of the last postcards made of Keyport's business district was this one, issued in the early 1960s. It was published by the Color Photo Co. of Toms River.

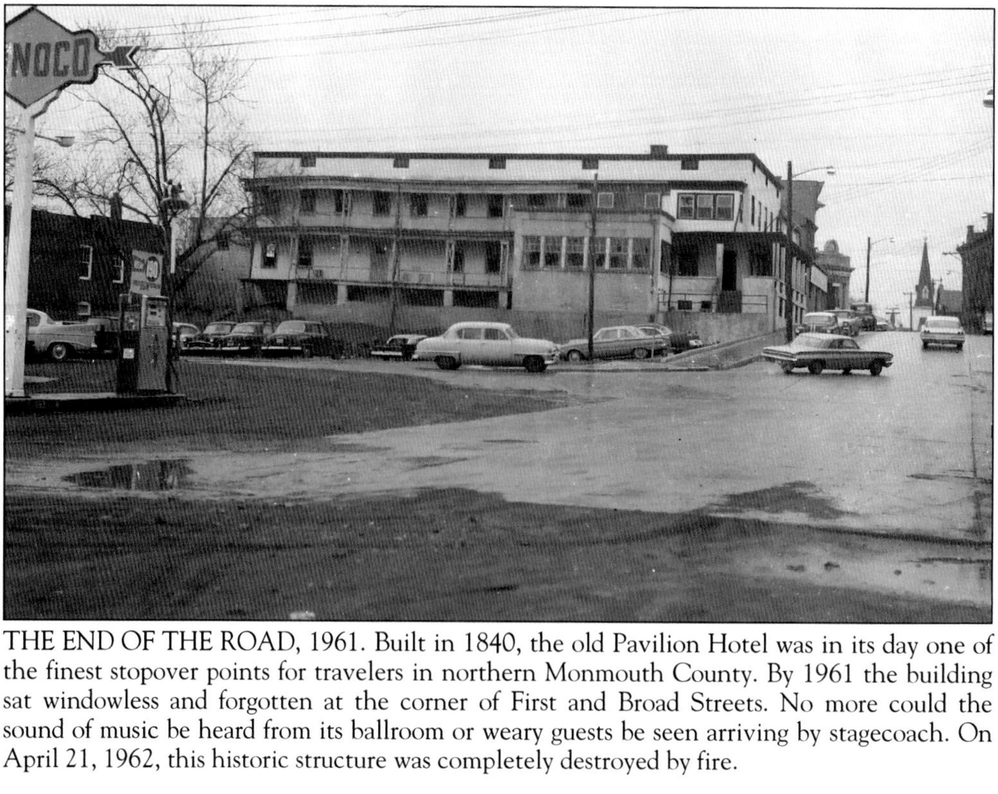

THE END OF THE ROAD, 1961. Built in 1840, the old Pavilion Hotel was in its day one of the finest stopover points for travelers in northern Monmouth County. By 1961 the building sat windowless and forgotten at the corner of First and Broad Streets. No more could the sound of music be heard from its ballroom or weary guests be seen arriving by stagecoach. On April 21, 1962, this historic structure was completely destroyed by fire.

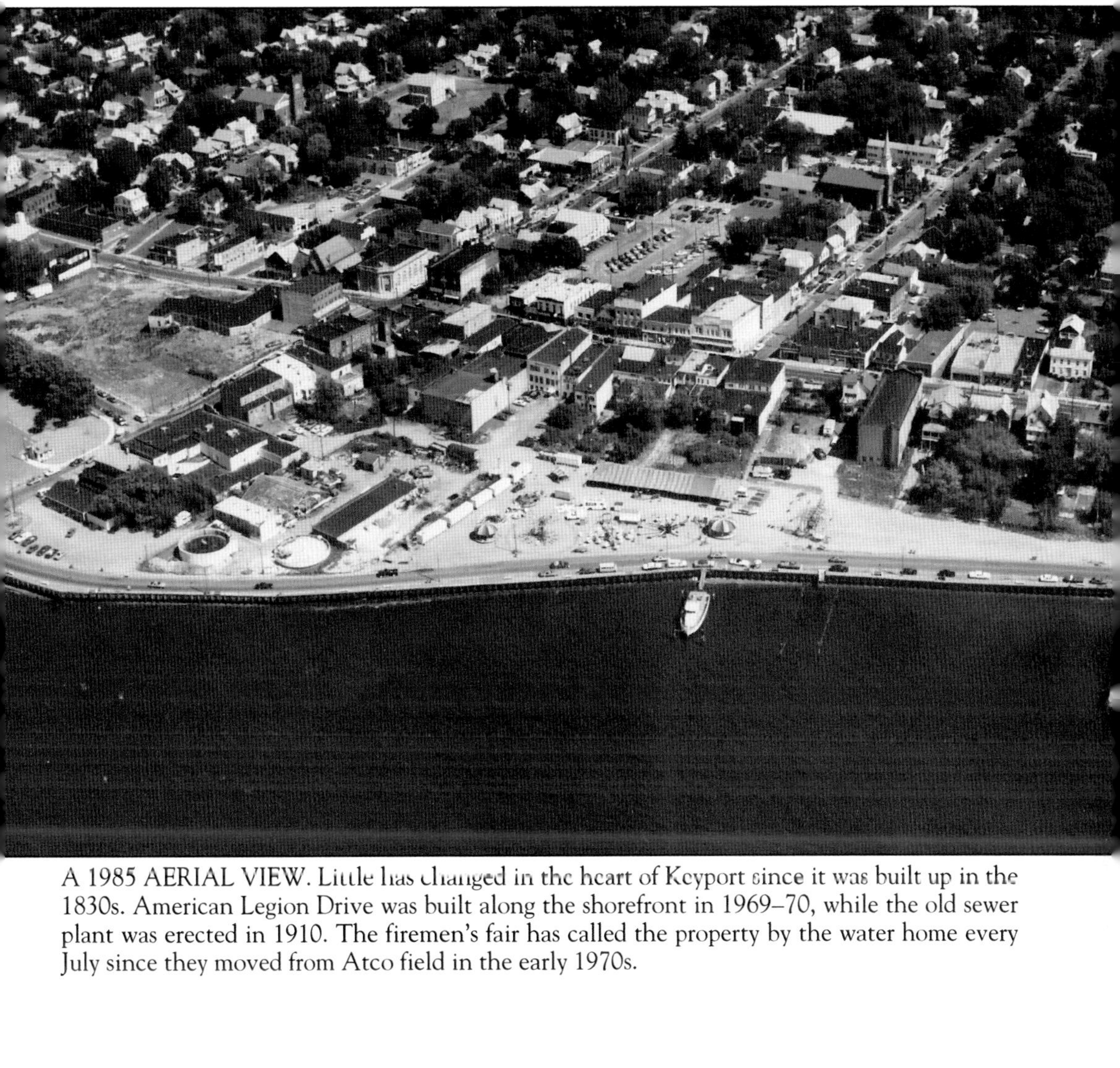

A 1985 AERIAL VIEW. Little has changed in the heart of Keyport since it was built up in the 1830s. American Legion Drive was built along the shorefront in 1969–70, while the old sewer plant was erected in 1910. The firemen's fair has called the property by the water home every July since they moved from Atco field in the early 1970s.

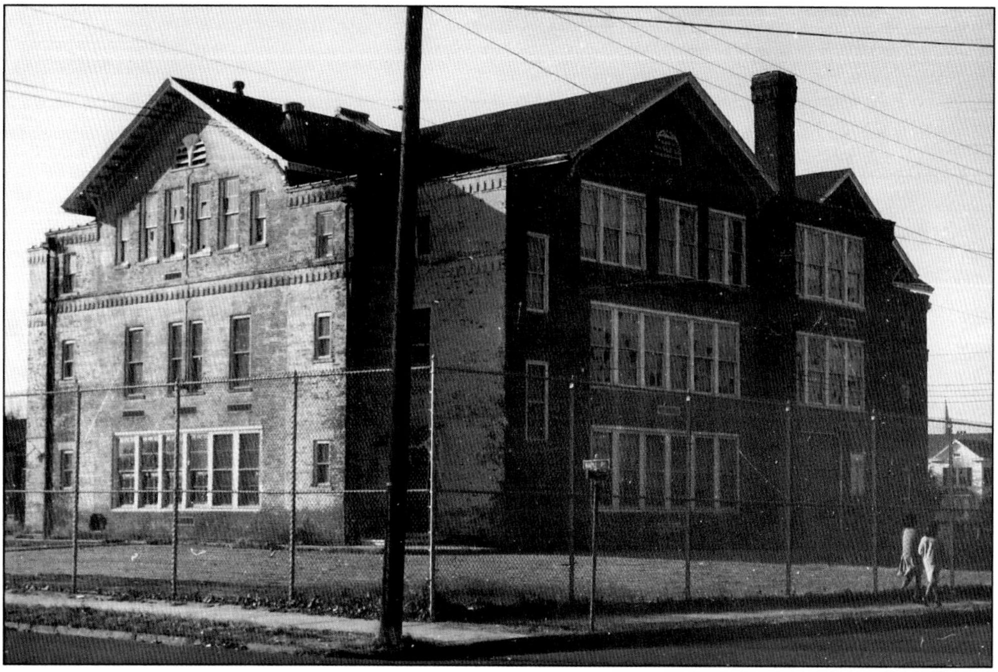

THE GRADED SCHOOL, 1967. I suppose every kid in town threw a rock at the old school building after it closed in 1965–66. For nearly one-hundred years the substantial brick structure was where most Keyporters were educated. Several months after this photograph was taken the building was demolished.

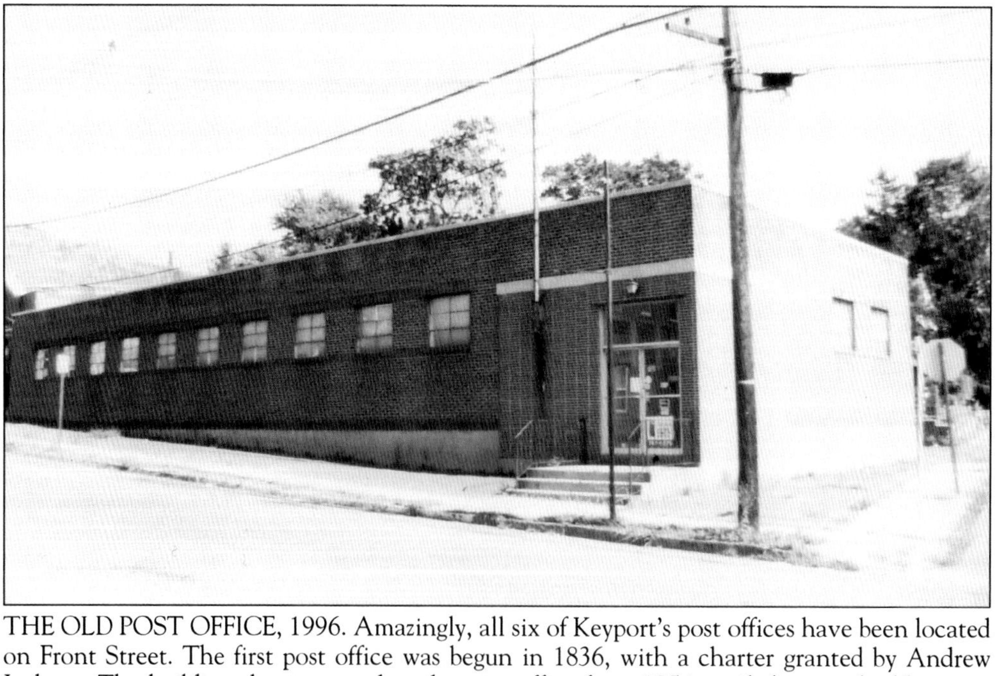

THE OLD POST OFFICE, 1996. Amazingly, all six of Keyport's post offices have been located on Front Street. The first post office was begun in 1836, with a charter granted by Andrew Jackson. The building shown served as the post office from 1954 until the new building was constructed in 1972. It was then purchased by the West Furniture Co, who used it until they closed in 1996.

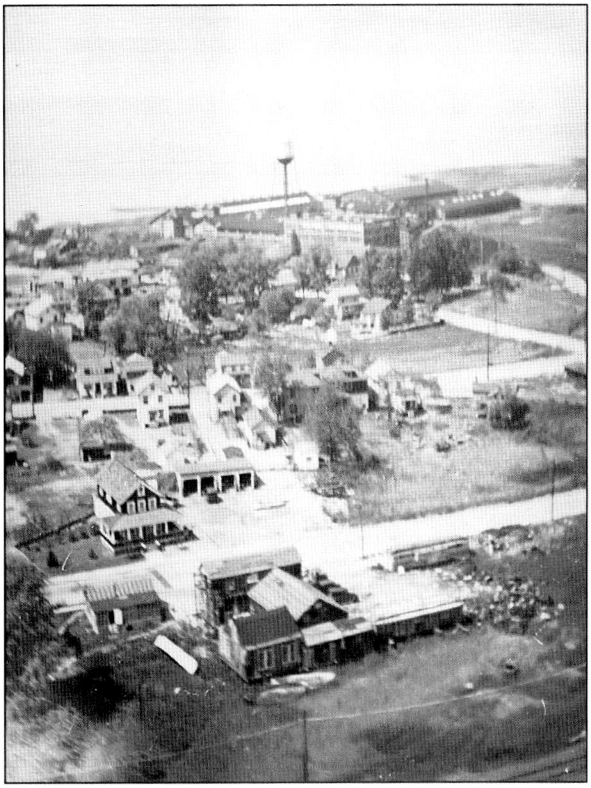

A 1930 AERIAL VIEW. Taken above the railroad tracks in Lockport, this photograph shows the industry which prospered in East Keyport in the mid-twentieth century. Aeromarine is to the right, while at the bottom is Alfred "Niffie" Poling's auto repair/welding/vulcanizing/junkyard complex.

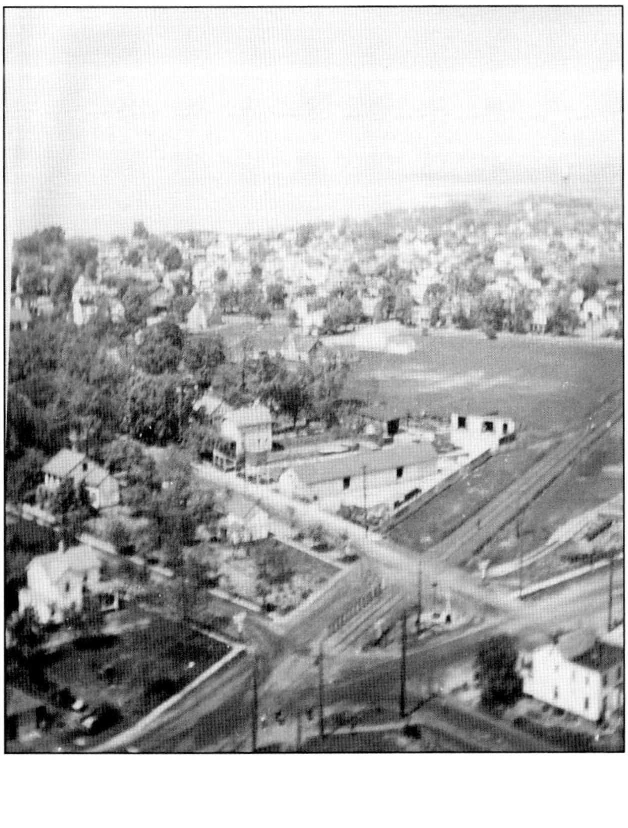

ANOTHER 1930 AERIAL VIEW. This photograph, also taken above the railroad, looks over the intersection of Maple Place, Church Street, and Atlantic Streets. The low sheds in the center were part of the Conover Lumber Co. and were used as their mill buildings. Houses were built on the site around 1984, after the mill was destroyed by fire.

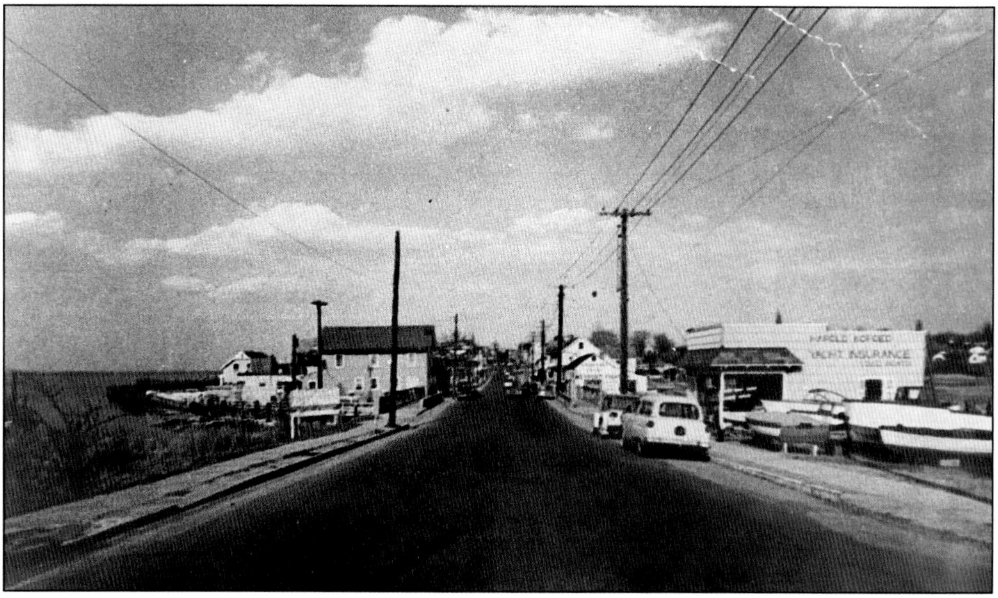

FRONT STREET, 1960. For many, this is one of the first places that catches your eye as you enter town. The area to the right was built up as Pedersen's Marina in the mid-1960s; since then no other changes have taken place along this street, although one may wonder if that is good or bad!

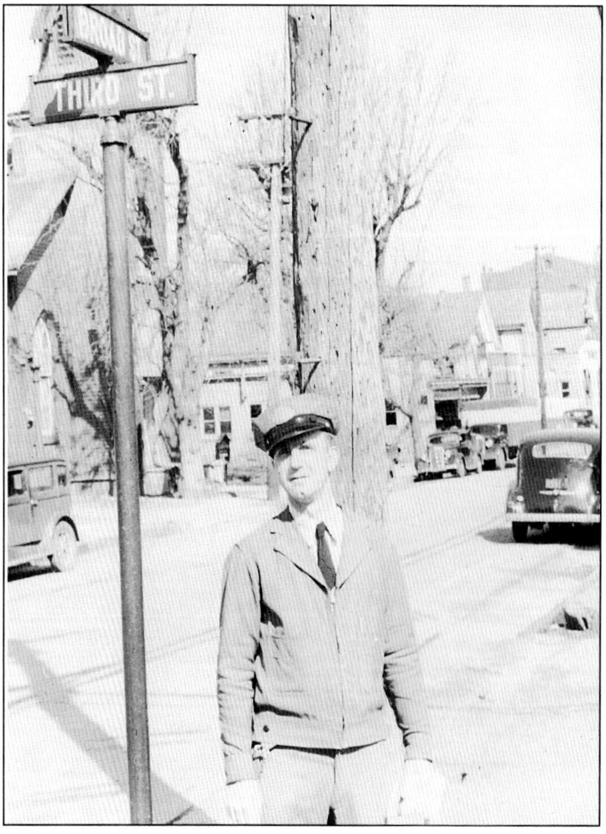

MR. COKELET. From 1836 to 1914 if you wanted your mail you had to go and pick it up at the post office. On June 1, 1914, W. Elmer Aumack became the borough's first mailman. He was followed by G.W. Walling, Stephen Ridgeway, and Mr. Cokelet, who is shown here posing at the corner of Broad and Third around 1940.

HERB DIETRICH, 1953. Until the 1970s, when Cedar Street Park was opened, Keyport had no public recreation facilities. If you wanted to shoot some hoops like Herbie did, you had better make friends with someone who had concrete driveway and a rim nailed above their garage door.

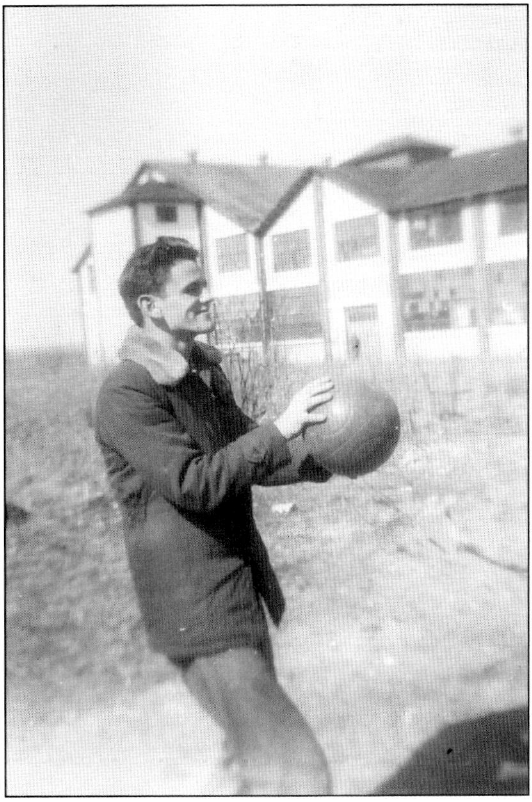

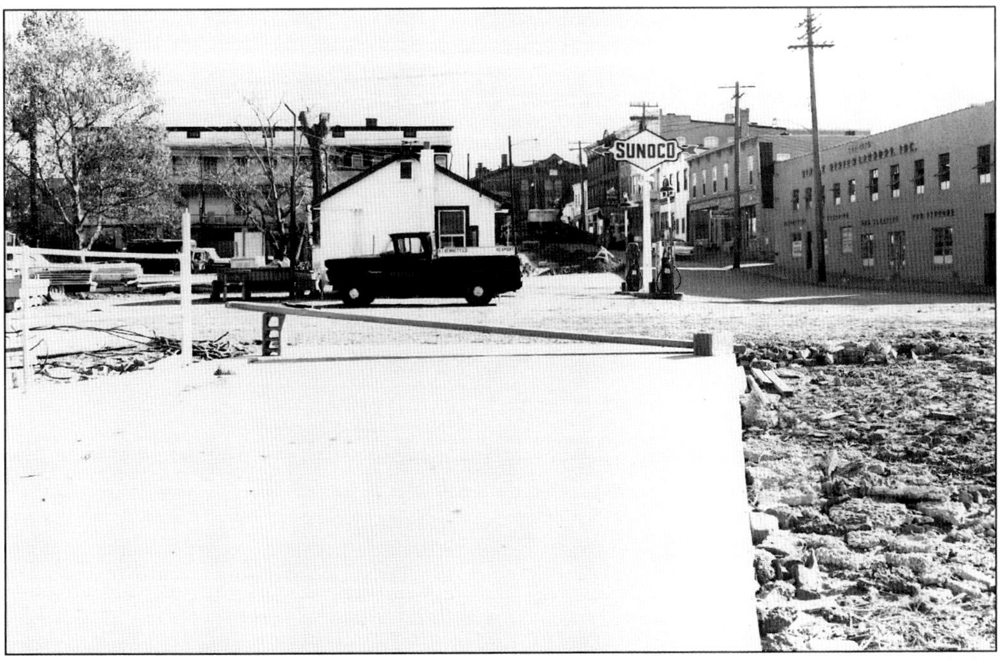

THE FOOT OF BROAD STREET, 1960. Keyport photographer Al Bennett captured the construction of the boat ramp around 1960. The Sunoco Station is now the office for the boat ramp tender.

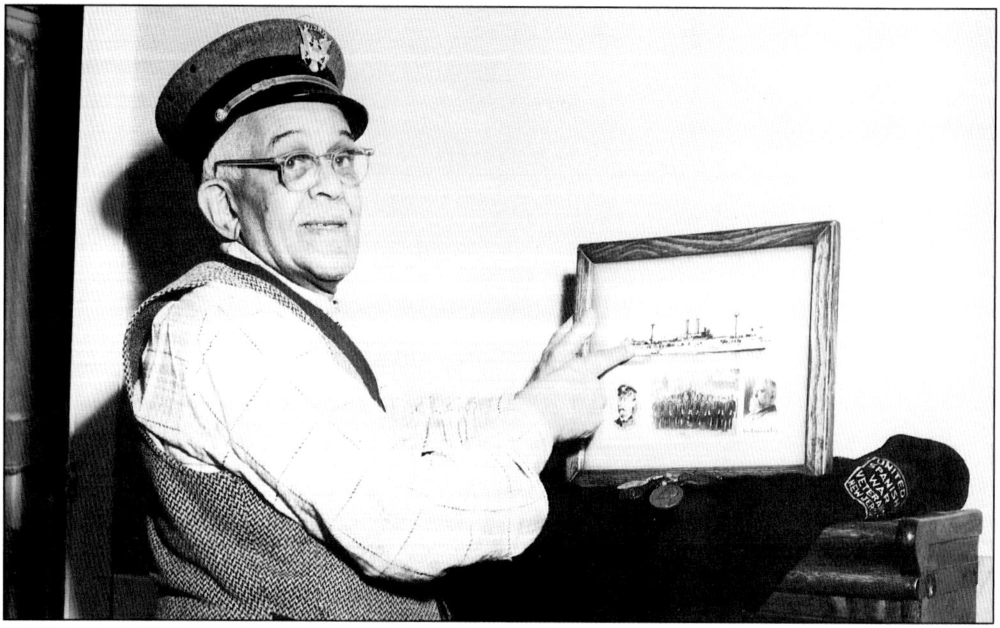

ALONZO WILLIS. The framed picture above is of the ill-fated battleship *Maine*, which was attacked at 9:40 pm on February 16, 1888, while anchored in the harbor of Havana, Cuba. Alonzo Willis was the only Afro-American to survive. Born on October 17, 1876, he returned to Keyport after the Spanish-American War, and soon married and raised a daughter at his house on Third Street. He passed away on July 3, 1959, at the age of eighty-two.

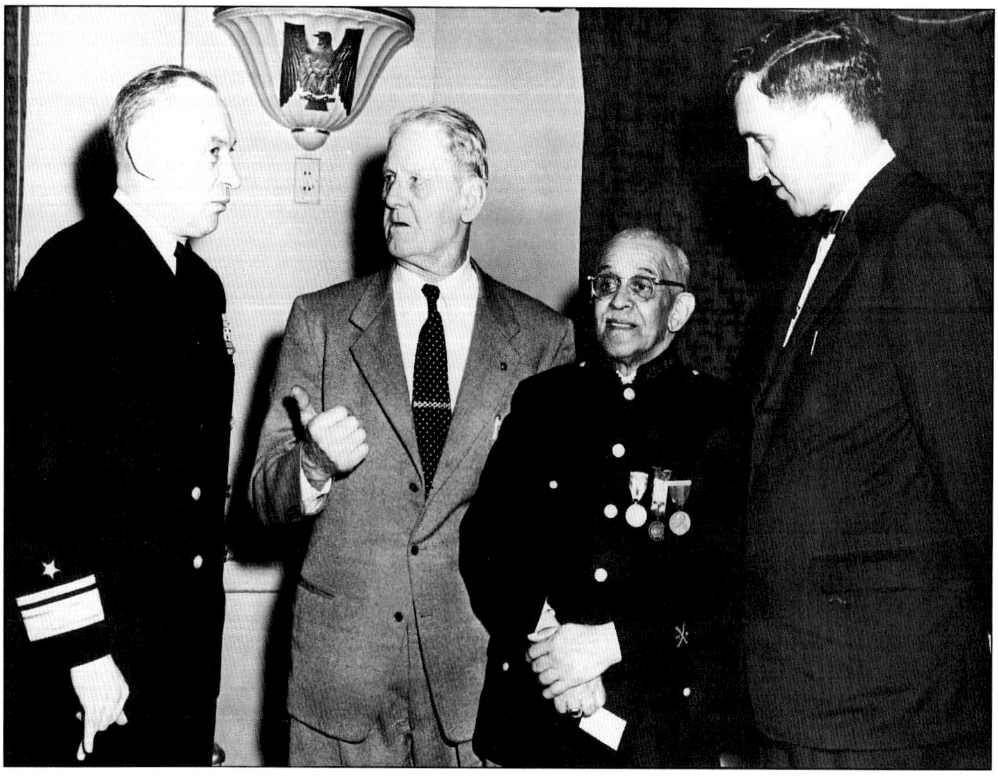

A LIFEGUARD, *c.* 1930. Bill Everhart is shown posing next to his tower along the Cliffwood beach in the 1930s. I'm sure many young women spent long summer days trying to get closer to this lifeguard.

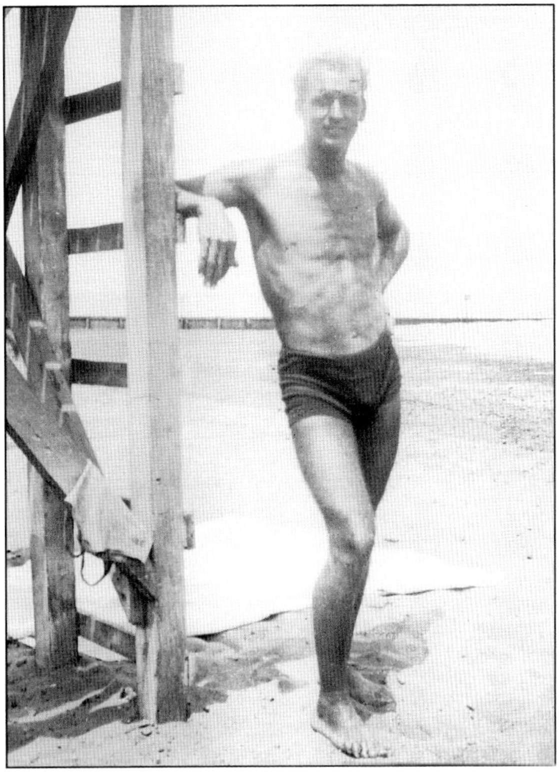

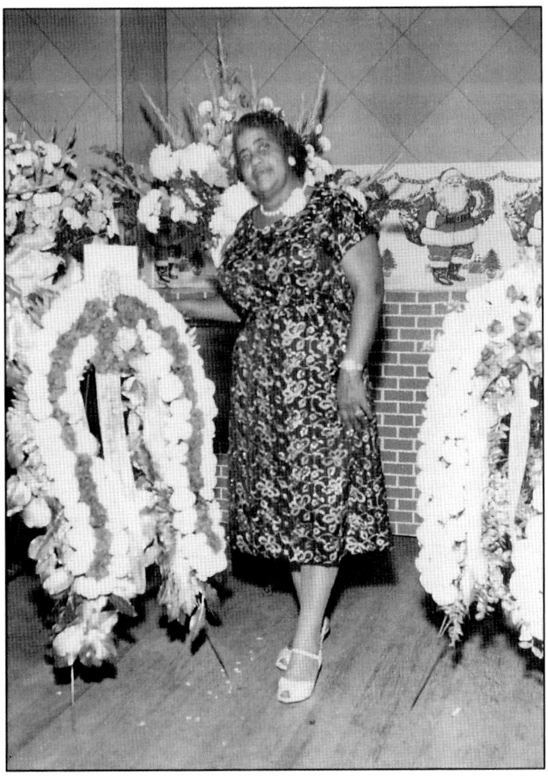

MARY ALICE MAJOR. In 1937 Mary came to Keyport with her brother, Frank Leroy, and her father, Frank. It was at this time that the old Green Grove Mansion was converted to Major's Bar and Grill. In this photograph, Mary Alice is shown inside the bar.

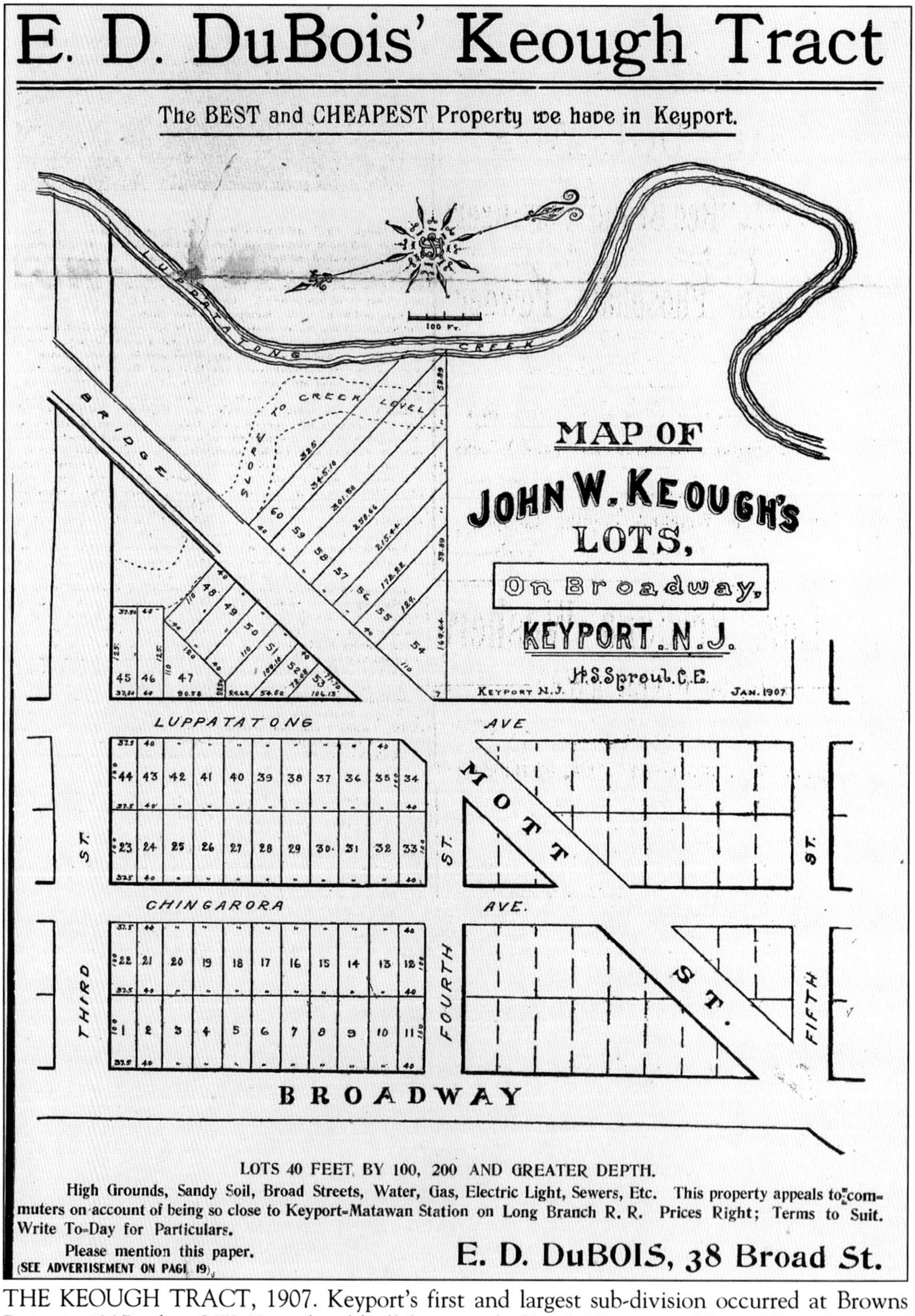

THE KEOUGH TRACT, 1907. Keyport's first and largest sub-division occurred at Browns Point in 1907, when J.W. Keough sold off this parcel of land. The area sold quickly and some of the finest Cape Cod-style homes in the region were built here.

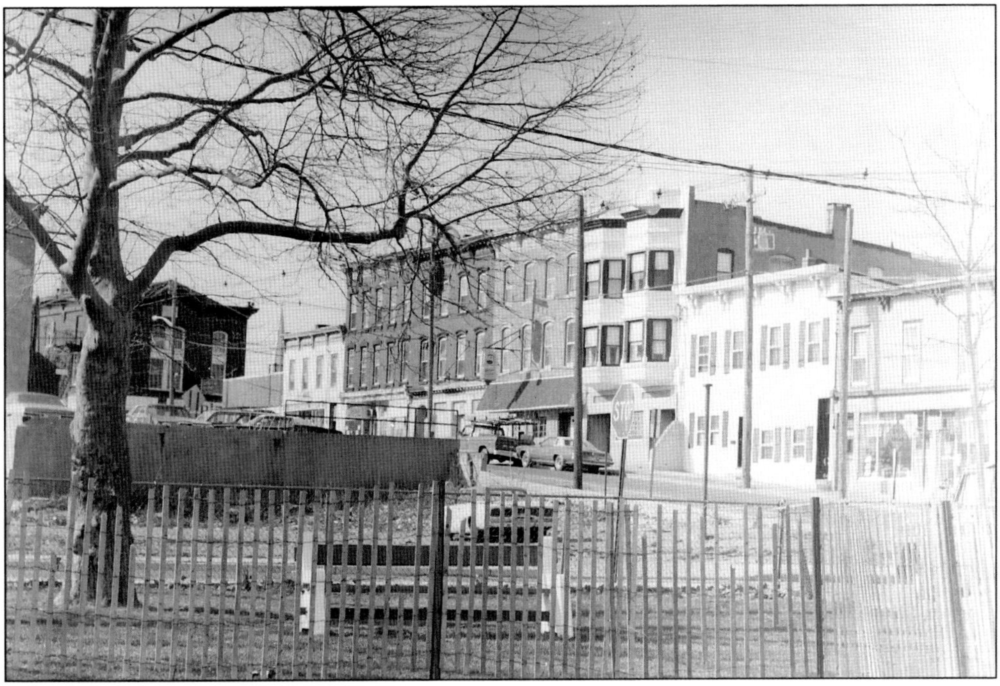

LOWER BROAD STREET, 1978. To the extreme right is the spot where Keyport's great fire began in 1877. After destroying most of the business district, it was checked on Front Street. All of the buildings pictured here were erected between 1877 and 1890. To the right is all that remained of the old Pavilion Hotel: a concrete wall and a metal railing.

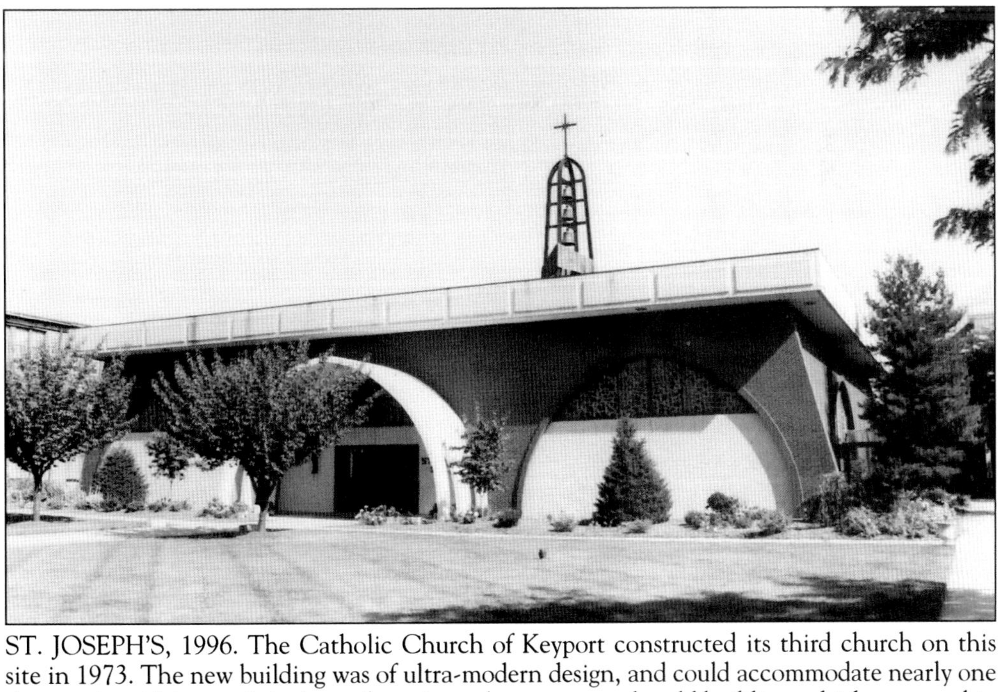

ST. JOSEPH'S, 1996. The Catholic Church of Keyport constructed its third church on this site in 1973. The new building was of ultra-modern design, and could accommodate nearly one thousand parishioners. It is shown here in stark contrast to the old building, which was razed in 1972 after nearly one hundred years of service. (see Volume I, p. 53)

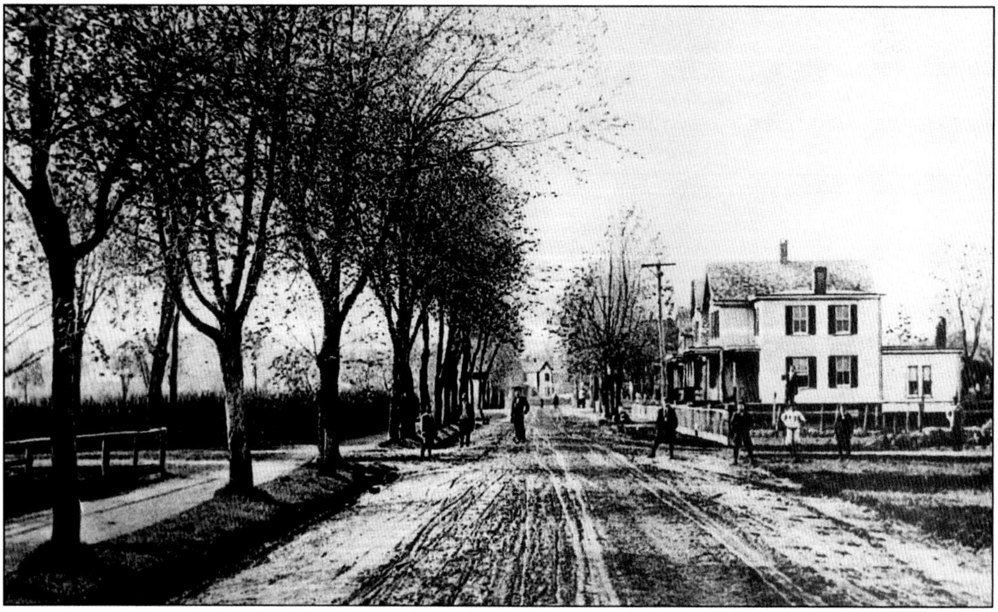

GREEN GROVE, LOOKING NORTH, *c.* 1905. Everyone seems to be so interested in the photographer. The land to the right has since been greatly developed, beginning in the late 1960s.

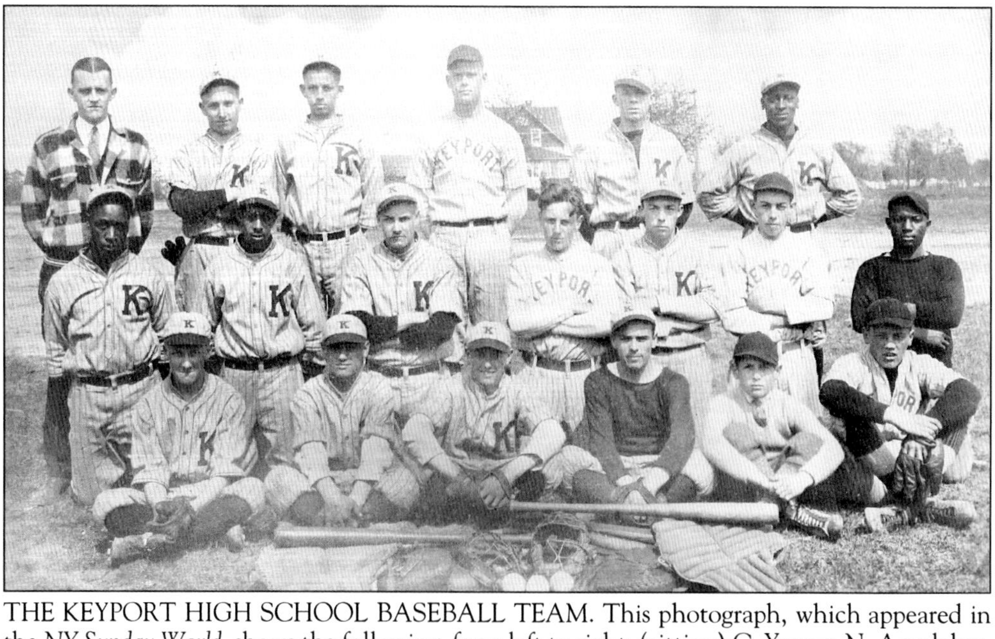

THE KEYPORT HIGH SCHOOL BASEBALL TEAM. This photograph, which appeared in the *NY Sunday World*, shows the following, from left to right: (sitting) C. Young, N. Aggelakos, J. Kennedy, J. Aggelakos, B. Sacks (the mascot), and D. Howard; (kneeling) W. Hall, V. Dandridge, A. Finger, H. Howard, J. Brady, C. Cherry, and P. Ball; (standing) Coach J. Hartzler, J. Jaffe, M. Walling, J. Loderman, R. Dane, and D. Banks.

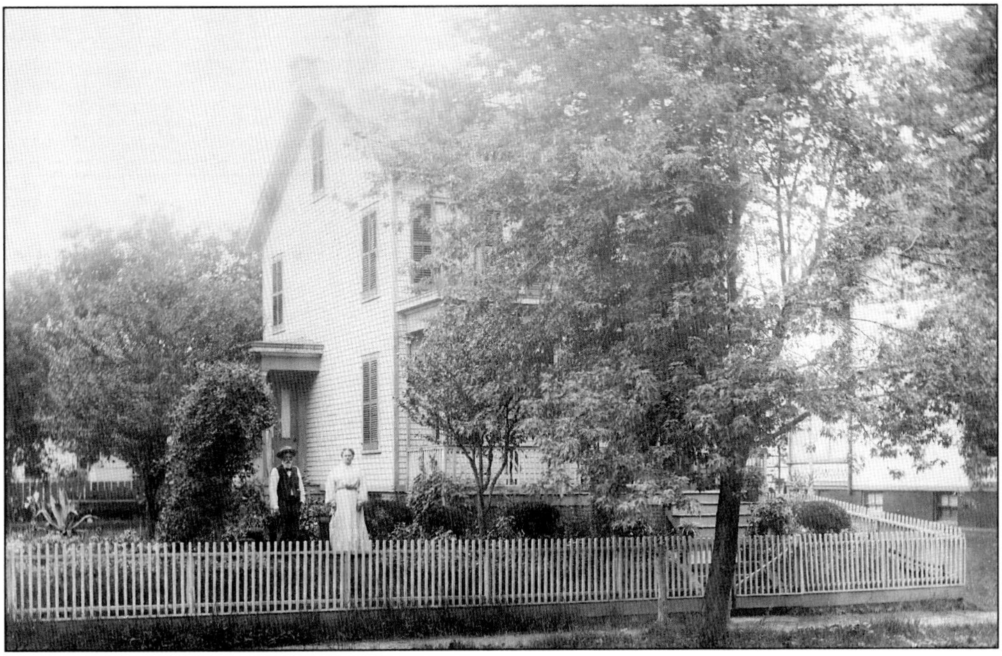

AN UNKNOWN HOUSE, *c.* 1900. This house is thought to have stood on Main Street but the large tree makes identification difficult. Regardless of where it stood its owners certainly maintained the property in a exquisite manner.

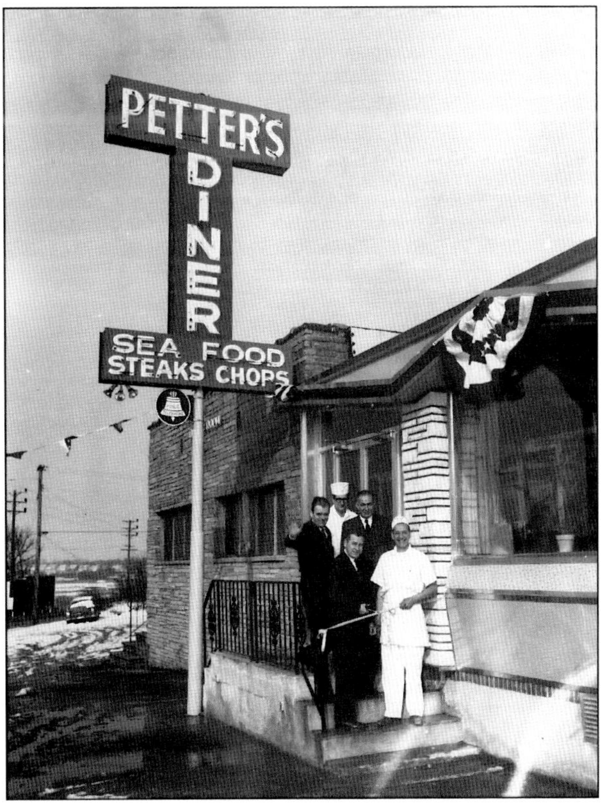

PETTER'S DINER, *c.* 1963. As the scissors slice through the red ribbon another diner officially opens upon the six corners in West Keyport. Petter's later became the Town and Country.

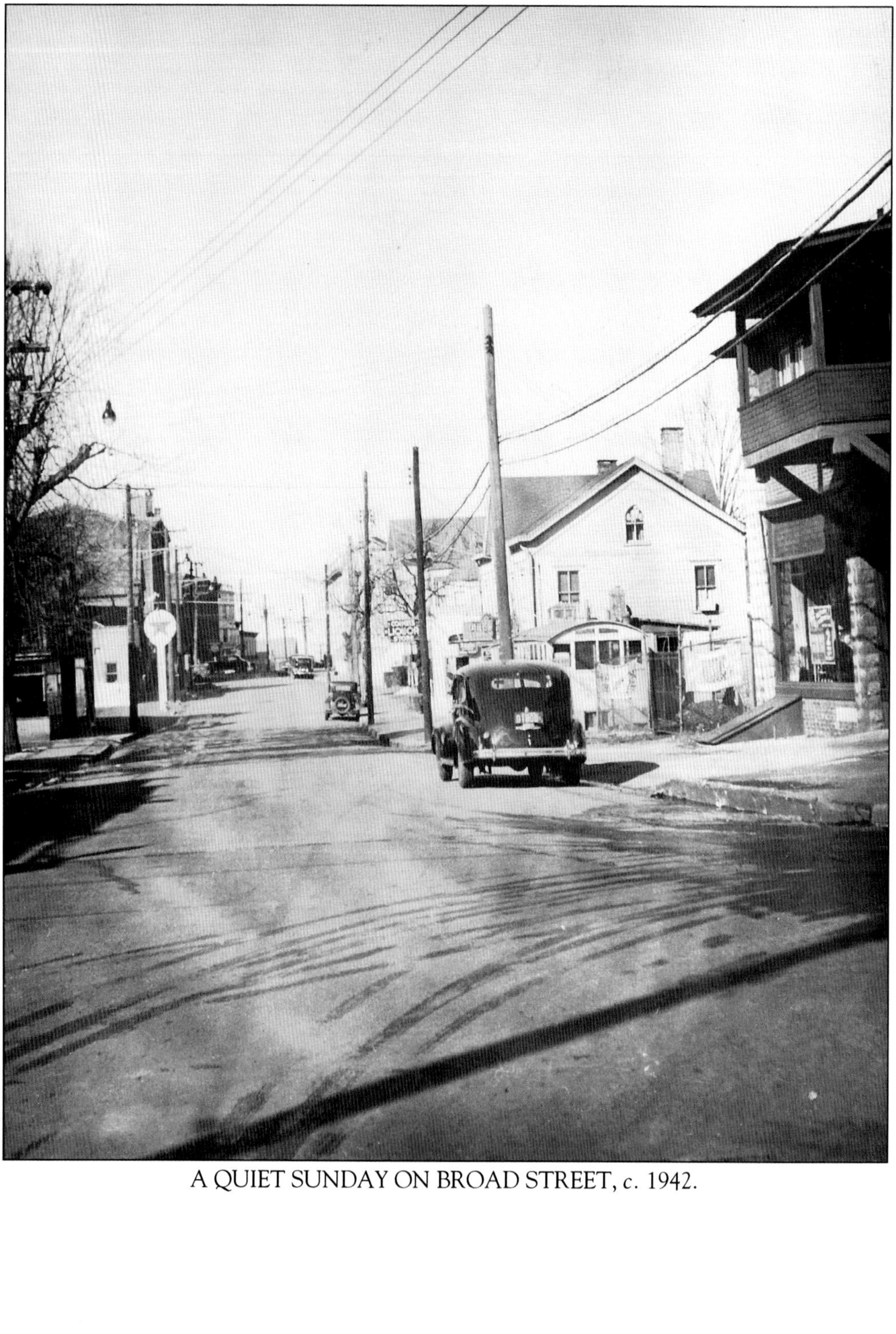

A QUIET SUNDAY ON BROAD STREET, *c.* 1942.